S0-BAC-120

Site	URL	Description
First Church of Cyberspace	www.godweb.org	Constructed by Charlie Henderson, the guide for general Christianity at About.com
Religious Shortwave Radio Stations	www.ping.be/tdp.com	Has links and live broadcasts to (mostly Christian) radio stations from Albania to Zimbabwe
Teach Me Online	www.utexas.edu/world/ lecture/rel	Over 40 courses, pitched at the 101 level, this site from the Distance Learning Center at the University of Texas, Austin, provides extensive syllabi, readings, and lectures online
A Riveting Monk	home.att.net/ ~PCasamento/ franciscans.htm	There is no better example of Catholic piety in cyberspace than this masterful Web site on a timeless and endearing Christlike figure, St. Francis of Assisi
A Hip Bishop	www.upenn.edu/almanac/ v42/n25/harris.html	A long URL, this site is worth the extra effort as it features the first African-American Episcopal Bishop in the U.S.
Kelly Lake COGIC	www.arrowweb.com/ klcogic/klcogic.htm	Another long URL, but again, it takes you to a site—in this case Pentecostal—where you will be dazzled by the graphics and intrigued by the content
A Trane That Never Stops	www.saintjohncoltrane.org	The home page for an African Orthodox Church in San Francisco dedicated to St. John Coltrane
The Grail for Techies	www.technosophy.com	You'd expect a lot from a home page dedicated to the coming together of technology and religion; you will not be disappointed
Wiccans Worship Here	www.witchvox.com	For both Wiccans and neopagan well-wishers, the Web is a boon, and here is the top religious site, with more than 70 million hits to date

continues

alpha books

continued

There is a tie for #10; you pick the winner.

The Jewish Internet Consortium Home Page	www.shamash.org	It's hard to find more thoughtful reflections on the many splendors of Judaism than those offered here
A Major Muslim Web Site	www.al-islam.org	It understates the difference between Shi'i and Sunni perspectives on Islam but projects a stunning tribute to Muslim piety

Five Search Engines with Great Stuff on Religion

Site	URL	Description
About.com	www.about.com	It's a big commercial search engine, with lots of info on stuff that has nothing to do with religion or spirituality, God or Truth. But it has a guide for many of the topics or groups clustered within religion, and you will not lack for the fun as well as the serious side of netaphysics.
Aphids Communications	www.aphids.com	No, this is not a search engine trying to locate insects, or the plants they eat, but it does have a HUGE appetite for religion. Click its religion megasite and you'll find over 4,000 Web sites on 177 topics, some of them spectacular, though not all are easy to find.
Lycos Directory	www.lycos.com	Lycos offers more than 22,000 sites on religion, so you have to know where you're going, or want to go, but if you do, you'll find a narrative summary of many sites, plus a bright button NEW!, telling you that an item has just been added.
Yahoo!	www.yahoo.com	Just when you thought you'd never get through Lycos and find what you want on a religious option or theme or group, you turn to Yahoo!, and wow! you find even more sites—27,000 and counting. It is a similar brochureware approach to the topic, but again, with patience, it can yield some good stuff.
AltaVista	www.altavista.com	Much more manageable than either Lycos or Yahoo!, AltaVista has a great keyword search engine, but you have to know what you want to find in order to get maximum benefit from it. Suppose your real interest is religious images or sound tracks, well, then, this might be the search engine for you: It has separate search options for images, video, and audio.

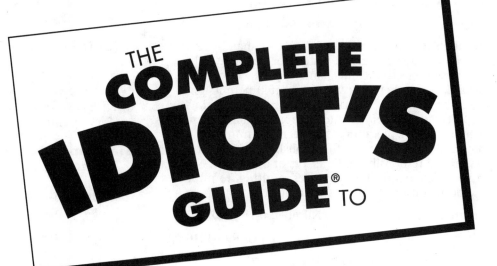

THE COMPLETE IDIOT'S GUIDE® TO

Religions Online

by Bruce B. Lawrence

alpha books

A Division of Macmillan USA
201 W. 103rd Street, Indianapolis, IN 46290

The Complete Idiot's Guide to Religions Online

Copyright © 2000 by Macmillan USA

International Standard Book Number: 0-7897-2209-7

Library of Congress Catalog Card Number: 99-64210

Printed in the United States of America

First Printing: December 1999

01   00   99   4   3   2   1

Trademarks

Warning and Disclaimer

Associate Publisher
Greg Wiegand

Acquisitions Editor
Angelina Ward

Development Editors
Nicholas Goetz
Gregory Harris

Managing Editor
Thomas F. Hayes

Project Editor
Tom Stevens

Copy Editors
Sossity Smith
Audra McFarland

Proofreader
Tricia Sterling

Technical Editor
Doug Dafforn

Illustrator
Judd Winick

Team Coordinator
Sharry Lee Gregory

Interior Designer
Nathan Clement

Cover Designer
Michael Freeland

Copy Writer
Eric Borgert

Layout Technician
Eric S. Miller

Contents at a Glance

Contents

About the Author

Bruce B. Lawrence is an Episcopal priest who is also Professor of Asian Religions and Chair of the Department of Religion at Duke University. He has written 10 books and over 130 published essays, chapters, and articles. He specializes in premodern South Asian Islam and modern-day religious movements. In addition to his prizewinning monograph, *Defenders of God: The Fundamentalist Revolt Against the Modern Age*, he has translated a major Persian Sufi manual into English (*Morals for the Heart*) and written an Asian-based defense of Islamic norms (*Shattering the Myth: Islam Beyond Violence*). A former President of the American Society for the Study of Religion, he was the American Academy of Religion's distinguished lecturer in History of Religions during 1998-1999. He used those lectures to create an undergraduate course: "God Online," and that course became the launch pad for this book. He lives with his wife, and co-teacher, Miriam Cooke, in Hillsborough, North Carolina.

Dedication

To St. Isidore of Seville, a sixth century monk who compiled a 20 volume encyclopedia, and is said to intercede on behalf of daunted cybernauts, whether geeks or idiots.

Acknowledgments

No book of this scope could have been written without several hands, and minds, at work. I am especially fortunate to have had resources from Duke University, and especially its Department of Religion. Both under-graduate and graduate students assisted. Aaron Reeves researched and assisted with some of the Protestant chapters, while Drew Michael pitched in with enthusiasm and insight to help research the chapter on Satanism. Ann Williams, also a Duke undergraduate and chair of the Majors Committee in the Religion Department, did extraordinary work. She was involved from the beginning in conceptualizing the project. She did prelim-inary scans of many kinds of Web sites. She met with others to discuss and edit several chapters. Hers was the guiding hand in most of the chap-ters in Parts 2 and 3, and she also helped with Chapter 26, "She Is God: Neopaganism and Wicca" as well as Chapter 30, "God Does Not Harm: Jains." Several of the smaller groups within Protestant Christianity were researched by her before becoming part of the chapters on Mainstream Protestants (14-17). I owe a major debt of gratitude to her, not only for her consistent high level of productivity but also for her willingness to crit-icize and give feedback to others.

Among graduate students, Rick Colby stands at the head of the class. Rick was involved in translating the chapters into HTML format, with the fig-ures included as appendices. Rick put in long hours in order to make this book happen over a period of four months. This project might have gotten started without Rick, but it would never have been possible to finish it without him. Alas, he had to leave before the end, and the translation work he performed was picked up and continued by Adam Porter. Adam also made the extra effort to meet deadlines, and he also did a superb job with both Chapter 9 "Chat Groups, Internet Newsgroups, and Email Lists" and Chapter 36, "New Religious Movements". Another graduate student, Rob Rozehnal, was also involved in the project at a crucial stage;

his was the guiding spirit and the major hand in both Chapter 27 "God's Many Prophets: Bahais" and Chapter 33, "God's Persian Prophet: Zoroastrians or Parsis."

As valuable as were students—both graduate and undergraduate—in assisting me, I would never have reached the end of this project without staff support. Lillian Spiller, as Administrative Assistant for the Department of Religion, ensured that the connections and exchanges with Macmillan Publishing USA editorial staff were facilitated, while Sandra Woods, the Undergraduate Staff Assistant for the Department, acted as the antenna for common sense. She checked all the Web sites and above all, she helped to guide each of the nearly weekly meetings throughout Summer 1999 to a happy conclusion. Her support was as crucial as it was superlative.

Finally, I'd like to thank all of the folk from Macmillan Publishing USA who helped. Angelina Ward was a stranger to me till she called my office way back in April and proposed that I consider doing The Complete Idiot's Guide to Religions Online. *She stayed with the project all the way through the mountain peaks and valley stops of the long summer, and then guided us through the last stages of completing the volume in early fall. Angelina was supported by a host of others at Macmillan, most of whom are names with email addresses, some of whom are names with voices, and all of whom helped this volume become an idea translated into a reality. Their names are listed on the inside of the title page, but I also want to express my gratitude to them for reshaping and improving the book now before you.*

I am also indebted to my colleague, and sometime biking companion, Claudia Koonz, for sharing with me a Newsweek *(12 July 1999) spot story on St. Isidore of Seville, who has now become the patron saint of this book as well as the last recourse for worried Web surfers. Another colleague, Kalman Bland, provided me with invaluable insight into Judaism (Chapter 21), and also read and critiqued my own efforts to make sense of the diverse Jewish presence in cyberspace. I owe Kalman an immense debt of gratitude.*

Tell Us What You Think!

As the reader of this book, *you* are our most important critic and commentator. We value your opinion and want to know what we're doing right, what we could do better, what areas you'd like to see us publish in, and any other words of wisdom you're willing to pass our way.

As an Associate Publisher for Alpha Books, I welcome your comments. You can fax, email, or write me directly to let me know what you did or didn't like about this book—as well as what we can do to make our books stronger.

Please note that I cannot help you with technical problems related to the topic of this book, and that due to the high volume of mail I receive, I might not be able to reply to every message.

When you write, please be sure to include this book's title and author as well as your name and phone or fax number. I will carefully review your comments and share them with the author and editors who worked on the book.

Fax: 317-581-4666

Email: consumer@mcp.com

Mail: Greg Wiegand, Associate Publisher
         Alpha Books
         201 West 103rd Street
         Indianapolis, IN 46290 USA

Introduction

Is the idea of *Religions Online* too good to be true...or is it a nightmare haunting our collective spiritual life?

For more and more folks, religions online *seems* too good to be true. After all, a mere 10 years ago, we were still limited to telephone, radio, and television for most of our indirect communications with other people. We could talk long distance, we could listen long distance, we could see long distance, but we could not interact long distance. Nor could we imagine interacting long distance with diverse groups whom we scarcely knew or learning about topics that we only dimly understood.

Today the global Net and the World Wide Web are part of our everyday experience. We can still talk to people by phone, we can still listen to programs on the radio, we can still watch news or sports or movies on television—but we can also do more on the cusp of a new millennium. We can buy a personal computer, get a Web browser, connect to the Internet, and enter a whole new set of conversations and relationships, some close, some distant, and all interactive, at least in principle.

With the World Wide Web, religion and ideas about spirituality can now be transmitted in cyberspace. Whether you want to connect to your own religious community, find out about someone else's, or research useful information such as the text of a holy book or the location of the nearest church, you are just a couple clicks away from stepping into other thought worlds, which are also vistas of religious imagination and spiritual expression. If you are a Protestant Christian, you have every resource from sermons to clip art that feeds your appetite for faith. If you are a Roman Catholic, you can find out more about saints and cycles of worship than was ever available to the pious, whether they were lay folk or priests or even bishops. (So popular is the Web for the current successor to St. Peter that he has been dubbed the first Cyber Pope!)

And others who are not Christian but are equally committed to a faith path can explore their options and connect to their spiritual cohorts through the Net. Jews and Muslims, Hindus, Buddhists and Sikhs, Zoroastrians and Taoists—all have found cybernauts, voyagers into cyberspace, who have created paths, or Web sites, for others to follow.

So why should anyone have a nightmare about the latest turn in modern-day technology and its inspired expansion of the spirit? Because some fear that the digital divine is not divine but demonic, or at least a block to true religious pursuits. After all, might online religious resources not become a substitute for the God of Abraham and Sarah, or the Holy Trinity, or Allah, or Vishnu, or the Buddha? Yes, one could worry that such a development might occur, and one might also worry that the pathways to techgnosis, or spiritual insight via the Web, might lead away from traditional structures of worship and the living communities supporting them.

One *could* have such nightmares, but instead of indulging them, one would be better off using this book. It is a manual that allows believers or explorers to enter the World Wide Web. It is a guide to finding other cybernauts and becoming a cybernaut yourself. You can begin slowly, or you can dive into the deep end.

Let's suppose you want to begin at the beginning and work your way into online religions. You should go to Part 1 and leaf through its three chapters. You will be told how to get started on the Web. You will find out to distinguish subject directories from search engines and use both to your advantage. You will come face-to-face with God.com and find hope, not horror, awaiting you.

Then you can move into Part 2 and imagine you are taking a journey. It will give you provisions for the road. It will tell you what is free and what isn't. It will show you where to find RealAudio and RealVideo assets to enhance your faith and ease your journey. It will even give you some clues on learning about religions without going back to school or into the classroom.

After you have gleaned what you need from Parts 1 and 2, you can start to get personal in Part 3. Getting personal means learning about friendship, romance, and maybe even marriage by connecting to someone who is a soul mate, that special other person who shares your values, your worldview, your faith. But getting personal may also mean improving what you know about various religious issues, whether through chat groups or newsgroups. You can also keep abreast of current events via the Net, and you might even find that the most personal need of all is economic: getting a job by connecting to a future employer who shares your religious commitment.

Does all this sound easy? Well, it actually is, when you learn how to make the Net work for you and begin to explore the World Wide Web as an extension of your own world. This book will serve as your guide.

But let us suppose that you already know a ton about computers, that you have your whole life in order, and that you just want to roam, or surf, the Web to enhance what you do as a spiritually hip person. Well, then, you might just skim through much of Parts 1, 2, and 3 and head straight to Part 4. (The initial parts do, after all, contain valuable tips, insights, and Web addresses.) If you are like four out of five Americans, your world is shaped by that ancient Mesopotamian wanderer named Abraham. Abraham has become the symbol for Jewish, Christian, and Muslim belief in the One God of history and humankind. And in Part 4, you will see the digital drama of the divine writ large on the World Wide Web. It is a story that continues with Jesus and his followers and moves through all branches of Protestant and Catholic expression. It also encompasses the Orthodox and brings to light the cyber churches now dotting the Net. While not as numerous as Christians, Jews and Muslims have become eager explorers of cyberspace, and Part 4 closes by offering you some of their Web sites, which are little short of dazzling in color, scope, and ease of access.

If it happens that none of the Abrahamic saga interests you, but you still define yourself as spiritual, don't despair. Just thumb your way to Part 5. It offers a huge diversity of voices, all appealing to the basic human sensibility to explore, to test, and to invoke the Divine. Represented are Native American voices, Asian voices, satanic and atheist voices, Wiccan and Vodun voices. Even voices from Start Wars and Scientology are clamoring for attention as religious sites on the Web. You will find them all in Part 5.

If you are not too exhausted, or if you just want to see where it ends, you can go to the Conclusion, which offers a brief caution: Don't have nightmares about the Net. It is, like the telephone, radio, and television, an instrument for helping people, not depriving them. If you search for the spirit of the ages and you use the computer with care, you can become a netizen, that is, someone who uses the Net the way citizens use the state: You recognize its value, you depend on it, you even pay it some money, but you retain your own sense of what counts and what needs to be done. You will use the Web to connect to other folks, and you will discover that God requires worshipers on the ground as well as in cyberspace. No nightmare lasts when dawn breaks, and *The Complete Idiot's Guide to Religions Online* is designed to help you see the dawn that is breaking on the Net—with divine assistance.

Special Features

Throughout the book, I've scattered some sidebars and margin notes to define terms, point out interesting sidelights, and provide a few warnings.

Wired Monk

These boxes contain notes, tips, and asides that provide you with interesting and useful bits of information on religions, Web sites, and other matters of interest to the online pilgrim.

Food for Thought

This box contains the definitions of terms, both religious and technological.

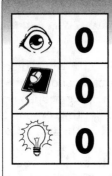

Rating

Occasionally, I'll use this box to point out some of the Web's truly outstanding religious sites.

Caution

The path of the online pilgrim can be beset on all sides by pitfalls. I'll use these notes to describe technical traps and sites or philosophies that may not be what they claim to be.

Part 1

Welcome to the World of Online Religion

Even if you are not a certifiable idiot, you might sometimes feel like one if a friend asks: "Gosh, did you see this terrific Web site? It's all about…." Fill in the blanks. And if you draw a blank at the idea of looking at a Web site, or surfing the Net, then you have come to the right book, and this is where you start to get on with a new life and a new life in cyberspace. Yes, cyberspace. It's just a fancy word for talking about all the data—gobs and gobs of it—that's being linked from one site to another in electrical bands that most people don't understand but more people are starting to use.

And religion is part of the new gold rush. Gold rush? Yes, because all this seems a bonanza for rethinking who we are and connecting to ideas, people, and options that we never imagined. Religion has been around for as long as people began populating the earth, and now what goes around comes around. It comes around in new forms but with old ideas, and they still have to do with life, death, meaning, hope, and celebration.

WAIT!

Chapter 1

Before You Get Started

In This Chapter

➤ Learn the basics about the Web: what it is, how it works, and how to get access to it

➤ Find out about the most popular Web browsers and their most important features

➤ Get an overview of the tools you'll need to explore religion on the Net, and other optional tools (such as plug-ins) that can come in handy

---

If you've never checked out the World Wide Web, you don't know what you've been missing! And it's never too late to start your very own Web adventure, You'll find that it's surprisingly simple to begin after you've learned a few basics.

Covering those basics is what this chapter is all about. While seasoned Web surfers might want to skim or skip this chapter, even those familiar with the Web might pick up a few useful pointers here. So without further ado, let's begin at the beginning.

What and Where Is the Web?

The World Wide Web (or simply the Web) is a collection of information stored on computers all around the world; the computers, in turn, are linked together to form a common network (the Internet or Net). The information on the Web comes to your screen in the form of an electronic page, sort of like a page in a book. The big difference, however, is that unlike a page in a book, a Web page contains highlighted items called hyperlinks, which allow you to move easily from one place to another on the Web—sometimes calling up entirely new pages on entirely different topics.

From Whence the Web?

What we today call the Internet originated in the late 1960s as a United States Defense Department project called ARPANET. It allowed scientists from all over to exchange data. By the late 1980s, you no longer had to be a rocket scientist—or a computer genius—to use the Net to exchange electronic letters or email, but the Internet was still out of the hands of the general public. The great advance brought about with the creation of the World Wide Web software in 1990, however, was the capability of vast numbers of people to exchange information in multimedia format (using words, pictures, and sounds). Although we don't have time here to go into further details of the history of the Web, if you are interested in finding out more about this fascinating subject you might check out the following sources:

➤ The Internet Society's Brief History of the Internet at
    `http://www.isoc.org/internet-history/brief.html`.

➤ The World Wide Web Consortium's Little History of the World Wide Web at
    `www.w3.org/History.html`.

➤ The Library of Congress' History of the Internet at
    `http://lcweb.loc.gov/global/internet/history.html`.

When you call up a Web page on your home computer, usually what happens is that your computer quickly begins to receive information from another computer that stores the electronic files making up that Web page. Your Web browser then interprets the page's instructions for displaying this information on your screen. Information stored on a computer half way around the world can appear on your screen in seconds. Amazing, isn't it?

However sometimes a page takes a long time to appear on your screen (or to "load up"). One reason such a delay can occur is that the files that make up the Web page might be very large. For instance, files that contain sounds, detailed graphics, or animated videos are often enormous (not physically, but electronically: they contain *lots* of bits of information). Loading a page with these types of elements on it can take a long time, because you have to wait while the information gets transferred from the other computer to your own before you can see it. If this is hard to picture right now, never fear; after you surf around on the Web a little while, you'll know only too well what we're talking about.

But enough techie talk. You're probably anxious to start exploring the Web (or in popular jargon, surfing the Web) on your own, so let's cut to the chase and zip through some of the basic things that you'll need to begin.

Surfing Supplies

Just as a surfer at a beach cannot catch the waves without her surfboard, a person cannot surf the Web without a few basic supplies. Whether you own these supplies yourself, or whether you use them at your place of employment, school, or public library, you'll find that the following are virtually indispensable for successful Web surfing.

The Basic Tools of the Trade

To surf the Web, first you'll need to own or have access either to a computer (the most common surfer's surfboard) or to a device that works like a computer terminal.

Wired Monk

Computer or No Computer?

That's a good question. Ever since the Internet became widely available to us common folk, common folk normally logged on to the Net via a personal computer or computer terminal that linked up to a larger computer elsewhere. These days it's more and more common for people to use other types of devices, such as ones that work through your TV set, to connect to the Internet. (For more on this technology, see *The Complete Idiot's Guide to Surfing the Internet with WebTV.*)

Experts predict that in the coming years, regular household appliances will be wired to the Net. Web telephones, Web thermostats...Web toasters? Strange days might be coming, but we all will be more and more wired.

We'll assume that you basically know how that device works. In what follows, we'll also assume that you're using a computer, because today that is by far the most common way to access the Web.

Although old computers often work just as well as new ones, keep in mind that a computer made this year has a much faster processor than one made just a few years ago. The faster your computer's processor (in megahertz, the higher the faster), the faster your computer will process information, which means the faster your Web pages will arrive onto your computer screen. But there is another important factor that influences the speed the Web pages arrive: the speed of your modem and the speed of your Internet connection.

Your computer may come with a mouse, but a mouse is not enough; to surf the Web, your computer needs to be hooked up the Internet somehow. Often, this requirement means the computer needs a modem, a device that the computer uses to dial up an Internet service provider (ISP) over your phone lines. Ideally the faster your modem is (measured in baud rate; again, the higher the faster), the faster your Internet connection will be.

How Fast Must My Modem Be?

Fast modems are often good to have, and faster and faster modems are designed every year. Unfortunately, many phone lines are only equipped to handle a certain limited baud rate, and so very fast modems will not be able to make your connection any better than those of medium speeds. The situation will improve as newer and better phone lines are installed, so when choosing a modem, be sure to check to see that its speed and the capacity of your phone line are in snyc; otherwise you might end up buying a faster modem than you really need. At present, a 56K modem should suit your purposes well.

Modems aren't the only way to connect to the Net, though. Cable companies are getting into the business of offering Internet connections through your cable TV connection, an even faster way to go. Finally, if you're lucky enough to be at a business, government, or educational institution that has its own computer network, you might be able to link into that network via a special cable connection called *ethernet*. Ethernet is about as fast as you can get these days. Whatever type of connection you have, once it's installed properly it should allow you to hook up to an ISP.

Finding a Good Provider: ISPs

If you connect to the Internet from a business, government, or educational institution that has its own network, you're probably in the enviable position of getting Internet access without having to pay for it. Others might be able to get free Internet access at their public library. In most other cases, however, you will probably need to sign up with an ISP to connect to the Internet and World Wide Web. Most (but not all) ISPs charge you on a monthly rate for their services. Examples of major ISPs include America Online, Compuserve, Prodigy, and probably even your long-distance company. Other, lesser-known companies can be quite good as well. Rates, accessibility, and reliability can vary quite a bit. Do some investigating before signing up with any particular ISP.

Browsing the Browsers

Now let's assume that you have Internet access and your connection is up and running smoothly. With some ISPs, you're now ready to get onto the World Wide Web. For instance, with America Online, you simply follow the onscreen instructions to connect to the Web: type a Web address into the proper text field and you're there. With some other ISPs, or at most businesses or educational institutions, you'll probably need to open up a program on your computer called a Web browser. Chances are your ISP will provide at least one browser with its software package.

Keep in mind that Web browser technology is changing all the time. Although your three-year-old browser might still work just fine, you might want to look into upgrading to a more recent version. One capability of recent browsers, the ability to display multiple windows known as frames on a single Web page is used on more and more sites. Having a browser able to display frames is a good idea.

Although there are many types of Web browsers, we'll limit our discussion here to two of the most popular: Netscape Navigator (the most recent version of which is called Communicator) and Microsoft Internet Explorer.

Wired Monk

Browser Wars

There continues to be immense competition for cybercommerce and cybertraffic. Which browser you choose might influence which site you choose as your Web home page, sometimes called your gateway. Dominating the gateways can spell big advertising bucks. The two largest rivals in recent years have been Netscape, which is now owned by America Online, and Microsoft. One benefit the competition has brought to the consumer is that Browser technology has been developing and improving rapidly. That trend is likely to continue in the near future.

Despite the competition between the companies that produce these browsers, the two browsers are in fact relatively similar, and they perform very similar tasks.

Netscape Navigator and Communicator

Netscape is a company that has been producing and circulating easy to use Web browsers for years. Free copies of the latest versions of this browser (version 4.61) can be downloaded onto your computer from the Netscape home page (go to **www.netscape.com**, then click the **Download** link at the top of the screen and choose the version that's right for your PC).

The Netscape browsers have a number of useful features. The main features you will use often as you explore the Web include the following:

➤ **The Location field**   This is a long text box near the top of the Netscape screen. It lists the Web address (URL) of the page you are currently viewing. You also can type an address directly into this field and hit **Enter** to jump to that location. (By the way, if terms like URL seem a bit confusing, don't worry; I'll define them later in the chapter.)

➤ **The Back button**   A large square button near the top-left of the Netscape toolbar, the Back button allows you to return to pages you've previously visited. Very useful for when you jump to a location that turns out to be different from what you wanted. You also can select **Back** from the **Go** menu at the top of the screen. This Go menu allows you to return quickly and easily to other pages you have visited previously (even several pages ago).

➤ **Bookmarks**   When you want to save the address of a site so that you can easily return to it at a later time, use the Bookmark function (click the word **Bookmark**, and then choose **Add Bookmark**, or press **Ctrl+D**) to add a virtual place marker on the site. When you want to return to that site, simply click **Bookmark** again, find the name of that page, and click it.

Each of these features is labeled on Figure 1.1, a picture of a Web page viewed with the Netscape browser.

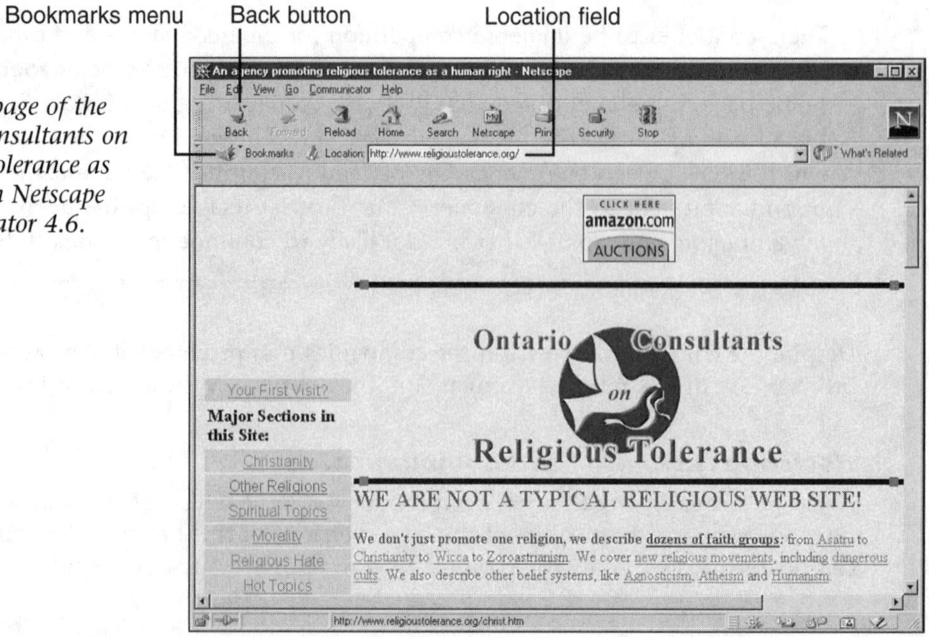

Bookmarks menu   Back button   Location field

Figure 1.1

The home page of the Ontario Consultants on Religious Tolerance as viewed with Netscape Communicator 4.6.

For a detailed explanation of all the features of the Netscape browser, go to the Netscape Help menu and skim through the Help Contents.

Microsoft Internet Explorer

Microsoft is the software giant whose programs are used on the vast majority of personal computers (does Microsoft Windows sound familiar?). In the latter half of the 1990s, Microsoft developed the Internet Explorer Web browser to rival Netscape's. Microsoft included the browser as a standard element of its newer versions of Windows. Despite the resulting antitrust lawsuits, the Internet Explorer browser has been very successful in gaining a vast portion of the browser market share. You can download the latest version of Internet Explorer (version 5) free from Microsoft at www.microsoft.com/windows/ie/.

Like Netscape Navigator, Microsoft's Internet Explorer is fairly easy to use. The following elements make up the basic tools you will use most frequently.

➤ **Address field**   Identical to Netscape's Location field, this text box displays the Internet address for the page you are viewing. As in Netscape, you can type an address into this field to jump directly to that location.

➤ **The Back button**   It works exactly the same as in Netscape. Click this button to return to the previous location you've visited. You can click the button called **History** to see on the left side of the browser window a list of sites previously visited. Click any one of these sites to return to that location.

➤ **Favorites**   These are identical to what Netscape calls Bookmarks. Add a site to your list of favorites to be able to return to that site later quickly and easily. Click the **Favorites** button to view your list of favorites and links; whenever you want, you can select from it a location to jump to. You can easily group a bunch of related favorite sites together in their own folder.

These features are labeled on Figure 1.2, a picture of the same Web page illustrated above but viewed with the Internet Explorer browser.

Not that different, huh? Didn't I say that the two browsers are very similar? You may be wondering where I stand on each of these two browsers, and what I recommend to those who want to surf the waves of pages about religion on the Web. I would be less than truthful if I didn't come right out and admit it: I like Netscape better. Netscape was around long before Internet Explorer, and there's something to be said for the benefit of experience. I'm also convinced that Netscape is a bit easier to use. And yes, the romantic in us is cheering for the tiny David company struggling against the giant Goliath company. But make up your own mind—you can make do with either.

The terminology and figures that you'll find throughout this book refer to features and images from Netscape browsers. But if you're not using Netscape, have no fear. Whatever browser or ISP you're using will probably look similar and will function in a similar fashion to the Netscape examples I use in this book.

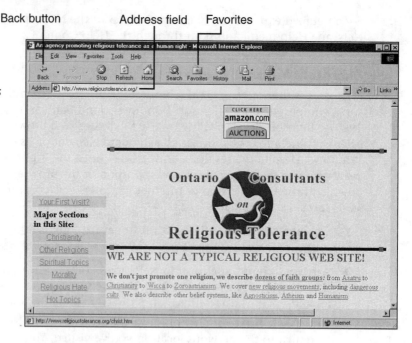

Figure 1.2

Once again the home page of the Ontario Consultants on Religious Tolerance, this time viewed with Microsoft Internet Explorer 5.

Basic Terminology and Techniques

Now that you are hooked up to the Web and equipped with the proper tools, it's time to discuss some Web basics that will make your Web adventure a more productive one.

Web Address = URL

Earlier I mentioned in passing that each Web page has an address, called a URL. URL is short for *Uniform Resource Locator*, and it's just another fancy way to say Web page address. Each page has its own unique URL that specifically describes its location. Enter that address in the **Location** (or Address) field of your browser, hit **Enter**, and with a bit of luck you will find yourself at the page you wanted. Didn't get there? Make sure that you typed the address *exactly* right. You usually even need to make sure that you capitalize the capital letters that happen to be in a URL, although thankfully most URLs are made up of lowercase letters. Always keep in mind that Web browsers are not very forgiving when you make a typo, so accuracy is important to your surfing happiness.

Now some of these URLs can get really long and complicated. For example, in a later chapter, I might suggest that you check out the Web page at the following address:

```
http://yahoo.com/Society_and_Culture/Religion_and_Spirituality/
Faiths_and_Practices/Afro_Caribbean_Religions/
```

Seeing such a long address might make you scream, "Do I have to type all that stuff? Type all of it in without a single typo? Give me a break!" It's enough to make you want to give up then and there, or at least move on to a more simple URL such as www.vodou.org. The good news is that you don't always have to type long URLs. You can often get there instead by a few button clicks. For instance in the previous long example you could get to the same page by first going to yahoo.com, and jumping to the desired page by first clicking **Society & Culture** (using your mouse or pointing device), then **Religion & Spirituality**, then **Faiths & Practices**, and finally clicking **Afro-Caribbean Religions**. Now wasn't that a bit easier? Such a shortcut will not always work, but it's often worth trying, especially if you hate to type.

Server and Pathnames

Most URLs in this book begin either with the prefix http:// or www. (or both: http://www.). What follows immediately after this prefix is called the *server name*; for example, yahoo.com or vodou.org. Now you don't need to memorize server names, but keep in mind that you might find it helpful to get used to recognizing some of the most common server names and their endings (.com is usually a commercial site, .edu often is related to an educational institution, .org is frequently used for non-profit organizations, and the list goes on and on).

The server name is sometimes followed by one or more of what are called *pathnames*, each pathname coming after a single slash (in our example, Society_and_Culture is a pathname, as are the other elements that follow it). Sometimes you can try leaving out a pathname or two from the end of a long address, and if you're lucky you could end up at another page associated with the same site.

Clicking around in this way illustrates the great advantage of the World Wide Web over a printed text such as a book. Web pages almost always contain text that is underlined, and this underlining is usually an important signal to all who visit that page. A signal for what? Glad you asked! Read on....

Hyperlinking Through Cyberspace

Underlined text on a Web page is usually a clue that the text represents what is called a *hyperlink*.

What's a Hyperlink?

A hyperlink is like a gateway to a new location: Click the hyperlink and it will jump you, almost like through hyperspace, to the Web site that the hyperlink connects to. Don't like your new location? Click the **Back** button and you will find yourself back where you were. By jumping around on hyperlinks, you can explore cyberspace without hardly having to type at all!

In addition to underlining, these hyperlinks are also often set apart by being a different color from other text on a Web page. Not only underlined text can be a hyperlink; a picture or menu item can be a hyperlink as well (sometimes indicated by a colored border).

With all the different appearances a link can take, how can you tell if something is a hyperlink? One sure-fire method is by moving around a Web page with your mouse or similar pointing device. When you move your cursor on top of a hyperlink, your cursor should change from an arrow to a hand with a pointing index finger. In addition, most browsers (including both Netscape Navigator and Microsoft Internet Explorer) will display at the bottom of their browser window the Web address (URL) that the hyperlink connects to, or some text describing the link. If you decide you want to go to that location, click the button and the hyperlink will take you there.

Or at least it will try to take you there. The unfortunate reality is that the Web changes every minute of every day, and sometimes hyperlinks (known commonly as *links* for short) try to jump you to a page that no longer exists on the Web. Chances are, the person who created that page in the first place has since deleted it. You might even find this to be the case—gasp—for some of the Web addresses that we list in this book! We have carefully checked out each URL up through the time that the book went to press, so we hope you don't find too many so-called *broken links*. But the Web changes every minute; constant flux is the rule. If you arrive at an address that is no longer valid, try not to get too discouraged. There are millions of pages out there, and if you keep trying you're bound to find what you're looking for.

In addition, even if the page you visit is no longer valid, pages sometimes leave a link as a forwarding address. Click the link and you travel to the page's new home. Some savvy Webmasters even arrange for their old page to transport you automatically to the new one.

Pulling Things Out of the Net: Downloading

Downloading means bringing files from a computer server down onto your own machine, so that you have a copy of the program or files on your computer's hard drive. Usually the process is straightforward, and instructions will be given at sites where downloading is available. To download a program, simply follow the instructions on the screen. Often, the most you will need to do is to select a location on your computer's hard drive where you would like the files to go. This process is identical to the one you use for saving any other file.

Pitfalls in Downloading

You might want to consider a few things before deciding to download every program you come across. First, depending on the size of the file you are downloading and the speed of your Internet connection, downloading can take a long time. Try to get an idea of how big the file is and how long the process will take. You can usually cancel in the middle of downloading if it's taking too long. Either that or go make yourself a snack.

Second, keep in mind that your hard drive has only a finite amount of storage space available, and some files take up a lot of room. Do you really need to download all 50 volumes of that Bible commentary? If you do, and if you run short of space on your hard drive, consider deleting the things that you no longer need.

Finally, be on guard against computer viruses. Viruses are little programs that attach themselves to other programs to cause mischief. Sometimes the mischief is relatively harmless, other times it can wipe out all the information on your computer. To protect yourself against computer viruses, be selective in what you download and from where, and use a virus scan program to check for viruses each time you download files. One of the most popular virus protection companies is McAfee; to see what they have available go to `www.mcafee.com/centers/clinic/`.

Plugging Into Plug-Ins

Now that you're familiar with URLs, hyperlinks, and downloading, you're fairly well equipped to begin exploring the vast world of online religion. Sooner or later, however, you'll come to a Web site that cheerfully informs you that you cannot enjoy the site to its full potential (if at all) without having certain programs attached to your Web browser. Do you want the music to play or the images to dance before your eyes? Then you might consider downloading the required helper programs and plugging them into your Web browser. Such programs are called *plug-ins*, and they come in many varieties.

Where's My Plug-In?

For a current description of many of the latest in plug-ins, visit the Browser Plugins page at http://home.netscape.com/plugins/. This site also allows you to download and plug in many of these plug-ins with the click of a button.

Most Web pages that make use of plug-ins will give you a message telling you when you need a certain plug-in to experience all they have to offer. Upon delivering such a message, many pages will give you the option to download whatever plug-in you need. This being the case, don't worry too much about downloading all these plug-ins now. Use the following list as an introduction to the most common plug-ins, and download what you need when you need it. Although we can't possibly list all the plug-ins you will encounter, the following are some of the most popular and useful.

World Wide Web Virtual Video

In recent years, Web pages have become more and more sophisticated, and one of the latest trends has been to include not only pretty, still pictures but also pictures with moving graphics on them. To be able to view those moving graphics, you will need to add one or more of the following plug-ins to your browser.

Shockwave and Flash Player

These useful plug-ins are by Macromedia. They allow you to view animated images on Web pages. Both plug-ins are available at the Macromedia Web site: www.macromedia.com/shockwave/download/.

QuickTime

This plug-in by Apple allows you to view video images and movies on the Web. Download a copy at http://apple.com/quicktime/download/.

Virtual Bells and Whistles

To hear the music and sound effects available on many Web sites, you'll need to have some plug-ins. In addition, a pair of speakers attached to your computer wouldn't hurt. While there are many audio plug-ins out there (see http://home.netscape.com/plugins/audio-video.html) RealAudio is one of the most popular.

RealAudio

This is a system developed by Progressive Networks to play music and sounds on the Web. You can download a free version, or pay for a more advanced edition with even more bells and whistles. Both are available at `http://home.netscape.com/plugins/get_real.html`.

WWW: What? We Worry?

All of this computer information might seem overwhelming. We have covered a lot in this chapter, and you don't need to master it all to be able to successfully explore religion on the Web. I have tried to present the most basic and helpful information you'll need to make your Web adventure a rewarding one, and I hope you have found this information clear.

Perhaps, however, you find yourself identifying with Groucho Marx in the movie *Duck Soup* when he said: "Clear? Huh! Why, a four-year-old child could understand this…. Run out and find me a four-year-old child. I can't make head or tail out of it." If you find the Web a bit bewildering, join the crowd. The irony is that some four-year-olds truly do know more about the Web than most adults!

Yet with a little practice you'll find that surfing the Web isn't so tricky after all. If and when you do get stuck, don't be afraid to ask for help from someone who is more experienced than you (no matter how old they are). While patience is sometimes required, you'll soon be amazed at the variety and detail of religion pages on the Web. Good luck, and happy surfing!

Rest and Remember

➤ You'll need to have access to certain supplies to use the Web, such as a computer. You might not have to buy a computer, however; you might be able to get access at your work, school, or public library.

➤ There are many different Internet service providers and Web browsers out there to help you get connected to the Web. Although they often have similar features, do a little investigating before you choose which one to use.

➤ Plug-ins are additional helper programs that are useful for hearing music and seeing animation on the Web. They let you realize the full potential of fancy Web pages.

Chapter 2

Your First Surfing on the Net

In This Chapter

➤ Search engines are *not* subject directories, and it is crucial to know how to use each to get what you want on religious topics and issues, options and activities

➤ Search engines give you a broad range of choices, only some of which can help you; a lot of them can waste your time, and even fizzle your brain, but a couple are really good

➤ Subject directories tend to have a narrower range. Sometimes they have a hidden agenda that can be detected if you know who put the directory together and why

---

Your best bet—and it is just that, a bet, so don't put too much on it—is to try a really good commercial search engine that covers the waterfront on a lot of themes, but also includes religion as one of those hot button themes. There is a lot to choose from. For instance you might go to *AltaVista* (www.altavista.com). Either search for a specific topic or use their subject index: find the category Religion and Belief under Society and Politics. Alternatively try *Lycos* (www.lycos.com) or *Yahoo!* (www.yahoo.com), both of which will be discussed in detail later in this chapter. All of these sites are huge, and they direct you from very general to more and more specific categories. Not a bad place to begin. But if you would like a little more guidance we would recommend that you start with a commercial site called *About.com*.

About.com

Here's how it works. Go to www.about.com, click the link to **society/culture**, and then you will see a side box of guide sites on the left. Second from the bottom it lists **religion/spirituality**. Click that, and let the fun begin!

Watch Out!

Religion/spirituality on About.com is right between two other sites. One is issues and causes. The other is sexuality. Either will find you trafficking in domains that have little to do with religion or spirituality, although if you happen to make a mistake, don't panic. You can almost always hit the Back button and return to where you were. Then you can click the *correct* button.

When you enter the religion/spirituality section of About.com, what you will see is a full page of menus, as seen in Figure 2.1.

Figure 2.1

This is a sample page of About.com's main page for religion/spirituality, but the featured guides change from day to day, as do many of the topics within the buttons you click. It is always good to bookmark what you find that is really helpful so that you can come right back to it at a later time.

You would think that a line up of 14 topics would give you everything you want, and on a platter. But it's not so simple. Some of these topics don't go very far. The one on Christian humor, for instance, leads to a lot of dead ends (no joke), while the one on Jehovah's Witnesses has a lot of jokes and cute stories.

One thing that makes About.com so nifty, however, is the information it gives on the major Christian groups. So, for example, you can click **Christianity-Protestantism**, and the guide for that subsection will take you through every topic. You will go from Advent, a key season in the Christian calendar, to War and Rumors of War, which deals with Christian perspectives on the UN sanctions hobbling Iraq. Or you can click **Christianity-General** and explore another hot overseas issue, Kosovo, under a section titled Kosovo List, or scroll all the way down to the biggest techie problem of our time, Y2K, and get a Christian perspective on that potential cyber saga of boom or bust.

Despite the benefits of About.com, there are also some down sides. I should let you know them even before you begin to surf and savor some of those sites for yourself. The first down side is the one that we can never escape, in virtual or real life, as turn-of-the-millennium Americans. We can't get around the fact that most of the religious traffic on the Web, like most American life, is shaped by Christian perspectives. The 14 major subtopics for About.com on religion/spirituality are all Christian, with two heavy-duty proselytizing denominations getting their own category: Mormons and, as we just saw, Jehovah's Witnesses. If you figure that Roman Catholics are over 60 million strong in the U.S., and that Mormons are maybe 6-7 million and Witnesses about the same, while Southern Baptists alone top 15 million, you begin to get the picture. But hey, those hip Buddhists don't even total a million on the ground in the U.S., at least not yet, but they still rate a whole category, right beside the Mormons and Witnesses. What's that mean? It means that neither the Web as a whole nor About.com in particular is about representing actual numbers of believers or would-be believers. It's about expectations and about projections, and both are very strong when it comes to Buddhists (see Chapter 28, "No Self, No God: Buddhists").

The second downside to note for About.com is the *.com* part. About.com is trying to become one of the heavy hitters who now rule the roost in Net company profit margins. It has a long way to go to catch the really big guys, like Yahoo!, which had 37 million visitors in June, or Lycos, which had a robust 30 million in the same month. By contrast, About.com allured but 7.2 million hits. It ranks twentieth on *Mediametrix*, the most respected commercial monitor of Net traffic, while Yahoo! ranks second, and Lycos ranks fourth (see http://www.mediametrix.com).

So About.com has to play catch up. It went public in March 1999, changing its name from the dull *Mining Co.* to the zippier About.com. It boasts 18 channels, of which society/culture is but one. It tries to outdo its competitors by making the Net personal. How? With guides. Yes guides, who are hired for their expertise in the field they traffic on the About.com site assigned to them. Not only do they post articles, they also answer FAQs.

What Is a FAQ?

Well, if you haven't been surfing the Net all your life, you might never have encountered a FAQ. But after you begin, the FAQs start flying. Yes, that *is* a pun, but it's still true. FAQs is shorthand for Frequently Asked Questions, and there's hardly a site worth its fiber weight that doesn't have FAQs.

Other Commercial Search Engines to Consider

Although you may have found everything—or just about everything—you think you needed to know about religions online from About.com, there is more to come. It comes in different packages, and with different accents, but it is still interesting, worthwhile, and maybe, just maybe it is that something extra you've been looking for on the Web.

Aphids.com

If you really enjoyed what you found in About.com, you might want to try an entirely different commercial search engine called *aphids.com*. After you're there, click **Religious Resources** on the Net, which is highlighted at the bottom of the home-page, or else just type the URL: `http://aphids.com/relres/` and you are there.

Aphids.com is even more heavily oriented to Christianity than is About.com. It is linked with special close ties to the Methodist Church. It has 4,002 listings in 177 categories, so be prepared for a lot of scrolling. It has very simple graphics. They seem almost like a cyber catalog in tone, so it is not a great eye-catching site. Nor is it that easy to get around, because it lists topics alphabetically from A-Z unless you elect to go through one of its major categories. The one that is named DIRECTORIES provides a convenient index to help you move to the subtopic that might really help you. It is a hands on way of discovering the warehouse of material you can get from the Web that relates to religion/spirituality in real life.

Lycos.com

If your interests are more cerebral, and you just haven't got everything you need or want from About.com, then you might try one other commercial search engine: *lycos.com*. Lycos is big time, as noted previously, so you would expect them to be thorough. They are, but they also lack guides, and their subdirectories are not as easy to traffic as About.com's. Still, suppose you wanted to see just how broad the spectrum of views about Catholicism on the Net is. If you go to `http://dir.lycos.com/Society/Religion/Faiths_and_Beliefs/Christianity/Denominations/` and click **Catholicism**, you will find many sites on all aspects and activities of the Roman Catholic faith. Also, you will find an awesome number of links for the Seventh Day Adventists. By contrast, the options for Mormons and Jehovah's Witnesses, which are so high in About.com, are much more modest in lycos.com.

Yahoo.com

Many people use yahoo.com as a general search engine. However, yahoo.com also offers lists of Web sites by categories, which can sometimes be a more useful way to find information quickly on a certain subject. While the presentation in yahoo.com is exclusively textual (don't expect pretty graphics), its outline approach to cataloging religion Web sites often can be quite useful for learning about religion on the Web. Check out its general list of different faiths and practices at `http://dir.yahoo.com/Society_and_Culture/Religion_and_Spirituality/Faiths_and_Practices/`. You'll probably be surprised how much is there.

Subject Directories

Subject directories are just that: grids of topics, with huge amounts of data, all related to one subject. The people who put together the directory want to get you to your destination as quickly as possible. Sometimes, though, they also want to make sure that you end up with an outlook close to their own.

Does that mean that subject directories are subtle ways of hooking you into one religious tradition or worldview and luring you away from another? Not exactly. They are more like an enormous maze of possibilities that offer you the best ones as the right ones. You can obviously disagree with, or leave aside, what you don't like, but you might be happier from the outset knowing what they aim to do.

The best subject directories on religion tell you right up front: "Hey, here is my take. This is what I think is important. This is why I put together the directory!"

Got the picture? This is *not* a commercial ploy. It is different from sites like about.com or aphids.com, which get you the message about religious resources or options in order to get your business. These sites are more genuinely interested in telling you why religion is important, and why thinking about it the right way is even more important. Most of the folks who put together subject directories make no money from their venture. Some of them even lose money, like the top subject directory on the entire Net (at least as of September 1999), OCRT.

Ontario Consultants on Religious Tolerance (OCRT)

Yes, you have to go north of the border, to Canada, to get the very best that the World Wide Web can offer on religious opportunities in cyberspace. Surf on over to OCRT at `www.religioustolerance.org` and see all that they have to offer.

Who are these folk? They are a group of four volunteers: two Unitarian Universalists (one agnostic and one atheist), one Wiccan, and one liberal but unaffiliated Christian. Three are female; one is male. They are mid-life heterosexual professionals, the oldest a retired electronics engineer, the youngest an unemployed waitress. The other two are a registered nurse and an urban planner. All do religion on the side because they live near Toronto with its tremendous libraries and educational facilities. What unites them? The desire to protect religious freedom, and to reduce religious hatred, misinformation, and discrimination. They have no underground, no secret agenda.

www.religioustolerance.org

There are only four consultants at this site, and they're all amateurs, but they do a professional job of putting together a user-friendly site with tremendous variety and depth on almost every aspect of contemporary religious life. The scary and the sacred, the small and the big, all get equal billing. Almost too fair? Maybe so, but it's a nice change from some of the aggressively self-boosting sites you find, even on a topic like religion.

How do we know so much about them? Because they tell us so on their splendidly crafted Web site. They also tell us that from their startup in spring 1995 till now, the site has continually grown. As of summer 1999 they have put together 860 essays and menus, and they get about 5.5 million hits per month.

They ought to be in the clover, right? Wrong. These gals and guy are losing money big time. They barely keep afloat through corporate sponsors and personal donations. Don't be put off by their poverty. This Web site repays your effort in spades. We give OCRT a lot of play in the pages that follow.

The one introductory step you might take is to click **Other Religions** in the sidebar to the left of the home page, which announces Major Sections in This Site. It has 18 colorful logos for specific religious traditions, including Christianity (ancient) and Christianity (modern). All you have to do is click one of those logos and you are off into the in-depth exploration—at once passionate and fair—of a major faith tradition. These gals and guy deserve their 5.5 million hits a month. They also deserve a more secure financial footing than has so far been possible.

Rutgers: Virtual Religion Index

You might be impressed with the flair and depth of OCRT but still want to find some site that gives you the academic scoop on religion. Then, you'll want to travel to New Jersey, or at least to the site that is maintained there at Rutgers University. You'll find it at `http://religion.rutgers.edu/links/vrindex.html`. It gives an up-to-date *Virtual Religion Index*, with frequent annotation, at once accurate and helpful.

And what is the *Virtual Religion Index*? It is as varied an effort as you will find to mark all aspects of the current religious scene, and it also gives you links to other sites. For instance, aphids.com, which we noted previously as a top religion search engine, is introduced here as the Mother of all searchable religion Web site directories. Unfortunately, that description was written back in March 1998, and that is one of the drawbacks to the *Virtual Religion Index*: it does not always give the most current information or evaluation of the fast changing religious scene in cyberspace.

Other University-Based Subject Directories

There are a number of other universities that maintain subject directories on religious topics. One of the most comprehensive of these directories, and one that also includes ratings of other sites, is maintained by Gene Thursby at the University of Florida, Gainesville. You might want to check it out at: `www.clas.ufl.edu/users/gthursby/rel/guides.htm`.

Or, if you prefer to get a West coast take on the vast array of religious sites, you can go visit the fine site of University of San Diego maintained by Doug Stewart at `http://www.acusd.edu/theo/ref-gen.html`. There is also a site with lots of bells and whistles but not as much substance further up the West coast at the University of Washington in Seattle. It is maintained by Mike Madin. The address for this site is `www.academicinfo.net/religindex.html`.

Finding God in Cyberspace: John Gresham's Site

Perhaps you feel that there's got to be more to see about religious life and possibilities of the spirit from overseas. Perhaps, for instance, you'd like to get a British perspective. Then you might check out John Gresham's site at `http://users.ox.ac.uk/~mikef/durham/gresham.html`. You'll find that it has a clutter-filled homepage, with links that are not easy to figure out. Its content on many Asian religions is little more than a link to information in a project called the *Virtual Religion Library* (`http://vlib.org/Religion.html`).

Interfaith Web Sites

Now that you've heard a lot about the *Virtual Religion Index* (not to be confused with the *Virtual Religion Library*), you might want to go to a site that gives you the whole nine yards—or, more accurately, the whole nine shelves—on religious resources available on the World Wide Web. A lot of this information comes up under the search engines and subject directories that we've already discussed. But if you want to go back to the sources for interfaith exploration, you'll want to visit a site maintained by a Bahai loyalist that is also the Mother of all interfaith Web sites, Facets of Religion.

Facets of Religion

`bounty.bcca.org/~cvoogt/Religion`

Maintained by Casper Voogt, a 21-year-old Dutch student of architecture at Georgia Tech, this site is housed under the Bahai Computer and Communication Association (BCCA). Its larger purpose is to introduce visitors to the structural delights and creedal truths of the Bahai tradition (see Chapter 27, "God's Many Prophets: Bahais").

But it also does much more. It has a list of five general sites on the top sidebar of its home page. They are: General, Interfaith, Cult Studies, Usenet, and email, as well as related sites. Most are useful. The interfaith sites, for instance, include those that accent pluralism such as the *Pluralism Project at Harvard University* (`www.fas.harvard.edu/~pluralsm`) and others that promote religious freedom, such as `www.religious-freedom.org`.

Guess who sponsors `religious-freedom.org`? It is sponsored by the First Church of Christ, Scientist (otherwise known as Christian Science; see Chapter 18, "Beyond Protestantism"). But why does this small Northeastern offshoot of nineteenth century American Protestantism, the Christian Scientists, merit a button on the *Facets of Religion* page as one of the 12 major world religions?

You might think it's no big deal to put one small denomination up there as equivalent to religions like Islam, Judaism and, yes, Christianity that have many divisions or denominations. Right, it's not a big deal...except that it indicates the way in which organizing data or putting something up front on the screen can subtly shift the way you think about small, breakaway groups becoming independent religions. That, of course, is what happened to the Bahais also, and it also happened to them in the second half of the nineteenth century, the same time as Christian Science came into existence. So by giving extra value to Christian Science as a group in its organizational scheme, this Web site also implies that other small groups should be viewed in a similar way. In short, how information is presented on the screen influences the way in which it is understood or valued by those who see it. This case is an example of what we will be calling *screen bias*.

There is nothing wrong with making choices. We all make choices. But when our choices are projected on the Net they can and do reflect a screen bias. Screen bias is a two way street. Someone chooses information or groups of information deemed important, and we often accept their choice at face value when we go to their site.

If screen bias is present in the listing religious groups, it is even more present in the numbers claimed by and for these groups. You might not have thought that much about numbers before, but if you want to get into it, go to the next section. It will change forever the way you read all those mind-numbing statistics about how big—or how small—a religious group is said to be.

Adherents.com

www.adherents.com

Adherents.com is a mind-numbing site found on the outer strands of the Web. It's a maze of statistics. It's certainly not for everybody, but it can sure help you get beyond the statistical nightmare lurking under the label *religion.*

Neither a search engine nor a subject directory, adherents.com is a summary survey. Preston Hunter, a computer science programmer at the University of Texas (Austin), has put together an impressive spreadsheet with statistics about *lots* of religions, churches, and belief systems.

Adherents.com provides over 33,000 adherent statistics and religious geography citations. It refers to published membership/adherent statistics and congregation statistics for over 3,000 religions, churches, denominations, religious bodies, faith groups, tribes, movements, and ultimate concerns.

What Are the Sources for Adherents.com?

The main sources for the statistics at adherents.com are the following:

➤ Organizational reporting, or what groups say their numbers are.

➤ Census records, and the last U.S. census that asked about religious preference was taken in 1936!

➤ Polls and surveys, which need to have extensive and consistent sample bases to be reliable; few are.

➤ Indirect data, which is data calculated by combining information from several different sources, like guessing that most Polish Americans are Roman Catholics just because they are Polish.

➤ Field work, which means going to some place and asking folk directly: What is your religious affiliation?

Would you believe that almost all reports on the number of religious adherents to a group come from the group itself? That means that most reports are guestimates, and the more evangelical the group the more likely it is to give high end, or even wildly inflated, numbers, at the same time that the more circumspect and traditional groups tend to make a low end, and sometimes a ridiculously undercounted estimate of their membership. Pentecostal Christians are over the top in the numbers parade. They might be three to four times greater in projections than in ground-level believers, while Unitarian Universalists tend to go the other way: Three times as many people claim to be Unitarian Universalists in the United States than are actually on church records! (Click `www.adherents.com/adhFAQ.html`, about half-way down the page under the query "Where do adherent statistics come from?")

The bottom line is to ignore statistics if you just want to get a spiritual home or a like-minded friend or a good song or a great course of study. All those are available in this book, but there is also a thirst in some of us to get it right. When we say that there are 40 million Baptists, we want to know that there are 40 million and not 100 million as is listed by Preston Hunter under the letter B. Check out `http://www.adherents.com/index_adherents_all.html#Letter_B` and you will see why *screen bias* is not just something that happens to those who create subject directories or search engines. Adherents.com is only as good as its sources, and 40 million Baptists (not 100 million) is much closer to the majority of sources, even though that number too is a conjecture not a firm figure.

The difficulty of screen bias is compounded when you get other sites that want to impress by giving statistics, and they cite the largest figure to be found from adherents.com as though it is factual, when it is not. These are conjectures or projections, not facts you can rely on.

Statistics from FECHA

`http://www.webstationone.com/fecha/religion.htm`

Ever heard of the First Electronic Church of America or FECHA? At its site, FECHA offers a summary of world religions. For its beneficial features, see Chapter 20. However, be forewarned that some of the statistics it gives can be quite misleading.

Funny Figures from FECHA

FECHA shies away from giving a gross figure for Baptists, listing them as a mere (!) 31 million, but it has less hesitation about Jews and Judaism. It gives the figure of 18 million followers of Judaism in the U.S. alone! Many Jewish groups would be astonished to hear such a figure. If they—or anyone else—wanted to find the source, all they would have to do is surf to adherents.com, and then click the letter **J** in the alphabetical index on the home page. Guess what you find? In the entire world there might be as many as 18 million Jews, but the more probable figure is 14 million (see Chapter 21, "God is g–d: Judaism"). The total number in all North America, including the U.S., is between six and seven million! FECHA got its inflated number by a simple screen bias error: Its creator probably clicked the world total from adherents.com, or some other source that used adherents.com, and entered it for the U.S. A conjecture? Yes. A fact? No.

If that sounds bad—and it is!—in this same essay the poor Anglican Communion is reduced to the Anglican Orthodox Church in the U.S., where its total is 6,000 (again from adherents.com) when in fact, the total for the Anglican Communion world-wide is probably 50 million (see Chapter 15)!

Rest and Remember

➤ Search engines and subject directories are terrific tools for finding out much, much more about religion than you can get from libraries, books, or even print media (see the next chapter).

➤ You would do well to start with just one search engine and one subject directory. They would be About.com (www.about.com) and OCRT or Ontario Consultants on Religious Tolerance (www.religioustolerance.org, who might run out of money but never out of ideas).

➤ The numbers game is as tricky on religion as it is in the stock market. You have to know where to invest your trust, and the sad truth is that most numbers just don't add up, especially those that make claims based on self-interested conjectures or misreadings of other sources.

Chapter 3

God.com

In This Chapter

➤ Why cyberspace is changing the way we think, plan, act...and believe

➤ How print media is trying to catch up, but doesn't quite stay abreast, of Netaphysics

➤ Where we go in this book toward having old-time religion in new forms

---

We are only now beginning to see how the Net is more than just a new phase of media development. It opens up ways that we think and feel and, yes, believe differently than we did a mere five years ago. How does the old connect to the new? That is what I will explore in this chapter.

The Continuing Appeal of Print Journalism

The time was December 1996. Most folk were thinking of Christmas—at least in the United States, where almost 9 out of every 10 people identify themselves as Christian, and in Japan, where there are fewer Christians, but Christmas is still a big commercial holiday.

So it's no big surprise to find an issue of *Time* magazine with the title God.com on the cover. After all, the year was 1996, a year when the impact of the Net/Internet and cyberspace communication was just beginning to be felt in its broad, seemingly global impact.

How Many Christians Are There in America?

No one really knows how many Christians there are in America, but a good place to start is with adults. Let's say that there were about 170–175 million adults in 1990 (out of a total population of 250 million). So how do these figures affect religion? One respected source gives 151 million as the number of adult Americans who believed in some form of Christianity back in 1990 (see `http://www.adherents.com/rel_USA.html`). The gross totals might go up, but the percentages will likely stay the same. What does that come to? About 87% of all adult Americans will consider themselves to be Christian.

The cover of *Time* actually mirrored a new dawn breaking. Under it was the simple but elegant God.com with an arrow pointing at the G, which was highlighted in Gothic floral relief, its yellow and purple hues offsetting the stark black of the letter G. You can see the cover as it appears on a Duke University Web site in Figure 3.1.

Figure 3.1

This Time *feature story is about Religion on the Internet. Will the Internet change the way Christians and others think about Christmas?*

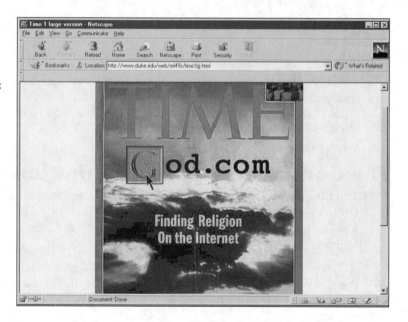

"Finding Religion on the Internet" is not only the subtitle, it is the focus of this *Time* feature essay in December 1996. That is what this book is all about, too: finding sources for religion in cyberspace, finding what you want—and maybe what you didn't know you wanted—by exploring the Net, by learning to surf the World Wide Web.

And so when push comes to shove, what's the real difference between the first and second information age? According to *Time*, and most other popular sources, the first Information Age was sparked by a religious document, the Gutenberg Bible of 1456. If that is so, then why should not the second Information Age be marked by a religious instrument, in this case, one that expands beyond any print or institutional boundaries, it is available to all who can find it. It is *Net* religion, the transformation made possible by the instrument which, five years ago, most folks didn't use, and no one, not even techies, knew would become as powerful as it now is.

Two Information Ages?

It might sound like an overload of data. Why do we need so much information? People were asking that question, too, back in the fifteenth century. It seemed as though the world changed just as people were getting over the Crusades, the plague, and some very nasty European wars, but you can't predict, or control, technological change. Sometimes it is small, like the zipper or can opener. Sometimes it is big, like electricity or the telephone. And sometimes it is huge, like the first *Information Age*, which started with the printing press, and now the second *Information Age*, which is marked by the World Wide Web. Don't be overwhelmed, but also, don't be too laid back. This is a turning point for the world as a whole, and you ought to get with it, rather than staying outside or resisting it. Go slow, especially with ideas about God, the universe, and human destiny, but keep going.

What's so different about the Net? Well, for one thing, it is truly interactive, as you'll see in Chapter 8, "Matchmakers," when I show you how to use the Net for meeting other like-minded folks, or maybe even a prospective mate, who shares your religious/spiritual outlook. Socializing through the Net was unimaginable five years ago; five years from now it will be commonplace.

Even just signing on to the Internet can be a transformative act for many folks. Sure, there is the fiber-optic cable that makes it all possible as a technical instrument and personal opportunity. Then there is the global tapestry of personal computers that tie together so many people from so many different places and cultural backgrounds. But there is also something more: the vast cathedral—or mosque or temple—of the mind.

The Net might be a virtual rather than a bricks-and-mortar place, but it is still a place where ideas about God and religion can resonate. It provides a space where faith can be shaped by individuals, and where groups can achieve a renewed sense of collective hope.

Okay, so you might not change the world, at least right away, but by logging on to your computer and surfing the Net you can discover a myriad of faith communities, which are also action nodes that will broaden your horizon and change your world. That is what used to be called *conversion*, and even if you are not prepared to make that step, this book can help you see how glimpses of many others at work on their life path and faith journey will make your own easier, lighter, and more exciting.

In its December 1996 issue, *Time* did a masterful job of surveying the history of communicating religious truths and spiritual quests via the media of the past and the media of the present. What Gutenberg was to the Reformation, the Net will be to what might be called *netaphysicians*, people charting their own way through the galaxies of divine-human interaction. It is not just for baby boomers or Generation Xers, but it is these two groups in particular—the over 35 but under 55 gang, and the 22-33 crowd—who will be using the Net to explore their own personal quest for spiritual connection.

Who Cares About Generations?

It is never easy to classify whole groups of people by their age, and you should always be suspicious when anyone uses phrases like Boomers and Xers. But on the other hand, you've got to account for taste and changes in taste. What is likely is that folks over 55 (especially over 60!) will find it harder to use the PC for as many different potentials as are now becoming available. Though they might not groove to a book like this with the same ease as Boomers, they will still benefit from using it, don't you think? As for the Xers, they will use it, but in different ways than the Boomers. They will see the opportunities for matchmaking and downloading as their first stops, but read less, and probably do less, about cyber courses on religious topics. And what about the Generation Yers, those under 22 (sometimes called Generation Next)? Hey, they're still trying to get through school, get their first car, their first job, or their first apartment, but shouldn't they also find time to explore cyberfaith?

The Cyber Sequel: *Time* Goes from Print to the Net

After *Time* editors saw the response to their December 1996 issue they realized that it was time (no pun intended!) to go to the next level. Where else but to cyberspace itself with the God.com story? God.com is the Web site pictured in Figure 3.2.

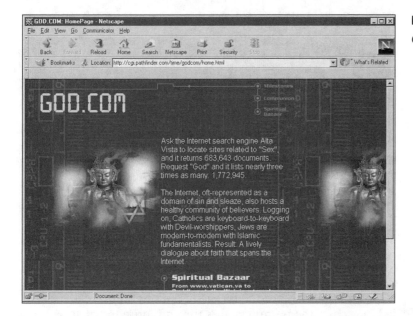

Figure 3.2

God.com on the Net.

It is a powerful tribute to the power of the World Wide Web that *Time* constructed this site to get its story across. It seems sleazy at first to compare the appeal of religion to the appeal of sex, as does God.com, but the two are often conjoined in the popular imagination. Both provide outlets, highs, connections, and both trade on the element of what is hidden, or little known, and always tantalizing! But wait a minute: there is more than a bit of hype here. Devout Catholics might be keyboard-to-keyboard with Devil worshippers, but is either likely to engage the other, except with a dismissive click to another site if they don't like what they see? And are observant Jews really modem-to-modem with observant Muslims? Are we going to see peace break out in the Middle East due to cybernaut gymnastics, netizens hurdling beyond ideologies toward the dawn of a lasting Christian-Jewish-Muslim lovefest? Don't hold your breath, or log on to that millennial dream, at least without a moment of hesitation or deeper reflection.

Still, the *Time* cyber site does do something that is consonant with the print media article: it points in the direction of a spiritual bazaar and a common table. The bazaar takes you into everyone's favorite set of Web sites that put a bright face on their religious tradition. Many of them we will explore in later chapters. Others are not so winsome, but still worth a brief click and fast look. It is a true smorgasbord or spiritual bazaar, where you can sample as little or as much as you want.

37

The common table, however, poses some thorny problems. As can be seen in Figure 3.3, the table sidebars six topics.

Figure 3.3

This portion of the God.com Web site invites discussion among the major religious communities, but will it succeed?

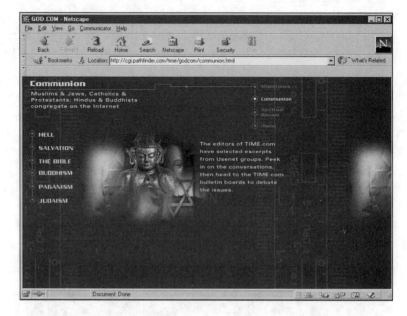

The problem with this option is the gap, the gap between what it promises and what it delivers. It is a huge gap. These six groups might find some basis for ongoing discussion, and they have tried in the past, but the meager amount of download, or threads, that is provided in each of the buttons makes the enterprise trivial at best, risky at worst. I mean: there are no Hindu voices in any of the excerpts, nor are there any Roman Catholic accents; Christianity appears as an intramural Protestant affair. Worse still, the link to other chat groups that foster a fuller, deeper discussion has lapsed since the Web page was constructed. Nowhere to go if you like the tease but want the full show, or at least a better show, of interfaith dialog. For an example of the possibilities of a different type of dialog, see the First Church of Cyberspace (www.godweb.org/library.html) discussed in Chapter 19, "The Orthodox Story."

> **Rest and Remember**

➤ Print and cyber media are both drawn to the power, the resilience, and the confusion of religious identities.

➤ *Time* offered a major feature story on the role of religion, and it shows how religion is being transformed through the Net at the end of the Second Christian millennium.

➤ Yet even *Time* can not offer the full range of options to expand your religious horizons that await you just ahead in this book.

Part 2

Getting Started

Now you know something about the Net, and you know that God.com is not a joke but just the first wave of a whole new way of trying to talk about religion. You can use Web sites, you can surf the Net, you can glide through cyberspace, and still be a believer! In fact, you might find ways to be a different, more effective believer in this part.

Much of what you might want is free, and you can find out how to get it in this part of The Complete Idiot's Guide to Religions Online. *You might even be in the mood for a course, something informative but not too heavy or exacting. You'll find lots of course information in the pages ahead, and if you're really eager to go back to school, there are even some sites that will help you ease toward that next stage of education, and also the satisfaction it brings.*

Chapter 4

On the Road and Ready to Go

In This Chapter

➤ Just because you're not at home doesn't mean your religious life has to suffer—you can find spiritual resources online

➤ Virtually anything you could want to find in print can be found on the Internet, and often for free!

➤ Internet resources for the traveling religious aren't limited to Christianity. Muslim and Jewish, Buddhist, Hindu, and Sikh, as well as other religious groups, also have resources on the Web for the traveler

When you're on a road trip, business trip, or vacation, keeping your religious life alive while on the road is not always easy. And goodness knows it's often when you're away from home that you need some religious guidance the most! Thankfully, the Internet has made this a whole lot easier, especially for Christians. Whether you're looking for scripture, sermons, or inspiration, you can find it anytime, as long as you have Internet access. And if you know that you won't have access while out of town, print out what you'll need and you're ready to go!

Multi-Resource Sites for the Multi-Needs Traveler

First, if you're looking for Christian resources in general or don't really know quite what you're looking for, there are a few sites out there that have links to just about whatever you want. Here are some of the best.

Serve Him: www.servehim.com

Wow! Talk about Christian resources at your fingertips! As the site suggests, this is a great start page for the Christian Internet surfer. Though it's low on graphics and simple in format, the simple format makes it simple to use. It is essentially a collection of links to the best Christian resources out there and the links are divided into helpful and clear categories. Find everything from online Bibles and Churches in your area to Christian magazines and radio broadcasts. All that a Christian could need off the Internet, at home or on the road, can be found here.

Goshen

www.goshen.net

The main feature of this site is a Web directory and search engine of Christian resource sites. It also provides a companion search engine for the Bible. In addition to these helpful features, there are a few other auxiliary features that are interesting as well. Here you can listen to a current news summary via RealAudio or send a greeting card to someone you're missing while on the road.

Christianity Online

www.christianity.net

In many ways, Christianity Online (shown in Figure 4.1) is similar to Servehim.com, though a bit flashier. They also have a little more of their own features and commentary which, though interesting, makes your search for information a little more cluttered. Nevertheless, there are great resources here as well. The menu offers links to everything from Books and Software to Fun and Games. You also can check out the Christianity Online Store or find advice on religious issues or even dating! Check out these resources and more at www.christianity.net.

Cybergrace

www.cybergrace.com

Here is yet another general resource page that can help the Christian on the road. Some of the most useful resources here for the Christian traveler are the Online Bible Study Tools and the radio broadcasts. Their cyber cards are also a fun way to stay in touch.

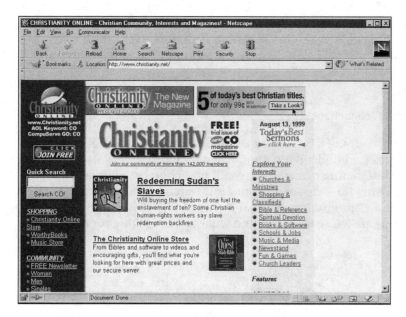

Figure 4.1
Christianity Online goes all out in providing resources for Christians at home and on the road.

Best of the Christian Web

www.botcw.com

Still can't find what you want? For some more suggestions, check out Best of the Christian Web. This site ranks various Christian sites and gives good descriptions of what they have to offer. You can't go wrong with the choices here!

Peter's Voice

www.petersvoice.org

For the Catholic traveler who hasn't found their niche in these largely Protestant sites, this one's for you. At Peter's Voice, you'll find Catholic radio online, loads of writings from the past and the present, and various audio files with discussions of current events and faith issues.

General resource pages are really the way to go for the Christian traveler. Just a warning: the Protestant sites claim to be nondenominational, but they tend to be more conservative and evangelical.

Church Locators

So, you're going to be in a strange town over the weekend and don't want to miss church on Sunday? You don't have anyone you can ask for a recommendation and don't have the time to drive around the town hoping to run into a church of your denomination. Just as many individual churches have their own Web sites, they also have listings on some of the bigger, and easier to find, national Web pages.

Church locators and directories can be found on a variety of Web sites and just as long as you're not looking for a very obscure denomination in a very small town, you'll probably find what you're looking for. Here are a couple good places to start.

Church Locator

www3.christianity.net/churchlocator/

This site is yet another service of Christianity Online. Using a great search engine that lets you search by keyword (denomination, name, or location) or just look at listings by city or state. By searching by keyword, you'll find churches with actual Web pages. If you're just looking for a church in your area, search by location and you'll find both Protestant and Catholic churches that are wired along with those who haven't yet made that leap. You're bound to find what you're looking for here, quickly and easily.

Food for Thought

Finding a Church

Who knows how many thousands or millions of churches there are out there? How in the world are you going to find a church of a specific denomination in a specific town? While general Church Locators that cover all of Christianity are helpful, they might not have what you want. Your best bet is to go straight to the home page of your denomination (see Chapters 13-19). Most of these official sites offer a directory of affiliated churches. That way you'll know what you're getting and be sure you get it!

Christian Resources

www.webcom.com/~nlnnet/xiancus1.html

A little more homemade looking than the snazzy Christianity Online Church Locator, this site looks only at those churches with Web pages. Its listings are relatively large though not complete by any stretch of the imagination. However, one interesting feature is the links to Christian Churches in foreign countries.

Sermons, Bibles, and Literature

If you don't think you'll make it to a service, or if you need some guidance and inspiration between services, several sites have been created for the sole purpose of providing organized and comprehensive resources for the inquiring Christian mind.

Biblical Text and Criticism

Don't have room in your suitcase for your Bible? If you are looking for the actual text of the Bible, here are some sites to try.

The Christian Pulpit

`www.talkingbible.com/`

Want to listen to the Bible as well as read it? The Christian Pulpit includes a feature called the RealAudio Bible, which can be accessed if you have the RealAudio plug-in (see Chapter 1, "Before You Get Started"). You can listen to or read the chapter or verse of your choice.

The World Wide Study Bible

`ccel.wheaton.edu/wwsb/`

This site, shown in Figure 4.2, is a service of Wheaton College, a source of many great online resources. This site in particular provides the text of the Bible itself as well as commentary, literature, and sermons for each chapter and verse.

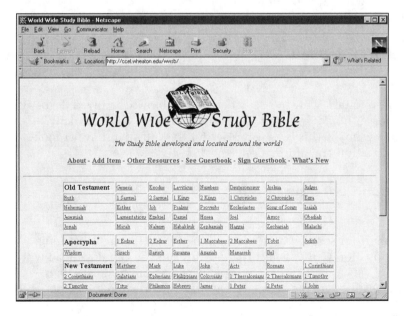

Figure 4.2

Easy to navigate and full of information, the World Wide Study Bible provides text and commentary on every chapter and verse in the Bible.

Audio Bible Online

www.audio-bible.com/Bible/Bible.html

A service of Goshen, this site lets you search for a particular chapter or verse and listen to it with RealAudio (which can be downloaded from this site). Keep in mind, though, that the version of the Bible used at this site is the King James Version.

Sermon Central

www.sermoncentral.com

While Sermon Central does not actually provide the text of the Bible, it has many related features. It includes the text of sermons on particular chapters or verses from a variety of ministers from a variety of denominations.

Official Writings and Daily Readings

If you're looking for more general Christian writings, devotionals, and works of patriarchs of the past, there are a few sites for that purpose as well.

The Ethereal Library

ccel.wheaton.edu

The Ethereal Library, again from Wheaton College, is the place to go to find any sort of Christian writings. Whether you want to read some of St. Augustine's Confessions or more recent Christian writings, you can find them here. They're all free to download and good reading material for that long plane ride!

Christian Fellowship Devotional

www.cfdevotionals.org

This site is all about devotionals. View the daily devotional, browse archived devotionals by topic, date, or author, or even get a free subscription to have the daily devotional sent to you by email! This is a great place for the Christian traveler looking for a little daily inspiration and affirmation.

Catholic Information Center on Internet

www.catholic.net

Are you a Catholic looking for some written material to get you through that long trip? The Catholic Information Center is just that. At this site you can download written statements from the Vatican, articles from Catholic periodicals to devotionals. Some other interesting features are the movie review section and church locator.

These sites are only a sampling of the Christian resources available on the Net. If you don't find what you want here, take a look at some of the more general sites and they will more than likely point you in the right direction. The road away from home might be lonely, but the Internet certainly makes things easier! You might not be able to be at home but you can find some of the comforts of home over the Internet. So, leave that space in your suitcase for something else and bon voyage!

Jews Looking for Synagogues, Torah Translations, or Other Resources

Christians aren't the only ones who travel or who need religious inspiration and guidance while out of town. Though the resources for the Jewish community aren't quite as extensive, they are out there! Here are some of the more useful and interesting.

Making Travel a Little Easier

Do Jews travel more than other religious folk? I don't know about that, but unlike other religious communities the Jewish community seems to offer a lot of resources specifically for the traveler. Check out these sites and you'll find information to make your trip easier and more compatible with your beliefs and customs. For more information on the religion of Judaism and Jewish Resources on the Net, check out Chapter 21, "God Is G-d: Judaism."

Jewish Travel: Your World Wide Guide

www.jewishtravel.com

This site is worth visiting before you make a big trip. It features articles on a variety of cities and has links to helpful sites on finding kosher restaurants and Jewish communities world wide. Much of the information is available via links to other sites. Nevertheless, this is a helpful collection of articles and links related to the concerns of the Jewish traveler.

Shamash's Kosher Restaurant Database

One of the biggest problems with leaving home is finding Kosher foods, especially when eating out is the only option. This site will help make that a little easier. Select from a long list of metropolitan areas throughout the world and narrow your search with the type of food you're interested in and you'll find quite a few matches! The search results list not only the name and location of the restaurant but a description of the cuisine offered and a price range, if available. This site is a must for any Jewish traveler! You can find it at shamash.org/kosher/.

Jewish Travel Network

www.jewish-travel-net.com

Do you travel a lot but are tired of staying places that don't click with your religious practices? Would you like to stay with like-minded people with whom you can share your customs while on the road? Would you want to host a Jewish traveler yourself? The Jewish Travel Network is a group that facilitates such exchanges world wide. You can register yourself as a host for free or look for a host in the town to which you are visiting for an annual fee of $24.95. The hosts themselves might charge a small gratuity but the cost is comparable or even much less than a hotel stay. Though many are reluctant to pay at all for Internet resources, the comfort of staying in a home-like environment might be well worth it!

Finding a Synagogue

www.jewishtravel.com/travelinks/shuls.html

Just as there are church locators on the Net, there are also synagogue locators. This site is more a place to start than an answer. Here you'll find links to sites with listings of synagogues throughout the country, organized by type of Judaism. Some sites are stronger in some regions than others but, through a little trial and error, you should be able to find what you're searching for.

Finding Texts, Literature, and Inspiration

If you want inspiration or encouragement from Jewish scripture and writings, here are a few sites that'll keep you from lugging around those heavy books.

Navigating the Bible

www.bible.ort.org

Like the Christian Bible Study sites, this is a site where the religious traveler can find inspiration. Here you can read the text of the Hebrew Bible while reading interpretations and essays on the different sections if you want. This is the site to visit if the actual text of the Bible is what you are looking for.

Jewish Torah Audio

www.613.org

This site claims to be "the first world wide Jewish audio since Mt. Sinai." And it does provide a lot of teaching and some noise as well! This is a pretty full resource page for anyone interested in getting a little Jewish education over the Internet. You can take RealAudio classes or simply listen to different texts over RealAudio. There is also an online book and other similar features. After you have RealAudio, you're ready to go!

Torah Fax in Cyberspace

www.netaxis.qc.ca/torahfax

This project was begun by using fax machines. Now it uses email! This service is made for the traveling business person or anybody on the go. Join for free and you'll receive daily emails with passages from the Torah and accompanying lessons. This is a great way to stay spiritual, even when on the road.

Muslims Looking for Mosques, Qur'an Translations, and So On

Are you a Muslim traveler? The following are some of the best resources for you while on the road. For more information on Islam and Islamic Resources on the Web, see Chapter 22, "There Is No god but God: Islam."

Religious Texts Online

In the following sites you'll find not only the Qur'an but also other Islamic religious texts and writings.

Al-Qur'an

www.islam-quran.org/frame.htm

Whether you are more comfortable with Arabic or English, reading or hearing, you can find the text of the Qur'an here. Choose a particular chapter in either Arabic or English, and then keep clicking if you want to hear the text you're viewing. It might take a little time to download but it's well worth the wait!

Voice of Islam

www.islam.org/voi/

As the site advertises, here you can find English lectures, Friday sermons, and current news in RealAudio format. Download the software from this site, if necessary, and you're ready to go! You can find more traditional stuff like holy texts, or more popular, modern stuff like lectures and current events. This site has a lot to offer for those who have ears to hear!

Finding Mosques and Other Muslim Resources

Looking for a mosque or other Muslim organization or business in a particular area? These sites are for you.

Islamic Finder

If you're travelling and want to find a mosque in the town you're visiting, you can do no better than this site. While it is currently limited to the United States, it is comprehensive! You can search either by zip code or by state. What comes up is all the mosques and places of worship in that area, complete with address, times of worship, and a phone number, if available. If you have any questions about how to use this service, check out the FAQs link under the title. This is a fabulous resource and a must see for any Muslim on the road! Visit it at `www.islamicfinder.org/finder/`.

Masjid Addresses in the United States

`www.msa-natl.org/resources/IS_USA.html`

While this site isn't quite as comprehensive as Islamic Finder, it does offer a broader range of information. Along with locating places of worship in your area, you also can find Islamic book-sellers or Islamic schools in a particular region. Though certainly not a complete listing, this can get you started if you are interested in Islamic resources in a particular area.

Buddhists, Hindus, and Sikhs Finding Their Niche

While these groups and the others not included in this chapter do not have as extensive resources as other groups like Christianity, they do have their share. Let's start with a couple sites that will help you find local places of worship for a variety of faiths.

Pluralism Project

`www.fas.harvard.edu/~pluralsm/`

Harvard's Pluralism project has a lot to offer. One of the most impressive features is one that's helpful for the religious traveler! Here you'll find an online directory of religious centers across the United States. It's so huge it might take a minute to download but it's worth it! Limit the search to your area and you'll find a list of centers, labeled with the religion they serve. The main focus is on Islam, Hinduism, Sikhism, and Buddhism. But be careful! When typing this address, leave out the "i" in pluralism or you'll find yourself in a dead-end!

Temple Reference Center

www.mandirnet.org/temple_list.html

Although this site is a subset of a Hindu site, one of its directories lists Hindu, Buddhism, Jain, and Sikh temples from around the world. You also can look for those temples that have Web sites, or view pictures of some of the more impressive temples. Be forewarned, the directory is not recently updated and not totally comprehensive.

Now on to the sites specific to each tradition.

Buddhists

Looking for enlightenment on the road? These Buddhist sites will help you continue your journey while away from home. For more information on Buddhism in general and its presence on the Web in particular, see Chapter 28, "No Self, No God: Buddhists."

BuddhaNet

www.buddhanet.net

This is the ultimate site for Buddhism online. Though it's a good resource for those interested in learning about the religion, it's also got some great stuff for the Buddhism traveler. If you go into the site index, you'll find some e-books, some of the main teachings and writings of the Buddhist masters, and lessons that might help you maintain your practice over a long trip. But if you don't find what you want here, for Therevada, Mahayana, Tibetan, and Zen Buddhism or BuddhaNet's Top 10 List, check out the links page. At BuddhaNet, you'll not only find great resources but also some great pictures. You can see BhuddaNet's main screen in Figure 4.3.

Buddhist Reading Room

www.geocities.com/~wtwilson3/

Looking for Buddhist literature or lessons? You'll find it here! Find the texts of different talks, stories, and lessons at this site. There's also a great links page that will help you if you still seek more!

Figure 4.3

BuddhaNet is Buddhism's center for resources on the Web. Here you'll find anything and everything for your education and religious practice.

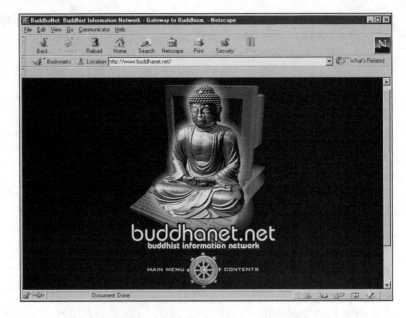

Hindus

It is said that there are as many Hinduisms as there are Hindus. You might also say that there are as many Hindu scriptures as there are Hindus! With so many sacred texts, Hindu travelers couldn't possibly carry it all with them! Here are a couple sites that'll help lighten that load and give you other sources of inspiration and community while on the road. For more information on the Hindu tradition, see Chapter 29, "God Lives on the Ganges: Hindus."

The Hindu Universe

www.hindunet.org

Looking a lot like a regular search engine, this is the home for Hindu resources. Of particular use to the Hindu traveler are their complete texts of the scriptures and links to temple directories. You also can find a Hindu calendar, chat online, read some Hindu news, or find a Hindu book.

Bhavagad Gita

www.the-gita.net

This is a flashy site with a lot to offer! This interactive page lets you read the Gita in English or Sanskrit and study it bit by bit. Choose your method of study. Perfect for the Hindu on the road looking for inspiration from this Hindu classic, this site is a must-see.

Sikhs

Sikhs have also found a place on the Web and the Sikh traveler will not be disappointed. Check out these sites for scriptures and inspiration for the trip. For more information on Sikhism on the Web, see Chapter 31, "God Loves Long Hair: Sikhs."

Sikhnet

www.sikhnet.com

Just as BuddhaNet is Buddhism's center on the Web, so is Sikhnet for the Sikhs. The Sikh traveler can listen to Sikh radio, read news from the Sikh community and even send Sikh greeting cards to those at home. You can read the holy texts of Sikhism and even receive daily readings via email. This site is a must see for Sikhs on the road or at home! Beware: this site is run by the 3HO sect, not a mainstream Sikh group. Even so, the site includes resources for all of Sikhism.

Gurudwara Net

www.gurudwara.net

This site claims to be a virtual Gurudwara on the Net. It truly is like a virtual temple and, therefore, the perfect home away from home for the Sikh traveler. Search the Global Gurudwara database or read the results from the community poll. You can also join discussion groups or hear the latest Indian news. This is a great meeting place for Sikhs from all over the globe.

While not all religions have been covered in this chapter, most have similar resources out there. The best bet for finding these is to go to the more general resource pages for the religion and go from there. The moral of the story is no matter what your religion or how far you're traveling, you don't have to leave your religious life behind. The Internet makes it possible for all religions to reach their followers, be they at home or on the road.

Wired Monk

Listen to the Baghavad Gita

Have you ever heard the Bhagavad Gita in RealAudio? Well, you might want to try it. There is a tone of authenticity here that would be of value even to a non-Hindu or a casual surfer! Check out www.the-gita.net.

Rest and Remember

➤ Though far from home, religious travelers need not be far from their spiritual home!

➤ Christian resources for the person on the road might be the most prevalent, but they are not the only resources out there. Jews, Muslims, Hindus, Buddhists, Sikhs, and other religious folk have their share of cyberspace.

➤ The Internet can never replace the comfort and resources of home, but it can make your trip less lonely and more tuned in and turned on to spiritual options.

COOL!

Chapter 5

You Want It All for Free? You Got It!

In This Chapter

➤ Although many services are for sale on the Internet, even more are available for free, especially on religious sites

➤ You'll find everything from religious electronic greeting cards to clip art to software programs free on the Net

➤ Sifting through the trash, the treasures, the free, and the expensive can be tiring. Check out some good sites to get you started

---

Almost no one can pass up a bargain—that is, if it *really* is a bargain—and fortunately for bargain hunters, there are some amazing giveaways on the Net. In this chapter I have tried to highlight religious sites that offer not just bargains but *great* bargains, giveaways that help you move ahead with your life on a religious plane and provide you spiritual resources that you might not have imagined possible, especially for free.

Finding the Freebies

These days, you can't go online without seeing tons of offers and ads. Most of them claim to offer freebies, if you'll only visit their site. Needless to say, this no-cost promise isn't always true. It's often a ploy to bring in customers.

Religious sites also offer stuff for free. The difference is that a lot of it is actually free. The beauty of the Internet is that it offers not only loads of free information, but also free services, images, and tools. For virtually every religion, you'll find loads of freebies from clip art to screen savers to email services. Check out the variety of options listed in the following sections. To start, go to CNet's Downloads and see some of the features of the AltaVista search engine.

AltaVista: www.altavista.com

The search engine at AltaVista hasn't made my list of favorites so far, but here is an exception. From the main page, you can limit your search to a particular media type, such as "Images." If you then type the religion you're interested in and hit **Enter**, a variety of images will appear! For Islamic images alone, more than 500 are listed. You can also try searching for electronic video and audio files.

CNet's Download.com

www.download.com/mac/list/0,339,0-d-27-36-d-1,00.html

The Religion and Spirituality section of CNet's massive Web page has more than 20 sites of interest. The page offers links and descriptions of the features of these sites. Before you follow the links, make sure you check to see whether the service is free or requires a fee.

Catholic Sites

Although Catholics can find many useful items on Protestant sites, a few sites cater specifically to members of the Church of Rome. Here are a couple of the best.

Children's Christian Videos and Software

www.guidinglightvideo.com/

Don't miss this one! This site features many Catholic videos and children's music videos. It promises "entertainment that kids love, biblical values that parents applaud." Also check out the online games and monthly contests as well as a variety of other freebies.

Christianbook.com—Books, Music, and More

www.christianbook.com

Well, maybe this one isn't completely free, but hey, at a 70–90% discount, this site is really aiming for your business if you are a devout Catholic. Christian Book Distributors has been providing books, music, and other goodies for 20 years, and the large discounts make this a site worth checking out.

Protestant Sites

Not surprisingly, Protestant-oriented sites offer a great deal of resources on the Net. These are just a few of the many freebies available, from greeting cards to software.

Cybergrace Electronic Greeting Card Center

www.cybergrace.com/html/cards.html

This site is a lot of fun, even if you or your intended recipient aren't Christian! By selecting a picture, caption, and message for your card, you can create a personalized electronic card to send to anyone you wish! What better way to brighten someone's day and, if you so choose, include a little inspiration.

Wired Monk

In a Hurry? Don't Miss This

Check out a site called Christian Freebies at www.tagnet.org/freebies/. The resources on this site are unending. Just a few of the attractions are books, bookmarks, clip art, email cards, email accounts, and even recipes—all for free!

Christian Shareware

www.christianshareware.net/

This site is a service of Goshen, one of the bigwigs in Christian cyberspace. Here you'll find Christian and Bible downloads, from games to study tools to Bible translations.

Christian Graphics Gallery

www.njwebworks.com/churchweb/gallery

Here you'll find mainly clip art, but with a Christian twist—from Jesus to crosses to angels. If you don't find what you want here, check out the Christian Graphics Hotlist at www.njwebworks.com/chrgraph.html.

Christian Postcards

www.ChristianPostcards.com

Choose the picture and message, and send someone a postcard with the click of a button. This is a free way to send some inspiration or greetings! Check out its offerings, shown in Figure 5.1.

Figure 5.1

Sending a quick, inspirational greeting to a friend, co-worker, or family member is easy at Christian Postcards.

Sermon Central: Free Bible Software Download Page

www.sermoncentral.com/bibkey.htm

Sermon Central has great features—as a matter of fact, this page is up there with the best. It includes links to various sites with free software. Each link has a brief description and is easy to use. The sites include sermons, illustrations, and hymn sites. Most sites are Baptist.

Jewish Sites

Christians aren't the only ones offering freebies over the Web! Many Jewish-oriented sites offer great software and clip art, among other things.

Chanukah Clip Art from Kid's Domain

www.kidsdomain.com/holiday/
chanukah/clip.html

Here's the site for any kind of Chanukah clip art. If you don't find exactly what you want here, check out the listing of links to other clip art pages.

Muslim Sites

Islamic goodies for free? You got it! Check out these two sites to get you started.

Muslims Online

www.muslimsonline.com

For Muslims looking to find their place on the Web, this is the place to start. It offers free email and free home pages hosted from this site.

Islamic Gateway

www.ummah.net

Here's the hub of Islamic freebies, and it projects itself to an open, non-partisan audience, although certain groups, such as the Ahmadis or Qadiyanis, are mentioned by name as excluded. Here you will find downloads, pictures, articles, software, and audio programs, all for free.

Wired Monk

Virtual Jerusalem: Software Library: www.software.
virtual.co.il/

This site claims to be "the largest collection of Hebrew and Jewish software on the Net," and that may not be an overstatement! It includes software clip art, fonts, calendars, and music of interest to the Jewish community.

Food for Thought

Uncle Debi's Jewish Clip Art:
home.wnm.net/~debi/jart.htm

Can a non-Jewish person provide good Jewish resources? When it's something like clip art, the answer seems to be "just maybe." Even though Uncle Debi makes it known he isn't Jewish, his pages have attractive clip art that's free for public use. Also check out his Jewish Bordered Backgrounds at home.wnm.net/~debi/
jewish.htm.

What's with the Ahmadis?

The Ahmadis or Qadiyanis trace their origins to nineteenth century North India, and to a prophet-like figure named Ghulam Ahmad Qadiyani. Because he made many claims that link him to the Prophet Muhammad—the last, prophet in Sunni Muslim belief—his followers are often viewed as non-Muslims (see also Chapter 22, "There Is No god but God: Islam").

Free Muslim Resources

www.geocities.com/Athens/Agora/4229/

You will want to check out Free Muslim Resources. Why? Because Free Muslim Resources has an endless supply of links to every kind of Muslim freebie you could imagine. From copies of the Qur'an to scholarships to clip art to email, this site has it all! This URL is a must-see for cyber Muslims.

All the Rest

Nearly all religions have some free offerings on the Net. Here are some highlights of the most interesting and useful sites for those of other religions who are looking for freebies.

The Modern Witches Spellbook

www.flash.net/~hight1/tmws.htm

The Modern Witches Spellbook is a program you can download from this site. You can try it out for a trial period for free, but you must pay for full use. The program itself is remarkable. You can use it to organize the "tools of the trade" and keep track of spells, rituals, herbs, chants, and more.

Mohan's Hindu Image Gallery

www.geocities.com/SoHo/Lofts/6834/

Looking for pictures of the many Hindu deities? Here you'll find more than 100 beautiful downloadable images.

Sikhnet

www.sikhnet.com

Along with all its other features, Sikhnet offers much for free. Download Sikh screen savers, Gimbani fonts, wallpaper, Sikh art, and even the Siri Guru Granth Sahib, the mother of all scriptures for Sikhs.

Although the number of truly free items on the Net is far less than the number of items that appear to be free, a lot is available. Whether you're Christian or Jewish, Muslim or Hindu, Buddhist or Sikh, or even Wiccan, you can find sites with interesting and helpful items that are free. Take advantage of the marketplace of free images, software, and downloads on the religious Net.

Rest and Remember

➤ If the Internet is the information super highway, why not skip the tollbooths? Religious sites carry loads of freebies for your use.

➤ You can benefit from the many people and religious groups that use the Net to publish and spread their art, graphics, software, and other interesting items.

➤ Not all sites and services that claim to be free actually are. Some offer only trial periods, and others require straight out payment. Although some of these sites may be worth your money, plenty of free items are out there to meet the needs of most religious Web surfers.

Chapter 6

What's There to Hear? (Don't Forget That Plug-In)

In This Chapter

➤ The Internet is just as exciting for the ear as for the eye

➤ Although downloading programs like RealAudio and RealVideo might take a little time, when you have them, it's smooth sailing

➤ The Internet makes it easy for you to listen to radio programs and view television broadcasts from around the world

The Internet isn't just for your eyes anymore! The World Wide Web is becoming as much a feast for the ears as for the eyes. Because of this, you don't have to just choose between hearing your news or a sermon on television or in church, you can hear and even watch it on the Internet! In this chapter, I'll show you how the Internet audio revolution is helping to spread the word about religions online.

Hear the Good Word

So what is out there to hear? On religious sites, you'll often find a RealAudio broadcast of news programs. You'll also find religious talks, sermons, and lectures, as well as music. All you need to utilize these services is RealAudio and, in some cases, RealVideo. Don't have them? Don't worry! Check out Chapter 1, "Before You Get Started," to learn how to download these programs for free.

Knowing What to Look For

If you decide to do some searching on your own for things to hear on the Net, beware. Just because you find a sight for a radio station, for example, doesn't mean that you'll be able to hear anything at all! Often, it's just an information page. Look for the keywords RealAudio, and you'll know you're getting the real thing!

RealAudio

RealAudio enables Web surfers to listen to or view live or prerecorded audio and video over the Internet. It uses a technology known as *streaming media* that enables the viewer to watch a prerecorded video or even hear a live radio broadcast as it occurs. Find out more and download the free software at real.com.

Much of the online audio information comes through radio stations broadcasting over the Net. The nice thing about Internet radio is that you never have to worry about interference or fading signals due to distance or obstructions. You can tune in to any station, anywhere! Check out the site described next, which is full of shortwave radio stations with a religious focus from all over the world. Then, if you want more, check out the following pages for more specific sites offering audio entertainment and education for those of various religions.

Religious Shortwave Radio Stations

www.ping.be/tdp/stations2.html

Want to get a feel for all that's out there? This colorful site lists many links to shortwave radio stations around the world. The links are categorized by countries. Whereas some take you to the contact information for the station, others take you to the impressive sites of the radio stations themselves, most of which are complete with Internet broadcasts.

If You're Roman Catholic...

For the Roman Catholic looking for some cyber-sounds, here are a couple sites to send you on your way.

Vatican Radio

www.wrn.org/vatican-radio/

Vatican Radio itself has been around for about 65 years! Needless to say, it hasn't been on the Internet that long. It has a lot to offer: You can choose from shortwave or satellite broadcasts (depending on your location) or broadcasts in any of 37 languages. The broadcasts themselves attempt to be the voice of the Pope and the Catholic community. You'll hear papal pronouncements and news of the Catholic church, as well as music and other programming.

Global Catholic Radio Network

www.ewtn.com/wewn/index.htm

This site offers Catholicism with a practical and popular twist. The attractive Web site offers live Web broadcasts, an advice segment, and programs on family life in the Catholic community. You can download the RealAudio program from this site. Just check the program schedule to find out when you can listen.

If You're Protestant...

Once again, Protestant Christians have cornered the market on great resources. Those described here are only a fraction of the many impressive sites offering live radio and television broadcasts, sermons, and music over the Web.

The Omnilist of Christian Broadcasting:
`http://members.aol.com/clinksgold/omnbroad.htm`

Look no further than this list to find exactly what you're looking for. The links are organized into radio programs, radio stations, TV, and others, and within these categories, the links are given gold, silver, or bronze stars to guide you on your way.

Trinity Broadcasting Live Audio

`www.tbn.org`

It's not surprising that the largest Christian broadcasting network in the world has found a place on the Net! Go to TBN's home page, and you can watch a live broadcast at the click of a button.

Christian Internet Broadcasting Network: `http://cirnet.com`

This site promises everything Christian on RealAudio and RealVideo. It seems to do pretty well with sermons, news shows, music, radio programs, and many others. You must be a member to take full advantage of its resources, but the membership is free! You must supply a lot of personal information, sign up to receive a newsletter, and agree to possibly accept further contact from commercial groups. You'll have to consider in advance whether the access you'll receive is worth disclosing this information.

700 Club: "Watch Online"

www.cbn.org/the700club

The Christian Broadcasting Network is right up there with TBN. *The 700 Club* is one of its biggest successes, and here you'll find the program's Web site. From this site, you can easily watch the latest show or any show from a 30-day archive.

Audio Central

www.audiocentral.com

Radio broadcasts, music, speeches—you name it, you'll find it on Audio Central (see Figure 6.1). Beware, though, that this site has a rather evangelical twist. But if you're interested in themes of prophecy, the second coming of Jesus, and energetic and passionate expressions of faith, you'll find them all here.

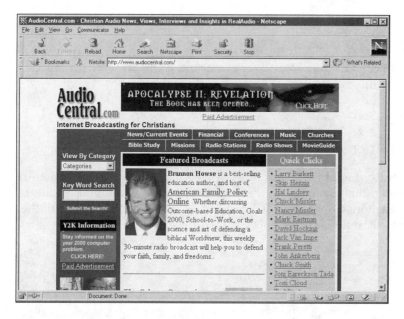

Figure 6.1

If evangelical Christianity is your thing, AudioCentral is an incredible resource for anything you can hear in the Christian Internet community.

If You're Jewish...

The Jewish Web surfer can find some great audio resources as well. Some radio stations broadcasting from Jerusalem can be heard over the Web. In addition, you can listen to particular religious writings and speeches.

Radio 10

www.radio10.co.il

Want to feel close to Israel without leaving your home? Check out this site and listen to live broadcasts from Jerusalem! The station offers an "Ask the Rabbi" segment, as well as more traditional radio programs. The makers of the site hope to add live video broadcasts of the Rabbi's lectures in the future, so keep an eye out!

Shalom America

shalom-am.com

This is the Web site of WELW 1330 AM in Cleveland, Ohio. But you don't have to be in Ohio to enjoy the show! Daily Internet broadcasts feature everything from music to cooking shows to news programs. You can even check out new CDs featured on the station and listen to previews.

If You're Muslim...

Want to hear some of the Muslim prayers? Want to hear the Qur'an read, perhaps with commentary? The Internet provides these resources and more.

Radio Al-Islam

islam.org/radio/default.htm

Straight out of IslamiCity, one of the major Muslim Web sites, comes Radio Al-Islam, a serious resource for Muslim teachings on the Net. At this page, you'll find readings of the Qur'an and recitations of prayers. Click the **Links** button at the bottom of the page to find even more Islamic radio resources.

Voice of Islam: www.islam.org/voi

This subsite of IslamiCity may not be flashy, but it has some great content. Look at listings by date or subject and find lectures, news, and Friday sermons on RealAudio. Videos are also available. And for those not yet connected, there are instructions for first-time listeners.

The-Quran.com—Al-Huda.ca

www.the-quran.com/

Are your needs simple? Want to go back to the basics? Check out this site—accessible at either www.the-quran.com or al-huda.ca—and find a recitation of the entire Qur'an at the click of a button. Click on the icon on the main page, and you'll find yourself at an index of chapters listed in both Arabic and English.

English Narration of the Meaning of the Glorious Qur'an

salam.muslimsonline.com/~azahoor/acmqem.htm

Just a recitation isn't enough for you? If you want to hear a little commentary as well, check out this site, which contains the translation by Marmaduke Pickthall. It includes narration and commentary by Charles Gai Eaton, another European convert, also known as Hasan Abdul Hakim.

If You're Hindu...

Hinduism is often recognized for its visual appeal, especially through the elaborate artistic depictions of deities. Thanks to the Internet, devotees can now enjoy audio features as well. Some of the best offerings are described here.

Bhajanawali's Audio Collection

www.bhajanawali.com/audio.htm

Bhajanawali's Audio Collection features everything from interviews with saints to the best Bhajanas, and even information on coming fasts and festivals. This site is worth a visit for anyone who is Hindu or anyone seeking to experience the depth of Hindu culture.

Shri Hanuman Online

www.hanuman.com/

This site doesn't offer much explanation for those unfamiliar with Hinduism or Indian culture. But for those who know exactly what they're looking for, this site is likely to have it! I mean, if you like songs in Kannada or Telugu or Tamil or Sanskrit, they are all here, plus a Web site for Shirdi Sai Baba.

If You're Buddhist...

Think the Buddhists are quiet people? They may spend a lot of time meditating, but they've made their audio presence known on the Net! You'll find lectures, chants, and prayers, all at the click of a button.

Buddhist Spiritual Sound Recordings

`watthai.net/sounds.htm`

Straight out of Sydney, Australia, some Tibetan Buddhists from down under created this site. Most of the audio files are educational, such as lectures on the teachings and beliefs of Buddhism.

Buddhist Lectures and Chants (RealAudio)

`www.campuslife.utoronto.ca/groups/buddhist/lectures`

This site is a great resource out of the University of Toronto. It contains links to various RealAudio items of interest to Buddhists. It includes everything from discussions on National Public Radio to recitations of sacred texts to Buddhist music to chants. Whether it's Joseph Campbell or Bob Thurman, Thich Nhat Hanh or the Dalai Lama, you'll find material on all of them that you can download and listen to.

If You're Sikh...

The Sikhs have also found a place on the Audio Web. Check out these sites for the sounds of Sikh scriptures and prayers.

Audio Files of Sikh Prayers

`www.sikhs.org/audio.htm`

This site contains just what the title suggests! Click on the prayer you want to hear, and you're ready to go.

RealAudio Discourses: Guru Gobind Singh Sahib

`www.baisakhi1999.org/audio.htm`

This site, shown in Figure 6.2, contains RealAudio discourses on Guru Gobind Singh Sahib, the most sacred of Sikh scriptures, as well as other works. In addition, it's easy to navigate—if you are familiar with Sikh terms and scriptures.

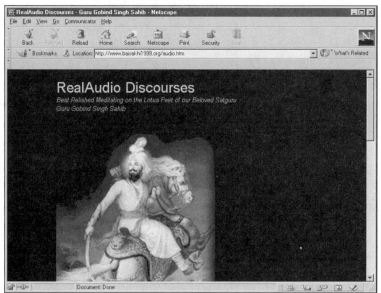

Figure 6.2

This Sikh site is pleasing to the eye and the ear. Take a look at the RealAudio discourses available, and get a feel for Sikh belief and culture.

As with most online resources, some religious groups are better represented than others. Nonetheless, most are beginning to make use of such programs as RealAudio to deepen and expand their presentations on the Web. The ability to touch people in a more personal and multi-leveled way with sound makes the Internet much more useful for those of any religion.

Rest and Remember

➤ As the Internet develops, more and more religious sites are offering audio features as a way of spreading their message.

➤ Using these features is as easy as installing RealAudio and RealVideo on your computer. And most sites offer a direct link to these downloads.

➤ The Internet no longer caters to the eyes only. People of almost any religion can find audio versions of teachings, news, and music, from within their tradition on the Net.

Chapter 7

Teach Me Online

In This Chapter

➤ You don't have to go to school to learn about religious history or ritual practices or spiritual perspectives; just get online

➤ In cyberspace, you'll find a lot of course material, ranging from the most general to the very particular

➤ The best way to explore what you can learn is to decide what you want or need—and then surf the sites that tend to have the highest profile in academic or educational circles

---

Not everyone who wants to go back to school can afford either the time or the money it takes. If you have a hankering for religious knowledge or spiritual options, then you can begin to satisfy it in this chapter. There are many, many more possibilities than those listed here, but at least you will get started, and you may even decide to earn a degree somewhere down the road on the information superhighway.

The Mega-Course Options

Long-distance learning is as much an option for religion as it is for history, philosophy, business, or law. The possibilities on the Net have never been greater. They increase by leaps and bounds every week, and when you get started with the menu here, you will find many more things to explore on your own. Buckle your seat belt (or rest your elbow), and let that mouse make you a cybernaut learning about religion.

Ontario Consultants on Religious Tolerance

www.religioustolerance.org

If you haven't already bookmarked this site, do it now. Here you will find the equivalent of a cybersource for revelation. Although it's not an actual online course, OCRT is a lodestone for anyone who wants to understand the fascinating complexity of religion. Here you can find out more about the diversity of religious outlooks, institutions, and movements, and at the same time, you can explore the quarrels, both historical and contemporary, between religious communities or between various religions and secular or anti-religious groups.

On its home page, OCRT calls itself "an agency promoting religious tolerance as a human right." That amounts to a crusade for broader appreciation of all religions without excluding or minimizing the value of embracing one. When you click on to this enormous and varied subject directory, you have to steer your way through the barcodes on the left of the home page.

Wired Monk

What Can I Learn from OCRT?

OCRT has more to offer than most of us could absorb in a lifetime of studying religion, spirituality, theology, or ethics. Its features are categorized in 7 major topics and 12 minor ones. Some of the major topics include:

➤ Historical, giving an in-depth coverage of both Christianity and 64 other religious and ethical traditions.

➤ Constructive, accenting spiritual topics that uplift and enhance human life.

➤ Ethical, exploring what is right and wrong and also what motivates those who hate others "in the name of God."

➤ Newsworthy, covering controversial topics from abortion to evolution to homosexuality to female clergy, as well as feature stories on cults and religious laws.

➤ Numerical, providing basic statistics on group membership and various religious holy days.

The 12 minor topics feature a mind-boggling table of contents, in itself a kind of course outline on religion today, plus a bar for hyperlinks and a bar for searching by topic, but there is a section on Internet censorship and an open appeal for funds. Why the need for money? Well, because OCRT has been running in debt every year for the past five years, despite getting more than five million hits a month!

Religious Topics on the Internet

http://www.wlv.ac.uk/sed/rsnet.htm

Maintained by George Chryssides of the University of Wolverhampton in England, this site is hyperlinked with OCRT. It amounts to a Rolodex-type serial listing of all the sites related to several religious communities. Although it's not exhaustive, it does overlap with some of the sites you will read about in other chapters of this book. It allows you to gauge how much can be learned from merely scrolling through random sites, either about multiple religious communities or the one of special interest to you. The hypertext links are of special value; they offer a non-traditional way to explore religious life in the New Information Age.

Interfaith Internet

www.godweb.org/library.html

Like OCRT, this site is not a traditional online distance-learning course; unlike OCRT, however, it is pitched to a specifically Christian audience. It is actually a downstream site for the First Church of Cyberspace, which is also linked to the Association for Religion and Intellectual Life (ARIL) at Columbia University. Figure 7.1 shows the welcome screen for this site.

Figure 7.1

The First Church of Cyberspace provides bells and whistles along with its cybersavvy approach to distance learning. Its pastor, Charles Henderson, also subs as a guide for About.com.

In promoting Interfaith Internet, ARIL lists several reasons why Christians should study other religious traditions. As one of the appeals, it even includes the proverb to "know your enemy before you make her or him your convert." In other words, if you want to convert people, you had better learn about their outlook before you try to change it! The principal benefit of this site is its simplicity. It lays out an annotated list of hyperlinks for each of six categories: World Religions, Christianity, Judaism, Buddhism, Islam, and Biblical Resources.

Online Study with a Real-World Counterpart

You don't want to explore a virtual library without a real-life classroom? Well, then maybe you ought to apply to the Association for Religion and Intellectual Life (ARIL) and participate in their research colloquium in July, 2000. All you need to do is propose a project that relates religion to an important issue, problem, threat, or possibility that people of faith will encounter in the new millennium. Interested? Click over to www.aril.org. There you will find the home pages for both ARIL and its ezine, *Cross Currents Online*. Scroll down to find the invitation for the July 2000 colloquium.

Encyclopaedia Britannica Online

www.eb.com

There's one way you can make a *big* leap into distance learning about religion without going to school or to the library: Bring the library to you. Get the best academic writing on the Net from Britannica Online. You can use this amazing reference resource for distance learning about religion in two ways. One way is to go to this awesome bank of articles and do a search on any given topic, such as the Reformation or the Dalai Lama. You'll find lots to ponder. The other way is to use Britannica's Internet Guide to find out what Web sites on religion it recommends and also how it ranks them.

Browse Britannica?

You must think I'm joking. After all, the world's largest reference work may seem too huge to give you any useful tidbits on religion or spirituality. Well, maybe it once seemed that way, but that's no longer the case. If you go to `www.britannica.com/philosophy/index.html`, you can skip the philosophy segments and have a feast on religious topics! In the menu on the left of the home page, click **General Religion** to find more than 20 sites on religious studies not just in the US, but also in Canada and Britain. For each one, you'll see a rating and a brief annotation. In addition, 15 other bars point you to specific traditions, from those of Bahais and Buddhists to Santerians and Sikhs. Although they're weighted more toward history and scripture than experience and ritual, these segments of the Britannica library still offer a boon for cybersurfers looking to learn more about religion without taking an actual course.

Distance Learning About Particular Religions

By now you've done all the homework you need to do on religion in general or surfing through general sites, whether they are subject directories like OCRT or reference resources like Encyclopaedia Britannica. Now you are ready for actual courses on particular traditions. So many are available in cyberspace that you'll see 101s all the way down the screen. From Buddhism to Paganism, you can find the 101 course that suits your interest.

Buddhist Meditation 101

`www.nashville.net/~kaldari/meditate.html`

Maybe your goal is to learn to meditate, and you've heard that Buddhists have some hot tips and cool ways to get into that silent side of the self. I don't usually recommend commercial home pages, but this one, from a Buddhist-inclined music studio in Nashville, Tennessee, is so good on the basics that I post it here as the first step into the practice of Buddhism. If you want to read more about Buddhism, go to Chapter 28, "No Self, No God: Buddhists."

Yoga Meditation 101

www.nashville.net/~yoga/yogapath.htm

While you're visiting Nashville in cyberspace, why not make it a double stop? This site is a simple, straightforward introduction to different kinds of yoga, again with an accent on the experiential. You will not know everything there is to know about Hinduism after you visit this site, but that's why this book provides an independent chapter on the primary Indian religion in the world. If yoga is not your thing, go visit the later chapter.

Sympathy for the Devil

Whoa! Okay, you don't want to practice Satanism, but you'd like to know what all those Satanists are up to. Well, in that case, you might want to cruise over to Satanism 101. Billed as a straightforward look at Satanic religion, this bells and whistles site gives you everything from the essential articles of Satanist beliefs to books, magazines, and art. It also has a chat room, located at www.satanism101.com.

Bible Mysteries 101

www.biblemysteries.com

After a few light readings on Eastern religious practice, (and perhaps a speedy plunge into Satanism), you might be ready to pull back and go into the deeper truths of Biblical stories via distance learning. If so, you will enjoy this site. It comes from a Rocky Mountain technology firm called WIT. WIT "has what it takes," or at least that is its slogan, and this site takes an open-ended but evangelical approach to scriptural resources. You can scroll through back lectures, look at the current one, and participate in discussion groups.

Christian Theology 101

www.goldenstate.org/

Evangelical, nondenominational, distance learning—if that is what you want from a 101 class, you might try this home page for distance learning, offered by the Golden State School of Theology. It is not free, and you do have to pay $45 per independent course, but if you apply effort, you can earn a degree via cyberspace. Other sites, whether for mainstream Protestant groups or for Roman Catholics, are also increasingly using the Web to supplement the real student body with *virtual learners*, that is, cybernauts geared to religion.

Judaism 101

www.jewishstudies.org

Not only distance learning, but also full-course study programs, are available at this site—the home page for Jewish Interactive Studies. It has been up and running for more than three years, it boasts more than 1,500 students, and it offers a range of possibilities (from basic courses on the Bible to exploration of Jewish belief to the basis of Jewish ethics to the cycle of Jewish holy days). In other words, if you are an adult Jewish learner, you can go back to school at this site and be rewarded with a deeper understanding of Judaism, free of charge.

Islam 101

www.iiu.edu.nd/studyislam.htm

In the past, you might have wanted to take a college course, but discovered it was offered only at a remote campus at inconvenient times. Well, this site is not next door either—unless you happen to have a personal computer and be hooked up to the World Wide Web, in which case it's as accessible as your front door.

Islam 101 comes from Malaysia, and the International Islamic University (IIU) provides it in Kuala Lumpur, Malaysia's capital. IIU offers not just one course, but a huge menu for online Islamic distance learning. You can register for these courses online. Then you can explore, learn, and get credit for everything from Muslim history to Islamic medicine. Many courses are framed in a sequence so that you can explore a subfield of the rich Islamic past through several related courses.

Everything 101

http://www.utexas.edu/world/lecture/rel/

By now you might feel like you've tapped into all the Internet sources for the study of religion. But actually, you have yet to see a mega-site that will leave you gasping by the time you've scrolled through its offerings. This is the home page for the World Lecture Hall, a cybersite on religious studies that's maintained by the University of Texas in Austin. It begins with a course on Anthropological Approaches to the Study of Religion and ends with a survey course on World Religions. Many of these courses convey a strongly evangelical, or Protestant Christian, approach to the topic they survey. But they are pitched to the 101 level, and so even those would-be distance learners who do not share that perspective might benefit from some of the courses. You do have to pay if you want to register for credit, but most of the syllabi and even some assigned books are posted free for those who want to explore among the 40-plus courses offered from this site.

Alternative Religions Via Distance Learning

It's hard to imagine a more hip source of the alternative press than *The Utne Reader*. For example, in its 18 September 1999 online issue, it explored the topic of sacred travel. This issue covered the places you might expect: Mecca, Jerusalem, China, and Scotland—all as pilgrimage sites with traditional religious foci. However, there was also an essay on Graceland as a pilgrimage site. After all, millions of Elvis fans stream there, as you can read about in *The Utne Reader Essay Online*.

Wired Monk

The Utne Reader

The Utne Reader provides just about the best of the shrinking alternative press in the United States. Of its many features, the essay online helps you to get into a little known topic and explore it more fully than you would in most mainstream journalism, whether you prefer daily newspapers or monthly magazines.

You can also visit the home page of Tammy Todd, the Alternative Religions guide for About.com. She has posted an essay from 11 February 1999, which she titles "The Church Of ... What?!?! : Joke Religions." In that essay, she describes some very unlikely churches, including those dedicated to the most loved and worshipped celebrity of them all: the mighty Elvis. No less than three major (and many minor) churches to the King grace the annals of the Internet, including the mesmerizing 24 Hour Church of Elvis, The First Church of Jesus Christ, Elvis, and the First Presbyterian Church of Elvis the Divine (which may be serious—I'm not sure). Figure 7.2 shows one such site.

Now, you won't find a single course that will give you all you need or want to learn about alternative religions online. But I suggest that you explore both the online versions of print sources (like *The Utne Reader*) and the several postings of Tammy Todd, an Alternative Religions guide with About.com. You may not have one-stop shopping, but the truth—at least as it's believed by various religions—*is* out there.

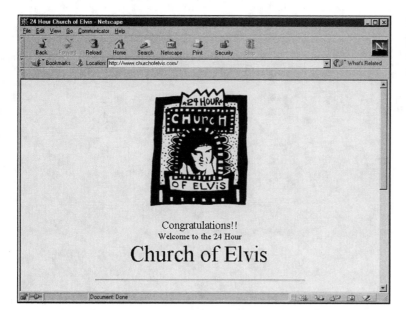

Figure 7.2
Elvis fandom has trans-muted into a religion online.

Rest and Remember

➤ Distance learning is no substitute for face-to-face instruction or classroom interaction with other students, but it does have the double merit of being both instantly available and easily adaptable to other time constraints.

➤ You can construct your own course from materials available on the Web, or you can take the packaged courses offered by a wide range of educational institutions.

➤ The best teachers and the most fun courses are often those that you stumble across when surfing the Web. But if you need some guidance, you might take a guide from the only search engine with announced guides: About.com.

Part 3

Using Religion to Socialize in Cyberspace

So you have religion but you also want to get personal? Well, stop and linger on this part of The Complete Idiot's Guide to Religions Online. *You want to explore friendship? It's here. You want to find romance? Maybe it's here. You want something more, like marriage? Well, that's tougher to find, in cyber time or real time, but you can surf some sites that just might connect you to that special person who is not only a soul mate, but also your life's partner.*

Check out this part's sections for more on these topics, plus religious-oriented sites offering news, chat, discussion, and even job opportunities.

Chapter 8

Matchmakers

> ### In This Chapter
>
> ➤ The Internet offers a fun and easy way to meet interesting people within your faith from all over the world
>
> ➤ While some sites focus on both friendly and romantic introductions, others are explicitly intended to help a user find someone to marry
>
> ➤ Meeting people on the Internet does not substitute for meeting people in person. Use caution, but enjoy the freedom and confidence you'll get from cyber-relationships!

No one ever promised you that you'd find your ideal friend or partner just by day-dreaming or praying or making a wish list! But the Internet is one of the most rewarding, and most pleasurable, new options for exploring a larger social world. In this chapter I've tried to provide some tips on ways that a religious commitment or outlook will help you get to the next level in your personal life via the World Wide Web.

Finding Friendship and Love on the Internet

It's not always easy to find a friend or partner these days. It's especially hard if your standards include your particular religion and beliefs. Finding someone who shares your beliefs *and* has other things in common with you is a bit more of a challenge. The Internet offers ways to make this challenge a bit easier. Different world religions have created resources for just about everything on the Net. So why not love? In fact, many sites are devoted to just that purpose—uniting a person of a particular faith with someone who shares his or her values and outlook.

The Pros and Cons of Cyber-Relationships

Internet matchmaking services have the great advantage of being able to put you mouse to mouse with great people from all over the country, or even the world. That means you have more people to chose from. But, beware. That very fact could also create problems! You may find the mate of your dreams, but he might live hundreds of miles away! Yet, it doesn't hurt to try, and long distance relationships *can* work...if only for a little while! Another advantage of Internet relationships is the freedom and confidence to put your best foot forward and be who you want to be. Yet, this freedom has pitfalls, too. You'll never know how true a person's self-description is until you meet him or her, and that may be limited by distance and other factors. Proceed with caution, but have fun!

Interested? The good news is that with most sites you can browse around and read up without making any commitment, financial or otherwise. And what do you have to lose? Most sites let you casually enter your ad or description and browse those of others. You may receive messages from interested people or send some to those you'd like to meet.

Now these sites aren't exclusively for those looking for love. If you just want to find a like-minded friend or email pal, there are sites for you, too. Just make sure you are clear about your intentions when you start...and beware of those sites with the words matrimonial, marriage, or love in the title! They are not always free, and they may sometimes be deceptive.

If you're looking for love within your religion, you have two options for how to start. Many of the general matchmaking sites let you limit your search by religion, ethnicity, and other factors. However, you'll find more variety and more specific and in-depth services by going straight to a matchmaking service within your religion. But if you are open to meeting someone *outside* your tradition, those sites aren't for you. Many of them limit use to those who are serious about their religious beliefs, namely the beliefs of that particular tradition.

Christian—Roman Catholic

There are an incredible number of Protestant Christian sites (covered next), but Catholics might want some sites that cater to their specific interests. If you're a Catholic single looking for another Catholic, these sites are for you.

Catholic Singles

www.catholicsingles.com

Catholic Singles claims to be the original Catholic matchmaking service on the Net. It has been around for several years and has served a good number of people. Like other such sites, they do charge a membership fee. The nice thing is, they also offer a free one-month trial. So if you're Catholic and single, you have nothing to lose! After you post your profile, you can view others' profiles and send emails to those who catch your interest. The email system and chat rooms are a great way to interact with others within the site.

Catholic Introductions

www.catholicintroductions.com

Having been around for 12 years, Catholic Introductions' success can be seen in its strong history. Yet, matchmaking on the Internet hasn't been around that long. So what kind of service is this? Well, the service doesn't exist only on the Internet, but is accessible online. You can join through the Web or by mail or phone, and they call for an interview and proceed to send you profiles of those you might like to meet. The fees start at $495 for six months—rather high, but the services seem to be of high quality and very personal. If you do marry as a result of this service, they'll even send you a wedding present.

Christian—Nondenominational Protestant

Are you Protestant, single, and looking? The following sites serve the general Christian community, though most seem to be mainly oriented toward Protestants. The number of quality and interesting sites is remarkable, so finding the one for you may take a little time and browsing. Give them a try, and you just might find a match made in heaven. Here are some of the best, along with their key features.

Christian Dating

www.christian-dating.com

Hundreds of marriages and tens of thousands of relationships have come out of this service over its 18 years of service. Claiming to be the original Christian dating service, they serve all sorts of Christians and see this service as a type of ministry to the Christian community. The site offers similar services to others mentioned in this chapter, with annual membership rates of $125. The claims of experience and success speak for themselves! You can see the site in Figure 8.1.

Figure 8.1

Enter this page and you're greeted with pictures of beautiful people who were supposedly happily united through this service. The Christian Dating service has been around for 17 years and boasts many happy unions.

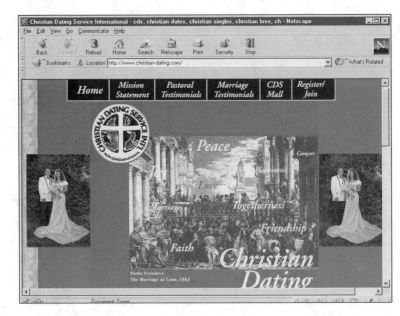

Christian Singles Connection

www.cybergrace.com/html/singles.html

This site is great for those who don't have a lot of money to spend but would like to be a part of a service that'll help them meet other Christians. The fees, which come to $36 for a year's membership, are very modest, and what you get is access to more than 5,000 member profiles of people you can email at the click of a button. The profiles ask basic questions but also leave room for a free response of what the person is looking for. The members tend to be devoted Christians who are relatively conservative politically and morally. Most are between ages 20 and 40.

African Wedding Guide

Found that perfect mate? Want a distinctive wedding that reflects your culture? For African-Americans that are looking to make their wedding different, this is the guide for you. This rather extensive site (at melanet.com/awg/) lets the user browse all sorts of resources useful for everything from finding African fabrics for wedding apparel to learning how to finance the wedding with the help of a wedding planner. For the African-American couple looking to make their wedding perfect, this site might help add some spice and culture to their ceremony.

Singles Christian Network

www.singlec.com

The Singles Christian Network is the top dating site in the religion section of www.hitbox.com, and with good reason. Whether you want to chat, send someone a Christian greeting card over the Net, get dating advice, or find out what's happening in religious news, this is the place for you. Oh yeah! And you can find the love of your life, too! As a member, you can search through more than 8,000 personal ads or look at the personal Web pages of single Christians, complete with photos. Although you can use many of the services without membership, you must pay a monthly fee ($9.95) to enjoy all the member services. If you don't want to search through all the ads yourself, you can use the matchmaking service as well. This site is so full of resources that you can create a program that works for you. However, if it's personal attention you want, without all the bells and whistles, you might get lost in this site.

Christian Singles Online

www.creativeye.com/singles/

Celebrating the 11th wedding of couples who met through its services, Christian Singles Online offers more than just personal ads you search through on your own. After paying a modest one-time membership fee (usually $39.95, but occasionally reduced to $25), you are a member for as long as you need the services. A match-maker takes your profile and searches the other profiles to find a match. The match-maker then sends that matching profile to you and yours to your match, and then it's up to you and your match to contact one another.

Christian (Mormon) Matchmakers

The Mormons seem to be everywhere on the Web! Their matchmaking sites are just as impressive as their more general sites. With their emphasis on marrying within the faith, it's no wonder the Mormons have quickly provided some great resources to help single Mormons find other like-minded people.

LDS Singles Connection

lds.e-match.net

This user-friendly site will help facilitate any Mormon match! You can post your pro-file and picture for free and specify what you're looking for. The only catch is that a lifetime subscription is $32. It is implied that in order to browse the listings or receive services, you must join. However, it may well be worth it. Not only can you browse through other listings looking for potential mates, but you will be notified by email every time someone who meets your specifications joins. This site also offers a chat room.

LDS Weddings: www.ldsweddings.com

Leave it to the Mormons to cover it all! If you've found your Mormon match and are ready to tie the knot, this site has everything you need to plan your wedding. From wedding planners to temple directories to advice on the perfect bridal shower, this site will answer many of your questions. This is a must-see for anyone planning an LDS wedding.

LDS Singles Online

www.ldssingles.com

For this service, you can pay a monthly membership price of $7, or pay $60 for an entire year. The services are similar to those mentioned for the previous site, but the questions in the profile section are more specific. The answers you can choose from are multiple choice more than open ended like those of the LDS Singles Connection. Nevertheless, this seems to be a quality and successful service. The long list of successful marriages resulting from this site is impressive!

Jewish

For devout Jews, finding a mate of the same religion is of vital importance. The following sites are geared to making this priority a little easier to meet. Some allow you to choose among the different branches of Judaism, but all promise to get you connected with some potential friends and partners.

Jmates

www.jmates.com

Jmates claims to be "the most exciting Jewish Dating Service on the Internet." Whether this claim is true or not, it is certainly worth visiting if you're a Jewish single. While membership is suggested if you want to fully utilize everything this site has to offer, it is not required for some resources. This site features profiles of various singles that you can view and contact. Some profiles even have sound bites, video clips, or both that you can tune into with your computer!

Zipple: www.zipple.com

Go to the Zipple home page and click **Jewish People**, and you'll find a wealth of resources for all age groups and interests. Click **Singles** to access the Zipple matchmaking service. Registration is free. You can also find links to other sites and services for Gen Xers, teens, and gay and lesbian Jews. This is only one of the many great resources at this site!

Your Ideal Date

www.yid.com

An international Jewish dating service, Your Ideal Date (YID) lets you limit your search by country and region. The system itself is a searchable database of member profiles. You can post a profile whether or not you are a paid member, but you cannot contact other members—they have to contact you. If that's too passive for you, become a full member, and you can participate as much or as little as possible. The site even offers a Dating Handbook to help you with online dating etiquette. Your Ideal Date is pleasing to the eye, as you can see in Figure 8.2, and to the heart.

Figure 8.2

At Your Ideal Date (YID), you can search as actively as you want to find a friend, a pen pal, or the love of your life within the Jewish community.

Jmatch

www.jmatch.com

Jmatch is similar to Your Ideal Date in format. It, too, is an international Jewish dating service. You can post your profile for free and browse those of others. A private membership is available for a fee for those who want more privacy than a free membership offers. If you opt for a private membership, you can view the profiles of others who have done the same, and your profile will be seen only by other paid members. Still, the site provides a lot of free services, so it's worth checking out!

Matchmaking for LGBT Jews

www.nuyenta.com

Are you a lesbian, gay, bisexual, or transsexual Jew looking for love or friendship? This site offers just that. Take a look at all it has to offer. You can create your own profile and browse those of others to find someone who shares your lifestyle and religious beliefs.

Muslim

For the Muslim looking for love, the Internet is a place to look. Several quality sites have detailed search engines that even let the Muslim Web surfer look for matches in other religions!

AlZafaf Matrimonials

www.alzafaf.com

AlZafaf is committed to making successful matches between single Muslims. They offer a free trial period after which you must pay a modest membership fee ($30 for 60 words for 6 months). With membership, you not only get to place an ad in the system but also get to search the almost 500 ads already in the database.

Muslim Marriage Lin

www.matrimony.org

This service is actually free! One of the few sites that can actually claim free services, the Muslim Marriage Link provides services similar to those of other sites that charge. It is a worldwide matchmaking service for Muslims, but it also allows Christian and Jewish women to place ads. The Web page also offers articles and books on Muslim marriage that can be purchased easily and delivered quickly.

To Pay or Not to Pay?

Most matchmaking sites do charge a fee for their services. While this charge might put some people off, don't turn to the personal ads in the paper right away. You just might get what you pay for. By charging a fee, even a modest one, services are able to better ensure that those who browse the ads and place them are serious about their religion and about finding a match. Those looking for a joke or trouble are often dissuaded by a fee. So although a free service is nice, it might not be as safe!

Zawaj.com

www.zawaj.com

Another free service, Zawaj.com not only allows Muslims to place matrimonial ads but also contains links to essays and Prophetic traditions about marriage in Islam.

Muslim Matrimonial Link

www.4you.com/MML

The Muslim Matrimonial Link charges a small fee to place an ad, but offers a great search engine for searching those ads in the database. You can search by type of Islam practiced, culture, job, and location all at the same time.

Others

Not just the mainstream religions have developed matchmaking services on the Net! Some smaller and less cyber-savvy religions have services to offer. From Sikhs to atheists, you'll find some of the most interesting sites here.

Sikh

www.sikhnet.com/matrimonials

A nice-looking site with lots to offer, Sikhnet's attempt to make matches in the Sikh community seems to be doing well! The site offers chats and discussions as well as matchmaking. There is no fee for posting or viewing ads, but membership is encouraged to help support the site. Some special opportunities are available for this fee, but you can certainly enjoy the site without forking over any money. Yet, beware that this sight is run by the 3HO group, which is not composed of mainstream Sikhs. Nevertheless, they strive to serve the entire Sikh community. Figure 8.3 shows the Sikhnet service, in all its glory.

Figure 8.3

This site enables Sikhs to network, make friends, and find love at the click of a button.

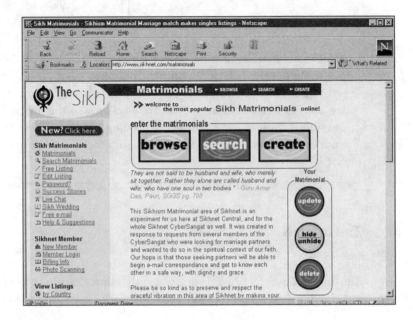

Indian Matrimonial Link

www.matrimonials.com/IML

Some sites for matchmaking are specific to the Sikh or other religious communities. Others serve a larger audience. The Indian Matrimonial Link serves all people of South Asian descent. You can place an ad for free or view others' ads by limiting your search by such criteria as religion and location.

The Pagan Webweaving Page

www.hue.org/paganww/

This free site is a great place to network. The Pagan Webweaving Page is not in the business of matchmaking, but the possibility is there. You can post and view listings for free and with ease. The profiles are freeform entries by the people themselves, usually describing the type of Paganism they practice. You can find those in your area by clicking on the country or state in which you live and scrolling through the entries with the cities highlighted. You then connect to people through direct links to their email addresses.

Venus Network

personal.redestb.es/albert.paloma/

The Venus group is a relationship agency based on astrology. The site provides two services: free astrological birth chart analysis and matchmaking. After you register your birth information and analysis, the site sends you an email with its most compatible entries based on astrology. If you believe the stars and planets determine your personality and are curious about which ones click with yours, this is a great free service to get things started!

Atheists

www.infidels.org/people/contacts.cgi

Sick of all this religious matchmaking? Atheists and freethinkers can find resources, too! At this subset of the renowned Infidels site, you can find atheists and freethinkers in your area. This isn't really a matchmaking site, but it provides a good way to find kindred spirits nearby whom you could contact. Who knows? Perhaps it could lead to love as well!

Rest and Remember

➤ It is important to know what you want before you sign up for any service. Are you looking for friendship or love? Do you want someone to search for you or do you want to do the searching?

➤ Because so many matchmaking services exist, you should take time to check out a few before you decide on one. No matter what your needs or your religion, what you're looking for is probably out there!

➤ Finding love and friendship through the Net is very different from finding it through traditional means. Courting in cyberspace allows you the freedom to be who you want to be, with a quick exit and no commitment. It also allows for deception and difficult long-distance relationships. Be careful what you claim, and be careful what you believe.

Chapter 9

Chat Groups, Internet Newsgroups, and Email Lists

In This Chapter

➤ Surfing the Web is like browsing in a bookstore: You can read and see a lot of stuff, but you can't contribute your views and opinions. On the other hand, chat rooms, newsgroups, and mailing lists foster group discussion and want your input!

➤ There are innumerable topics from which to choose—more than 90,000 mail lists, 17,000 newsgroups, and countless chat rooms!

➤ These interactive sites allow you to pose questions to the Internet community and share your insights and wisdom with others

There is so much on the Web that you have to pause, catch your breath, blink, and then move on. One way to begin to absorb all the information and opportunities within your grasp is to use interactive sites, and the purpose of this chapter is to move you along the information superhighway with a cellular phone!

What's on the Internet Besides the World Wide Web?

Believe it or not, the World Wide Web is not the whole Internet! The Web is a relatively recent creation. It dates back to the early 1990s. But before the World Wide Web existed, the Internet provided other ways for people to connect to one another. The older newsgroups and email lists are not as pretty as Web pages, but they offer a great way for individuals with common interests to communicate. In this chapter, you will look at email lists, Internet newsgroups, and chat rooms. You will also learn how to access them!

Email Lists

If you use the Web, you probably have an email account. You use it to send letters and notes to your friends and family, right? But you can also use your email account to access a huge number of email lists! Each list is dedicated to discussing a certain topic. Much like a newsletter, the list of emails is sent to everyone who subscribes. Some of the mail lists are fairly general and attract a wide audience; other lists are very specific. A list might have only 300 subscribers worldwide, or it might have thousands!

Mailing lists allow you to participate in discussions with other people on the list. Suppose someone asks a question or poses a query and sends it to the mail list. Everyone on the list receives the message. If you write an answer, it will be sent to everyone on the mailing list. Thus, mail lists offer subscribers a terrific way to have ongoing discussions about topics of interest. There are two steps to getting onto an email list: (1) find the list and (2) subscribe to it.

Finding Mail Lists

You might think it's easy to find mail lists on the Web, but it is not. Some are private and do not want to be listed on the Web. However, a few indexes do have information about mail lists. Perhaps the best is Liszt, the mailing list directory located at www.liszt.com.

Liszt, shown in Figure 9.1, catalogues more than 90,000 email lists. Many of these are organized into categories (Books, Computers, Humanities, and so on) in much the same way Yahoo! or other Web search engines are organized. So you can browse around and find an email list that might interest you, or you can search Liszt's entire database of email lists and find exactly what you are looking for. Liszt offers assistance to prospective mailing list users and is a good place to begin exploring mailing lists.

Subscribing to Email Lists

When you have identified an email list you are interested in, you need to subscribe to it. Don't get out your checkbook, though—this subscription is free! Some lists make this easy by providing Web pages and forms you can use to submit your name to the mailing list. If the list you are interested in supports this method, read no further!

However, many other mailing lists require you to submit an email request asking to be added to the mailing list. Subscription requests are sent to a mailer program, which adds, removes, and assists people using the mailing list. One thing you *must* remember about mailing lists is that they use two different addresses: an administrative address and a list address.

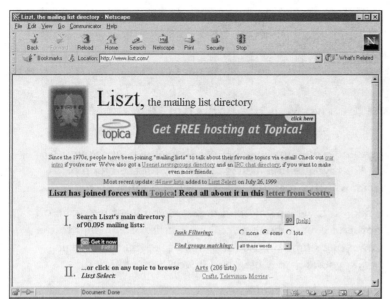

Figure 9.1

Liszt.com is a comprehensive guide to mail lists and chat rooms.

Keeping Your Wits on the Web

While surfing the Web, you will find that many sites ask for your email address. You should be careful about giving it out! Many vendors legitimately collect email addresses to send out information about their products, but some unscrupulous companies may sell their mailing lists to "spammers" who will send you junk email. One useful trick to get around this is to set up a free email account at Hotmail (www.hotmail.com) or Yahoo! (www.yahoo.com) or some other free service. You can then give this "dummy" address to questionable companies or individuals; should they begin "spamming" you, your main email account will remain unaffected, and you can just delete all the rubbish in your second account!

How Are the Two Mail List Addresses Different?

The *administrative* address is the address to which you send commands to the mailer program asking to subscribe, unsubscribe, or otherwise change your subscription to its mailing list. If you send a message intended for the group to read, the mailer program will choke and send you a lot of error messages!

The *list* address is the address to which you send messages you want everyone on the list to read. Do not send your "subscribe" or "unsubscribe" commands to the list address. It wastes everyone's time on the list to read that you are changing your subscription, it marks you as a "newbie," and it won't affect your subscription!

When you find the name of the mail list you are interested in joining, at Liszt.com or elsewhere, you will also find the address of its mailer program. The Web site that tells you about the name of the mail list usually tells you what commands you need to use to learn more about the list's main focus and also how to subscribe to the list.

Before you subscribe to any list, you should try to learn if it is really what you are interested in. The best way to do this is to send a one-line email to the administrative address for the mailer program. Your message should read "info *listname*" (where *listname* is the name of the list in which you are interested). (The administrative address is probably listserve@*somewhere*.com, majordomo@*somewhere*.com, or listproc@*somewhere*.com, where *somewhere* could stand for any domain name; the name of the mailer program appears before the "@" and the host computer's name follows the @.)

The mailer program will note the email address in the "From" field of your message and automatically send you information on the requested list. Most mail lists have fairly detailed information files, including information about who is on the list, who its intended audience is, and directions on how to subscribe, unsubscribe, and interact with the mailer program.

Can You Give Me an Example?

Say you are interested in paganism and go to Liszt.com. Liszt.com tells you about a mail list for the Covenant of UU Pagans: `cuups-1`. It also tells you that the administrative address for the `cuups-1` list is `listproc@uua.org`. So, to learn more about this list, you would send a one-line email to `listproc@uua.org` containing the words `info cuups-1`. The mailer program would then respond by sending you information about the cuups-l list and how to subscribe to it.

Practice Your Netiquette

Many mailing lists have a small cadre of users, and you should spend some time "lurking" (reading the email on the list without responding or initiating a message) to figure out the character of the list. Careless use of mailing lists can spark "flame wars," where one subscriber attacks another, making online time rather unpleasant. Please observe the "netiquette" for the list you want to participate in, lest the list administrators remove your name from the mailing list!

Internet Newsgroups

There is an enormous number of newsgroups on the Internet. Liszt.com lists more than 17,000! Many of these groups are dedicated to discussing religious topics, and they are easier to find and participate in than email lists. Unfortunately, newsgroups are completely unmoderated: Anyone can sign into them and write whatever he wants. Thus, "flame wars" are more likely to break out in newsgroups than in email lists.

To participate in a newsgroup, you can use your Web browser. If you're running Internet Explorer, select **Tools**, **Mail and News**, **Read News**. From the Netscape program window, go to **Communicator**, **Newsgroups**. The browser may ask you for some information about your email address and your news server; your Internet service provider (ISP) can provide you with this information. The browser will then download the lists of newsgroups your news server supports. During that time, go get a cup of coffee, because it can take a while to download all their names (although it is unlikely that your ISP will have all 17,000 groups available!). When you're ready to view a newsgroup, you'll see a list of topics like the one shown in Figure 9.2.

Figure 9.2

In a typical newsgroup, the upper part of the screen displays the message "headers" (or subject lines), and the bottom part displays the text of the message.

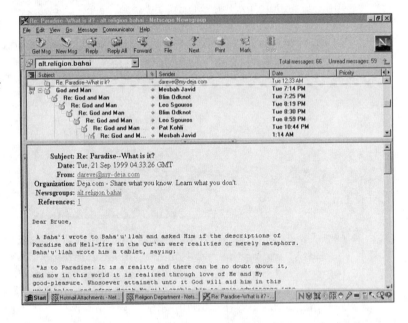

When you have a list of the newsgroups available to you, you can select the ones you want to subscribe to by searching the list, highlighting those of interest, and clicking the **Subscribe** button. Subscribing ensures that you'll always open these particular newsgroups when you access your browser's newsreader. You don't have to subscribe to a newsgroup to check its contents every now and then, though.

When you subscribe to a newsgroup, you will see a list of "headers" or "subjects" that briefly summarizes what the messages are about. For each message, you will also see the email address of the author, the date the note was sent, and the note's length. Click one of the headers to bring up the full text of the message. You can read the messages and respond as you feel appropriate. Be forewarned, though: A lot of people pass peculiar theories around on various newsgroups, and because the forum is completely unmoderated, you will learn some really interesting "facts."

How Are Newsgroups Organized?

Newsgroups are grouped by topic. Because newsgroups have been around since the days when the Internet was mainly used by academies, most topics of general interest fall under the alt or soc heading (short for *alternative* and *social issues*). This is especially true for newsgroups dedicated to discussing religious topics. Good places to start looking are alt.religion, soc.religion, and talk.religion. Each of these major headings has numerous subheadings: alt.religion.christian.baptist, alt.religion.christian.roman-catholic, and so forth.

A Few Newsgroup Caveats

Newsgroups should be approached with a certain amount of caution. Since there is usually no restriction on what can be posted, some posts are deliberately provocative—sometimes even hateful—or contain unwanted material like advertisements or even pornography. Some newsgroups are *moderated*—that is, someone removes offensive messages.

In addition, since an email address is part of the post, unscrupulous direct marketers often target these addresses for spam—unwanted direct email. You may see posters modify their email address in response by adding a key phrase like nospam. For example, `joeschmo@nospam.aol.com` is really `joeschmo@aol.com`; just remove nospam from the address to email the person.

Chat Rooms

Many ISPs offer chat rooms to their subscribers. The Internet offers an enormous number of chat rooms that are open to anyone. Chat rooms may be Virtual Places, or they may be rooms in CompuServe and AOL, but very often they take the form of Internet Relay Chat (IRC) channels, of which there are more than 37,000!

Conversations on IRC are a little strange because you typically have several people "talking" at one time; most messages are short, and the topic of conversation can change dramatically in a short period of time.

You can look in on one IRC chat in Figure 9.3. The upper part of the screen shows the status of the program—this is where you would subscribe or quit from a particular IRC. The lower part of the screen shows the actual chat room, with a conversation in progress!

Figure 9.3

A typical IRC chat room.

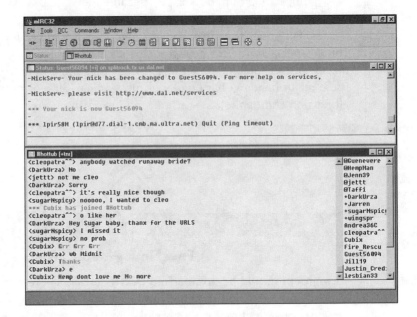

To participate in an IRC chat, you need to download an IRC *client*, a piece of software that allows you to enter the chat rooms. Of the many available clients, perhaps the most popular is "mIRC." A trial version is available at their Web site, www.mirc.com. After you download and install the IRC client, you are ready to chat!

When you have your IRC client up and running, you can join ongoing IRC chats. Most client software displays a "status" window and separate windows for each chat room you have joined. One cool feature is that you can participate in more than one chat at a time! mIRC divides each window. At the bottom of the status window, you time your commands to join or leave chat rooms. At the bottom of the chat room window, you enter the text you want to say to the rest of the chat participants.

Let's say you want to join the IRC called "chatcafe." You would open the status window on your IRC client. At the bottom of the window you would type /**join** #**chatcafe** and press **Enter**. The client would open up a new window for the #chatcafe chat room, and you would begin seeing the messages from other folks who are in the chat room already.

Some IRC Commands

All IRC commands begin with a "/" (a forward slash), and all IRC channels begin with a "#" (a pound sign). The most common commands are listed here:

JOIN	Join a channel
PART or LEAVE	Leave a channel
NICK	Change your nickname
QUIT or EXIT or BYE	Quit your IRC session
LIST	Access a list of all current channels

Again, as with mail lists and newsgroups, it is a good idea to "lurk" before posting messages in chat rooms. Most IRCs have rules about advertising, use of inappropriate language, and so forth. These rules will be displayed when you join the chat room; observe the rules, or you may be kicked out of the chat room! Also, you may just want to skip to America Online (AOL), and create your own special interest chat room there! The options abound.

Rest and Remember

➤ Web pages offer impressive graphics and lots of information, but they give you little opportunity for interactive communication. Mail lists, newsgroups, and chat rooms are interactive and encourage discussion.

➤ Always observe "netiquette" when posting messages in any of these areas.

➤ Interactive communication on the Internet is fun! Many people spend lots of time in chat rooms, sometimes sparking offline friendships or even romances.

CLINTON AND WHO?

Chapter 10

Are You Grooved on Current Events?

In This Chapter

➤ Whether you're looking for religion in the news or religious takes on the news, the Net has you covered

➤ It's important to know the source of the news you're reading. When dealing with religious news or moral issues, so-called "news stories" aren't always objective

➤ There is no better way to see how religion shapes the world or how religion is shaped by the world than by looking at religious news on the Net

News is everywhere on the Net, and every major news network, from NPR to CNN, seems to have its own Web site. But television and radio corporations aren't the only ones that have such Web sites. Religious groups are using the Internet to broadcast what's going on with their followers. Moreover, nonaffiliated groups are using the Internet to cover all sorts of religious news that affects the larger world.

What else can you find on the Net? Well, as you can see on the news, for every issue that's represented, there are hundreds of opinions. Religious groups are at the forefront of debates over moral issues such as abortion, the death penalty, and religious freedom. Because they care so much about these issues, religious groups are out to publicize their opinions. What better place for this than the Net?

For those looking for how religion affects the world and how religions view the world, the Net is a great place to get started. The following sites will help you explore these topics. If you want to learn more about the religions themselves and the issues of concern to them, consult the appropriate chapters in Parts 4 and 5 of this book.

Religion in the News

Religion is a big deal in people's lives. Few other forces shape the morality and actions of the world as much as religion does. But many of us think of religion as a private thing, right? Not so fast. Because religion makes such a difference in the way people see the world, it affects everything around it. Everything from an individual's personal actions to large-scale world events can be, and often are, motivated by religion. So, it's no surprise that religion makes its way into the news every now and then. Following are some of the sites that seek to track religion's place in current events.

Nonaffiliated Sites

Although most religious news comes from (where else?) religious groups, some non-religious groups have also entered the fray. They seek to study religion's involvement in the world by reporting on religion-related current news.

Pluralism Project

`www.fas.harvard.edu/~pluralsm/html/news.html`

One of the most useful features of the Harvard Pluralism Project's Web site is their "In the News" section. If you're looking for a relatively objective collection of the most current religious news, this is it. The news bits are categorized not by religion but by date. Read about everything from pagans in the military to religion-based hate crimes.

Religious News Service: `www.religionnews.com`

This is the mecca of Web sites for general religious news. The Religious News Service is up-to-date and full of interesting tidbits of information. The site features weekly top stories, a religious calendar including religious holidays of all religions, and a weekly commentary on a specific religious issue. This is a great place to keep updated on what's going on in the world of religion on a week-to-week basis.

Religion-Affiliated Sites

Secular groups aren't the only ones tapping into the "objective" presentation of religious news. Religious groups are also providing this service. The selection of stories often reflects the interests of the group and commentary usually follows.

Nevertheless, if you're looking for news stories more closely related to your particular religion, a site geared toward your audience is helpful.

The Catholic Register

www.catholicregister.org

The Catholic Register is actually a real newspaper published in Canada that has made its way onto the Web. This free site provides some great information. You can ready about the week's news—news from around the world that is important to the Catholic community, as well as news from within the Catholic community. The site also offers some special interest sections such as Arts and Culture and Youth.

Catholic World News: www.cwnews.com/

The Catholic World News is a great resource for Catholics who are willing to pay some money! The Catholic World News Service covers international news affecting the Catholic community. This site covers it all, from the latest word from the Vatican to decisions and opinions on moral and political issues in the Catholic interest. Catholic World News is updated frequently, and even the most recent news is posted. When you click the story you want to read, you're given the first paragraph, and then you're asked for your password. A 30-day trial period is free, but after that, you must pay $25 for a year's subscription.

Religion News Today (Christian)

www.religiontoday.com

From the title, you wouldn't know the affiliation on this site, but when you reach it, you'll find there isn't much question. This is an attractive and useful site for those looking for both Christians in the news and a Christian take on world news. You can even listen to a RealAudio reading of the day's news summary just by clicking a button! It's a colorful site with lots to offer, as you can see in Figure 10.1.

Figure 10.1

Religion News Today is a good everyday site for the Christian news buff. Here you can find daily news summaries, as well as links to devotionals, bible study tools, and other Christian sites of interest.

Jewish Communication Network

www.jcn18.com/default.asp?content=news

Want news that's relevant to the world's Jewish community? This is the place to start. Although the Jewish Communication Network does not actually run news stories, it offers links to the many Jewish news resources on the Net. Scroll down the list on the left and try out a few of the links, and you'll find a vast array of news stories and perspectives. If you want other takes on the news, check out the non-Jewish news sites listed on the right of its page.

Islamic Voice

www.islamicvoice.com

Here's the site you should use to find out about news of interest to the Muslim community. This is a monthly online publication with a variety of articles on topics ranging from political issues involving Muslims and Islamic countries to moral and social issues Muslims face. It also includes links to several sites focusing on children, book reviews, and other topics of special interest.

Hinduism Today

www.hinduismtoday.kauai.hi.us/htoday.html

Hinduism Today is the renowned magazine of the worldwide Hindu community. This site features the current issue online, as well as access to back issues. Download an issue to find stories on international news, lifestyles, and opinions. You can also fill out a form on this site to subscribe to the paper copy of *Hinduism Today* (for a fee of course!).

Bahai

www.onecountry.org/

The vision of the Bahai faith is a united world, an international community. This Web site reflects just that! This is the online newsletter for *One Country*, the international newsletter of the Bahai community. You'll find this news in all sorts of different languages. It covers United Nations activities, development and environmental issues, as well as issues related to women, human rights, and education. The site covers Bahais in the news and the Bahai take on international news.

Wired Monk

Internet Infidels Newswire: www.infidels.org/wire/

This sounds like a site that's just for infidels, right? Wrong. This is a great site not only for atheists but for anyone interested in issues of the separation of church and state. The stories included are taken from the larger newspapers of the country but are carefully selected for this particular audience. The articles cover such topics as school vouchers, teaching creationism in schools, and the encroachment of religion on public life. The page also features an "Eye on the Right" section, which features articles about the political and religious movements of the right-wing in America. There's even a newly drafted "Bill of Rights for Unbelievers" that you can sign if you're so moved. If you're looking for a non-religious take on how religion interacts with politics, this is the site for you.

Religious Takes on the News

If the previous sites weren't opinionated enough for you or didn't focus enough on your religion, this is the section for you. Many religious sites offer news that is either exclusively focused on their community and its activities or that provides extensive commentary and interpretation of the world's religious and non-religious news. Here are some of the best.

CBNnow: www.cbn.org/newsstand/

This site is the cyber-incarnation of Pat Robertson's powerful and influential Christian Broadcasting Network, or CBN. Looking at the headlines and main stories of this site, you'd think it was CNN! Look further, however, and you'll find commentary from a Christian perspective on the most recent of the world's news—from politics to culture. It also includes various "Channels" for learning more about lifestyle choices, the Bible, and outreach. By clicking **Christian World News**, you'll find out where Christians are making news—mission work, growth in members, and even churches on the Net!

LDS Church News

www.desnews.com/cn/home.html

Here you'll find the most recent news in the Mormon community—from recent trends in the religion to happenings in Salt Lake City, Utah (the hub of Mormon activity). In addition, an extensive section covers the most recent and upcoming LDS conferences. You can see this site in Figure 10.2.

Figure 10.2

The Latter-day Saints (Mormons) use this attractive and striking Web site to track the activities of Mormons worldwide.

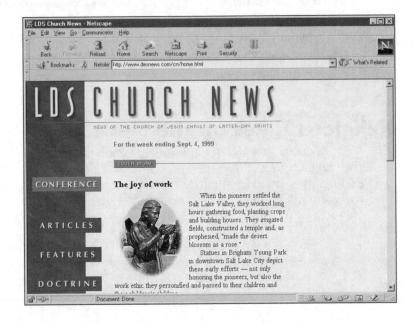

Screen It!: `www.screenit.com/search_movies.html`

Many of today's movies contain violence and adult themes inappropriate for kids. If you're not sure what your kids should watch, Screen It! is for you. Although this page is a link accessed from a Christian site, it does not appear to be directly affiliated with any particular religious denomination. In fact, it would be useful for any parents concerned about the media's influence on their children. A frequently updated site with inclusive reviews of most current movies, Screen It! provides some extensive rating systems. The categories it uses range from language to violence to drugs to "imitative behavior." It then follows with explanations of whether the lead characters can serve as role models, why the film was rated as it was, and long explanations of each of the rating categories. Beware: The evaluation of each movie is so extensive that it might just give away the ending! Read selectively if you plan to see the film yourself! This site also contains reviews of movies that are out on video.

iViews.com (Muslim)

www.iviews.com

This site is just about as comprehensive as CNN! If you're Muslim and want to read about world news that is relevant to your culture, life, and beliefs, this is the site for you. If you're not a Muslim but are interested in the Muslim take on world news, this site is also for you. At iViews.com, you can read about news from all over the world and get a variety of opinion articles that comment on events from an American-Muslim perspective. Because its news comes from Muslims themselves, iViews.com provides a more balanced view of Islam in the news than the mainstream media usually gives. Each analysis is detailed, and you can even give feedback on a particular analysis through the site.

The Muslim Observer

www.muslimobserver.com

The Muslim Observer mixes the reporting of world and Muslim news with strongly worded editorials about the news and daily life. At this site, you can choose from a variety of options from economic news to health or sports. Recipes are even posted regularly! The service does require a fee for full use. Nonetheless, you can read most of the information without actually joining. If you like what you see, it might be worth paying the fee!

NeoPagan and Wiccan Takes on the News

www.witchvox.com/xwrensnest.html

Pagans fall out of the realm of mainstream religion and, therefore, are often the subject of much scrutiny and persecution. So naturally, the best of the Pagan Web sites, Witchvox.com, has an entire section devoted to news relevant to Pagans and to giving the Pagan response to them. Here you'll find the full text of recent articles and a link at the end of the article to Wren's opinion on the subject. For Pagans looking to keep up with the news or non-pagans looking for the Pagan perspective, this is the place to start.

Church of Scientology

www.freedommag.org

This is the online version of the magazine published by the Church of Scientology. It's main focus is to conduct investigative reporting in the public interest. Although the site is trying to promote subscription to its magazine, you can read articles from the current issue on this site. The magazine covers worldwide issues, many of which are related to human rights, discrimination, and freedom.

Religion shapes the world around us and the lives of the people who practice it. It's no surprise then that religion has such a prominent place in the news, or that it has such strong views on the news. This is by no means an exhaustive list of sites, but it's a starting place. You might also want to check out one of the Web pages of a religious organization mentioned in the chapter covering that particular religion. You're likely to find not only news, but views on political and social issues and all the commentary you want! Check out About.com (www.about.com) for some guidance in this area.

From news to views, you can find it all on the Web. One of the biggest perks of a religious group's presence on the Web is its ability to publicize its religious, moral, and political views to the whole world. The result is almost overwhelming! There's a reason the Web's called the information superhighway!

Religious Views on Social Issues: www.about.com

Yes, it's About.com again! By going to the main page for **Society/Culture** and clicking **issues/causes**, you open the door to the vast array of opinions on everything from the death penalty to abortion. Alternatively, you can do a simple search for the issue you're interested in, and you'll find yourself with a long list of religious and non-religious sites taking a stance.

Rest and Remember

➤ Many nonreligious groups have created sites full of information on the activities of religious groups throughout the world.

➤ News services by religious organizations abound on the Net. You can find either religious takes on the news or religion in the news.

➤ Whether you're getting your information from a religious group or a nonaffiliated one, remember that few are truly objective in their services. Watch for bias, but delight in the focused and charged presentations.

Chapter 11

A Religious Job for Pay?

In This Chapter

➤ If you have a strong faith commitment, you can exercise it through your job as well as through your church (synagogue, mosque, or temple)

➤ The Net has exploded as a switchboard with options for job seekers, including those with religious commitments that don't always translate into the work place

➤ Some of your best options require a bit of surfing through several sites, but the results will pay off

One might not think of religious affiliation or faith commitment as the basis for getting employment, but in the fast expanding world of the Internet no stone is left unturned to make life easier for cybernauts. If you are among those who want to connect what you believe with where, and for whom, you work, then you might find a religious job that suits you, and you might find it through the several hints I try to provide in this chapter.

Brother, Can You Spare a Job?

The information superhighway is being built and rebuilt and *expanded* every day. It moves more and more data every day and at a faster and faster pace. Don't be overwhelmed. Because job listings are one of the most popular lanes on the information superhighway, cybersites compete to provide the best access. Each tries to outdo the others in connecting potential employees with potential employers all over the world.

Spend and You May Receive

Jobs mean money, but finding jobs also means money. To get some you have to spend some. In other words, almost every site has a commercial connection. You might get free data from the Web. You can even download lots of cool sounds and neat images from the Web, but to land the job you want, even the religiously connected job, you will have to pay some fee.

To see what is out there for career-related sites, you might want to visit the FastCompany home page at www.fastcompany.com. For even more specific information, visit their page at www.fastcompany.com/online/16/webjobs.html, where you'll find a lot of advice and info about landing a job online.

You have two basic options. The first is to post your résumé on the Web and wait for takers. The second is to use the Net to search thousands and thousands of listings available at the click of a button.

Whichever way you decide to go, the Web has a lot to offer for the religious-minded job seeker. Here's a general road map of some of the cyberpaths you might want to explore. Whether you have got a souped-up race car or just a second-hand putt putt, you can navigate the jobs superhighway and find what you want...without getting run over.

Résumés Online

Although the road to finding a religious job that's right for you might seem long, and you might already think you see some potholes, don't give up. Just keep moving, and you will find some helpful signs, road maps, and guide books. They are all provided on the Web, and if you put in a bit of effort, they will point you in the right direction.

Religious Jobs on About.com

For those contemplating their first trip into cyberspace job sleuthing, the most basic and certainly one of the friendliest guides is About.com. You can either click directly to the site or go to the link for creating and posting résumés. Here you will find general tips as well as links to some of the most popular databases on the Net.

If you haven't done so already, check out About.com for its job searching guide (http://jobsearch.about.com/). It is a how-to manual for electronic recruiting. It even has an index of the 28 million Internet job postings out there (and they stopped counting at the end of 1998). Chances are there may be closer to 40 or even 50 million Internet job postings by the time you read these words! But if you want the right religion-based job for you, and you happen to be Christian, you will find an amazing range of options at the About.com Religious Jobs page, `http://jobsearch.about.com/ msubreligion.htm`, shown in Figure 11.1.

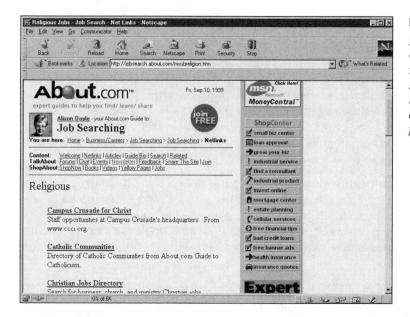

Figure 11.1

It begins with Campus Crusade for Christ. But if that's not your niche, keep scrolling. This site is truly loaded with prospects for a Christian motivated job seeker.

If you want to go the résumé route, it's also pretty simple. The main About.com job search page (again, `http://jobsearch.about.com/`) has a button on the left that can lead you to advice about constructing your résumé or cover letter. Then just click to an online résumé posting site and follow the steps for filling in their boilerplate forms. When you're all done, post the results and wait for good news.

Job databases go to the next level: They ask you some basic questions about what sort of job you might want and then ask you to submit a more streamlined résumé that will be posted for prospective employers or recruiters. Again, it's hard to best About.com. Follow the links on the job searching page to About.com's new service entitled Résumés Online (forthcoming).

Does that still sound too impersonal? Well then you can find an employer whose job looks attractive and email your résumé directly to his or her company (instead of just posting it online). In return, you will receive job lists, also by email. And you just might be invited to attend some career events, events that might be held close to home or might be in cyberspace!

Millions of Listings—Which to Choose?

You are entitled to be confused. With so much to choose from, how do you narrow your search to specify your religion or the desired religious outlook of your future employer? The key is the keyword. If you use a keyword search, you will save oodles of hours, and you might land that job you've been seeking even quicker than you imagined or prayed for!

Job Listings by Religion

Suppose you are a Christian and you have now figured out that one of the most popular online job databases is an enormous site aptly titled Monster.com (www.monster.com). So you go to Monster.com and go to the Quick Search navigational platform. Now you are in the fast lane on the information superhighway, so be sure you're buckled up before you enter the keyword *Christian* and click **Search**. Before you can check your speedometer, you're looking at all kinds of postings that have used the word Christian in their job descriptions.

Okay, now the hard part begins: How do you know what kind of Christian each description is referring to? That means downshifting into a slower lane. You have to check out some aspects of each self-profile, often going to the company's Web site before you make the leap of submitting your résumé or emailing the company site for more info and before you actually apply. Note that Monster.com does charge a fee for accepting your résumé.

But suppose you are Jewish, and you want to find a Jewish-oriented job. The Monster can still be your friend! All you have to do is follow the same procedures as above, entering the keyword *Jewish*. Before you know it, you will find a page like the one shown in Figure 11.2, which takes you everywhere from the West coast to the deep South, for every kind of job, from techie stuff to health care to education.

Search Engines and Metasearches

Even under the keyword Christian, there are so many jobs to consider that you may elect to go another route. You aren't sure whether to register or not register. You don't feel that the keyword *Christian*, or an even more restrictive keyword like *Protestant* or *Roman Catholic*, has given you the range of jobs you're seeking. One other way to streak along the information superhighway in the job search lane is to surf through a number of sites by using a search engine or a metasearch. The following sites are good places to start.

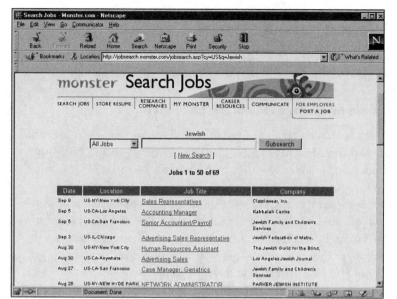

Figure 11.2

The Monster board lives up to its name: It has hundreds of names of both job openings and job seekers. You are included in the list for a year after you enter your résumé and pay a fee.

Jobs and Religion on Yahoo.com

www.yahoo.com

If you go to a large search engine like Yahoo.com and search under the keywords Religion and Jobs (type in those words and hit the **Search** button), you will find links to lots of specific Web pages that list religious jobs. For instance, this type of search might connect you to the Ministry Jobs page (www.ministryjobs.com), a Web site that posts Christian job openings across the U.S. Such a search will also yield a bunch of other sites for you to check out. Although this method takes a bit more Web surfing, who knows, you might find the site that's just right for you and your job search.

Careerbuilder.com

www.careerbuilder.com

Careerbuilder.com is a tool for making a metasearch. A metasearch allows you to send a search from a single site (in this case, Careerbuilder) through many other Web sites simultaneously (Monster.com and the rest). So Careerbuilder allows you to meta-search for jobs through its job search engine called Mega Job Search. On this navigational platform, you can specify location, job type, or a keyword (such as Christian).

Career Path: www.careerpath.com

You may find all this job searching a bit too fast. You still are not sure whether this is the way for you to find the ideal job. You'd like to slow down to the minimum speed on the information superhighway—or even pull into a rest stop! If you're beginning to feel this way, maybe what you need is a group called Career Path that's located at www.careerpath.com. Check it out, but be prepared for a slower pace. This is an online job site that lets you search through the classifieds section of most major U.S. newspapers. It allows you to use whatever keywords you want. It may take you a bit longer, but it also may get you where you *really* want to go. After seeing what Career Path has to offer, you might think twice before buying a newspaper simply to spend hours leafing through its job-related classifieds. Send the money to your favorite charity, or save it for a new power dress or business suit. But also remember what Henry David Thoreau said back in the nineteenth century about appearances. He warned his fellow Americans to beware of professions requiring new clothes. It may still be good advice for job seekers on the Net in this new cybercentury.

No one has ever found a job by just thinking about it. You may have to follow many links on the Net, experimenting by trial and error. But if you persist, you may not only find that you have more to offer a future employer that you ever imagined, you may also find that yourself in the religiously connected job that's right for you.

Rest and Remember

➤ The Internet isn't the only place to find a religious job, but it's one of the handiest and fastest.

➤ You'll find the best jobs by following a two-track policy: File your résumé, highlighting your own faith commitment, and at the same time, scan the lists of available jobs that connect to religious keywords that are important to you.

➤ If at first you don't find what you're looking for, keep at it; you will save time, labor, and money by going to one of the increasingly competitive career-related cybersites.

Part 4

Mainstream Religion—or What You'd Expect to Find on the Net

Would you believe that four out of every five Americans are either Christian, Jewish, or Muslim? All three groups trace their worldview and religious stance back to an ancient Mesopotamian wanderer named Abraham. Abraham has become the symbol for Jewish, for Christian, and for Muslim belief in the One God of history and humankind. In Part 4, you will see the digital drama of the divine writ large on the World Wide Web. It is a story that begins with Jesus and his followers, and then moves through all branches of Protestant and Catholic expression. It is a story that encompasses the Orthodox, including the Saint John Coltrane Church! And it is a story that features some of the cyber churches now dotting the Net.

Chapter 12

Making Sense of Jesus and His Followers

In This Chapter

➤ A CyberChrist was not in the minds—or hearts—of most believers before the Second Information Age

➤ Today, images of Jesus, and His followers, abound on the World Wide Web

➤ All the many branches of Christianity depend on telling—or retelling—the story of Jesus; now they use cyberspace

---

There was only one Jesus of Nazareth who now stands as the most revered teacher, and also the divine presence, in the world's largest religion, Christianity. While all Christians share common beliefs, they also have overlapping images of Jesus, and nowhere is this overlap more obvious than in pictures of Jesus.

Whose Jesus?

Still, you might ask yourself: How did a Protestant artist get a picture of Jesus that he drew posted on one of the most popular Roman Catholic Web sites, Catholic Information Center on the Internet (www.catholic.net)? Easy. Because Warner Sallman's Head of Christ is said to have included in its profile hidden images of the real meaning of Jesus. Look closely at the picture in Figure 12.1.

Figure 12.1

Warner Sallman's Head of Christ.

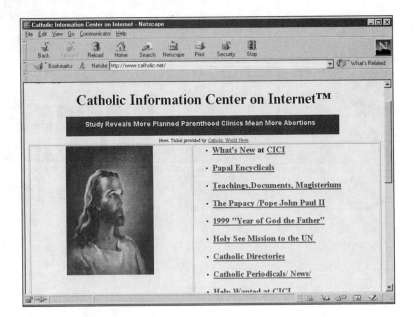

One hidden image is a light circle on the forehead. That's taken to be a symbol of the wafer used in the Eucharist or Holy Communion. Another hidden image is near the bright brow: It is the shining outline of a chalice. Then if you look carefully beneath the right eye, you will see a dove, symbolic of the Holy Spirit. By now, you might be scratching your head: Why did anyone go to this much trouble? He might not have, at least consciously, but others saw these images in his profile. Many of those who saw them were devout Catholics, so much so that to this day the Head of Christ by Warner Sallman, painted in 1940, is thought by both Catholics and Protestants to be a faithful representation of the real Jesus. But who was Jesus really? What was he all about? In this chapter you can learn about how to discover Jesus online, whether you're Catholic or not.

The Three in One, the One in Three

If there could be no Buddha without Hinduism, there could be no Jesus without Judaism. Just as Gautama, later the Buddha, was a rebellious noble from Northwest India, so Jesus of Nazareth, later Jesus Christ, was a rebel rabbi in Roman Palestine.

The life of this rebel rabbi has inspired the largest—and most contentious—religious tradition in world history. Jesus' life was remarkably simple: He left home at an early age, he drew disciples to himself, he preached great sermons, especially from high places, he found unusual ways of crossing water and providing food, he cared for the sick, the poor, the downcast, and he did not like official Judaism, also known at the time as Pharaseeism.

The Whole Life of Jesus in a Nutshell

If you have never heard a Sunday School version of the life of Jesus, or if you have but want to see a cyberversion, the Life of Christ page at www.lifeofchrist.com/ will be your answer. It is very simple, not much on visuals, but it is easy to navigate, and it does give you the basics.

If instead you want a scholarly approach, then you might try a site that's been very active, and reflects a coordinated effort to make sense of Jesus' life within the present day academic study of religion: the Jesus Seminar Forum at http://religion.rutgers.edu/jseminar/. You will need to buckle your seatbelt if you are a diehard believer, but it's still an exhilarating trip.

Jesus might have lived a much longer life, even married in time, as the Greek writer Nikos Kazansakis imagines he did in the notorious novel *The Last Temptation of Christ*, which later became a movie. Instead of a long, comfortable life, Jesus had a short, tumultuous life. He died when he was about 33 years old.

The beginning of the end for Jesus was his fascination with Jerusalem. He was drawn to this ancient city. The capital of Roman Palestine, it also was a sacred site for Jews, but it was off limits to rebels. It was there that authorities arrested, tried, and killed him. Jesus died by a means of execution common to Roman criminals called crucifixion. You can see a Salvador Dali rendition of the crucifixion in Figure 12.2. Dali believed that you had to electrify the senses to capture the inner sense of life's drama. He didn't paint as the eye sees but as the imagination plots. In the case of Jesus' death, Dali plotted a view from the top down, as if it were a sky-to-earth, God-to-man gaze at the body of Jesus slumped on the cross. The unexpected view forces you to see the tense shoulder muscles, and also the continuous shadow between the two outstretched hands.

What happened next is the basis of the Christian difference, not only from Judaism and Islam, its cousins via the Prophet and Patriarch Abraham, but also from all other religious traditions.

Jesus rose from the dead. Not right away but after three days, and in spite of a big rock that blocked anyone getting to him, and would've blocked his own escape (had he just come down from the Cross, as some have said he did). He then roamed the city, appearing to his relatives and disciples. And he kept appearing, right up to 40 days after his first sighting.

Figure 12.2

A Modern Painting of the Cruxifiction by the Spanish painter, Salvator Dali (d. 1989), at `http://sunsite.auc.dk/ cgfa/dali/p-dali18.htm.`

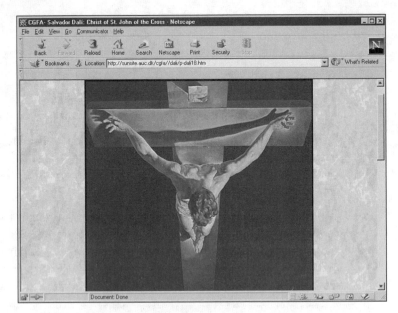

How Did Jesus Rise from the Dead?

It is much easier to describe how Jesus died than to pinpoint the exact nature of his resurrected being. One Roman Catholic site, `www.knight.org/advent/ cathen/08377a.htm`, lays out the basic story. Of course it was a miracle, but what a miracle! It is the miracle on which most Christians base their faith claim, so it is good to re-examine it in this sparse story form, yet it is also good to be wary of the notion that the historical Jesus must be different from the Jesus of the Gospels. For a no-holds-barred review of who Jesus was or was not, whether he was bodily resurrected or not, check out `www.pbs.org/wgbh/pages/frontline/ shows/religion/`. It's the 1998 PBS Frontline program "From Jesus to Christ," now available on the Web.

On the fortieth day it was not a bodily Jesus but a spirit-filled presence that inspired his followers. They even spoke in tongues, unable to contain what they felt on that first Pentecost some 2,000 years ago.

All the events after Jesus' death are so unlike the experience of other human beings that many have stopped short of even entertaining their possibility. One was Thomas Jefferson. Jefferson was a believer, but he believed in Jesus the Teacher, and made a special red-letter edition of the Bible that struck out the offensive parts about miracles during and after the life of Jesus. The Jesus whom Jefferson uncovered as the historical man named Jesus was, in his words, a man of illegitimate birth, of a benevolent heart, (and an) enthusiastic mind, who set out without pretensions of divinity, ended in believing them, and was punished capitally for sedition by being gibbeted according to the Roman law.

Other skeptics have claimed that Jesus, whether divine or human or both, was such an extraordinary figure that he could never be emulated. In other words, their skepticism shifts from Jesus himself to his followers: Because there could never be another like him, how can anyone truly claim to be his follower? One such skeptic was Oscar Wilde (d. 1900), the Irish poet whose own life was almost as notorious as Jesus'. Wilde once said that there have been no Christians since Jesus, with one exception, St. Francis of Assisi (the marvelous poet-saint of fourteenth century Italy, on whom you'll see more in the next chapter).

But most of the world's more than one billion Christians fall somewhere between Jefferson and Wilde. They do accept the basic gist of the four prose-poems about Jesus known as the Four Gospels. They also try to make sense of the letters about the Risen Christ written after his death by St. Paul and a few others who took St. Paul's name as their own. In other words, they try to wrest meaning from the New Testament, as well from the Old Testament, or Hebrew Bible, which preceded it and to which it makes numerous references or outright citations.

What Is the Bible?

For some the Bible is just the two Testaments, the Old and the New, and it is best read in English. But the Bible consists of another seven books called the Apocrypha or Deuterocanonicals, which are part and parcel of the Bible for Roman Catholics and some other mainstream Protestant churches. As to language, English, even King James Version (KJV) English, is a relative newcomer to the Bible. For over 1,500 years, it was read in its Latin version, especially in a translation made by a fifth-century monk named St. Jerome. Called the Latin Vulgate, it included all 73 books of the Bible, and stood the test of time until Luther challenged the worth of the Apocryphal books. His translation of the Latin Vulgate into German did not include these seven books, though others have challenged the wisdom of his decision. On how hot this issue can be, check out a Web page called The Deuterocanonicals found at `http://www.jps.net/bstanley/deuter.htm`.

The great stumbling block for many remains the concept of the Trinity. We cite it in the title of this section, the Three in One, and One in Three. It is taken from St. Patrick, another saint but not like St. Francis. He was more of a warrior-saint, who brought Christianity to the Irish isles in the fifth century, and he also wrote hymns. One such hymn begins

I bind unto myself today,

The strong Name of the Trinity.

By invocation of the same,

The Three in One, and One in Three.

Who Was the Real St. Patrick?

You've heard of St. Patrick's Day Parade, perhaps even St. Patrick's Cathedral in New York City? But you want to know more about the person who gave us both institutions, and much more? Well, you don't need to wait till the chapter on Catholicism or the subset on Catholic saints. You can visit Ireland, or at least a kind of virtual Ireland, at About.com's Ireland for Visitors pages: `http://goireland.about.com/`. Here you'll find out all about the real St. Patrick and also the many traditions that are linked to him, both in Ireland and among Irish Americans.

But how exactly do you make one of three, or three of one? It is a puzzle, or a mind-twister, that has occupied many Christian thinkers for almost 1,500 years, giving rise to creedal differences, even religious warfare. But in its simplest, it says that God was in effect the same as Jesus while Jesus lived; that is, Jesus was the perfect man-God, God-man. Beyond his death, with his rising and his final disappearing 40 days later, what God did, or tried to do, through Jesus, has been passed along as a super task, a monumental, unending labor, to another agent. That agent, also fully divine, like Jesus and like God Itself, is the Holy Spirit. The Holy Spirit inspired all the early Christians, from Peter, the chief narrator of the Book of Acts, a short version of the Christian story as told by one of its main participants, until the present day Peter, the current Pope, who by Roman Catholic tradition, is said to be the successor of the first Peter.

Are you confused? Well read on, because it is a story that unfolds into more stories, and they all go back to Jesus of Nazareth, the rebel rabbi, the miracle worker, and, for more than 2/5 of humankind, the Son of God.

The Church After Jesus

This is a story with many chapters. One could focus on the early controversies about the nature of Christ, or one could look at the institutional split between Rome and Byzantium, which gave rise to the Orthodox Church in the eleventh century. A Web site devoted to this issue is pictured in Figure 12.3.

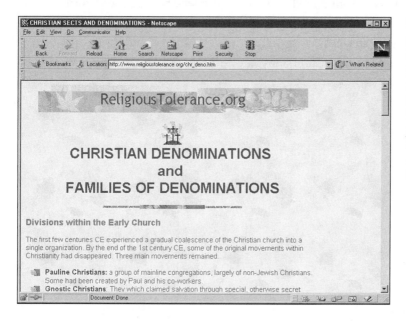

Figure 12.3

*How did the Christian Church become divided? For the best overview of debates within the Church, check out the Religious Tolerance page on Christian Denominations (*www. religioustolerance. org/chr_deno.htm*).*

Probably the most enduring split came with the Reformation. It reshaped the notion of Christianity as hierarchical or top down. It introduced the notion of the priesthood of all believers, and it backed it up with translations of the Bible into vernacular languages, which made God's word at once more accessible and more controversial.

There is a lot of information on the Net about the sixteenth century division within Christianity. Of the many sites that deal with this crucial fork in the road for Western Christians (but for the Eastern Orthodox Christians see Chapter 19, "The Orthodox Story"), we recommend starting with About.com's subsection on Protestantism. Just go to www.protestantism.about.com, and then to the subsection marked Church History, where you'll find a link to the Hall of Church History (http://www.gty.org/ ~phil/hall.htm). Its curator is Phil Johnson, and he has developed a comprehensive and enjoyable benchmark on the Reformation. It ranges from The Church Fathers to The Recent Stalwarts. He calls it "theology from a bunch of dead guys." Dead guys?! Yes, they are dead, but what they said can be funny, and here it is particularly accessible. Also remember: those dead guys had something to say for the rest of us who are still (barely!) living.

Rest and Remember

➤ Jesus was a Jew, and his Jewishness shapes much of what we know about him.

➤ Jesus' rising from the dead is a miracle for believers, a stumbling block for others. The Trinity is a tough sell, even for those who accept the Resurrection as fact.

➤ Not all historians tell the same story with the same skill; some of the best accounts of the history of Christianity, are to be found on the Internet.

Chapter 13

All Roads Lead to Rome

In This Chapter

➤ Roman Catholicism is the largest and most universal of the historical branches of Christianity

➤ The official story comes from Rome and from the Pope, but unofficial stories differ from, or flatly oppose, the official story

➤ You can find both stories and terrific resources about Roman Catholicism both on the Net and in this book

How could you miss him? How could you forget her? He, of course, is the current Pope, John Paul II, who is among the most traveled, the most telegenic, and now the most cybersavvy of all Popes. (Actually, the Net wasn't invented until *after* he became Pope in 1978, so it may take another millennium to update his scorecard as the pace-setter among media mavens in the Vatican's top seat.) She, of course, is Mother Teresa, the charity-driven Albanian nun who founded a global network of support for the poorest of the poor in Calcutta, India. She died in the same week (September 1997) as Princess Diana, who was also her great admirer.

The Pope and the Nun

If you are eager to find out more about the top two cybernauts in the Roman Church, but you don't want to wade through other sites on the Roman Catholic tradition, try these two sites:

➤ www.vatican.va/holy_father/john_paul_ii/

➤ www.catholic.net/RCC/people/mother/teresa/teresa.html

Each delivers an extraordinary profile of one of the most high-profile figures in contemporary Catholicism. Individual biographies never tell the whole story about any religious group, yet these snapshots of the top two Roman Catholic spiritual and media stars will give you a tone for the church as a whole.

But watch out for non-authorized stories about Mother Teresa. If you want an unofficial version of what happened to Mother Teresa *after* she died, check out the Ascension Research Center at www.ascension-research.org. It gives you an account of her reception into heaven by the Blessed Virgin Mary, the mother of Jesus! Although it may sound very Catholic, it does not come with the Pope's blessing as a Roman Catholic site!

Roman Catholic History

Roman Catholics, often called just plain "Catholics," represent the largest Christian community, with close to a billion members. Because they have been around so long, they can claim to be both universal and worldwide.

How long has the Roman church been around? A long, long time. The Roman Catholic church has been around almost 2,000 years and counting. It goes back to that fellow Peter who once fell asleep on the job ("Before the cock crows three times..." Matthew 26:75). But Peter was restored to favor, in part due to a word play. "Peter" also means "rock," and Jesus once declared: "You are Peter, and on this rock, I will found my church" (Matthew 16:18). Ever since then, the Roman Catholic church has traced itself back to Peter as the foremost of the first 12 disciples to follow Jesus.

Its history is as vast as it is old. From the fourth century on its Popes, bishops, and even priests dealt with the nitty-gritty details of everyday life. They plunged into the nasty stuff of politics, economics, and education. But the Church was also appealing to men—and women—who renounced the world, cloistering themselves in isolated communities. These were monks and nuns, and they developed monasteries and convents that were also part of the Roman Catholic Church. Some orders not only set themselves apart, but then took up the task of instilling a deeper respect for the Church among lay people. Notable among them were Benedictines, Dominicans, and Franciscans (which I'll describe in more detail shortly).

The really big decisions for the Church were made by councils called by Popes. But neither Popes nor councils, monks nor nuns, saints nor scholars could prevent the major developments that divided the Roman Catholic Church. First, Rome was split from Orthodoxy in the eleventh century, and then came the eruption of Protestantism in the sixteenth that has shaped the history of Christianity in the past millennium. For a synoptic history, you can do no better than to check out Ontario Consultants on Religious Tolerance (OCRT) at `www.religioustolerance.org/chr_hirc.htm` (see Figure 13.1).

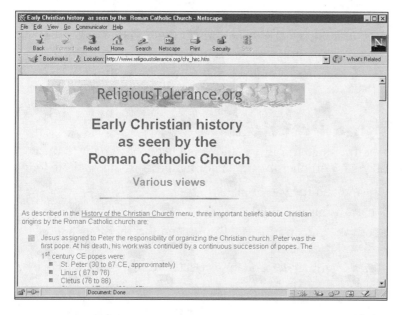

Figure 13.1

Here is church history, as told from Rome.

Do you want to learn more about what Catholics think of Catholicism? Well, then, go to the About.com site (`http://catholicism.about.com/`) monitored by a committed and well-read Roman Catholic guide, Joe Cece. Cece provides an accent on Vatican II, which is the latest of the 21 regional councils of bishops, also known as "ecumenical councils." These councils can only be convened by the Pope, and they are usually convened to settle doctrinal disputes. The results of Vatican II, for instance, were dramatic: to accent vernacular languages, to foster activity by lay persons, to recognize other non-Christian religions, to be more engaged by other non-Catholic Christians. All these conciliar decrees continue to be sources of controversy within the Roman Catholic Church, but they have permanently changed the way Catholics view themselves and others.

What Were the 21 Councils Convened by Popes?

If you want to find out about how controversy was handled within the official ranks of the Roman Catholic Church, visit the ecumenical councils page at http://www.catholicism.org/pages/ecumenic.htm. At this site, the Center of St. Benedict reviews all these decisions. Be prepared for a long, deep, technical (and sometimes tedious) read, but at the end of it, you'll know much more about the Roman Catholic Church's self-understanding than you'd get elsewhere. The only difficulty is that because the Center of St. Benedict does not itself represent official Catholic thinking, you have to go elsewhere to find out how these councils are currently understood in Rome. Your best bet? Try Catholic Resources on the Net, http://www.cs.cmu.edu/Web/People/spok/catholic.html.

Catholic Beliefs and Practices

So perhaps you aren't *that* interested in history, and you'd like to skip right to the beliefs and practices of Roman Catholicism. The major signposts would be these four:

➤ Jesus was the son of God and the son of man.

➤ Mary has a special place as his virgin mother.

➤ God acts through both the Son and the Holy Spirit, and together they are the Trinity.

➤ The Pope, who is Peter's spiritual descendant, is elected to that office for life by a college of Cardinals.

Who are the Cardinals? Cardinals rank above bishops. They are selected by the Pope, and a future Pope is usually one of their own. The Roman Catholic clergy are like a pyramid, with the Pope at the top and Cardinals just beneath him. Then come archbishops, bishops, priests, and deacons. There are also other special orders, of nuns as well as monks. But there are no women priests (or bishops or archbishops or cardinals). A woman pope? Don't bet on it, at least not for some time!

A Simple Catholic Catechism

If you find that there are too many qualifiers in Catholic teaching and you just want the nitty gritty, you might go to a site that is designed by Catholics to teach their children: the Keeping It Catholic page at http://members.tripod.com/

~catholic_homeschool/pit.html. It is easy to read, and it has terrific organization, good layout, and a clear writing style. It also counsels good Catholics against exploring common points with Protestants, especially on issues of the Holy Family, Bible study, and the role of saints.

Saints

Have you ever heard that popular spiritual "When the Saints Go Marching In?" It goes something like this:

> "Oh when the saints, Oh when the saints,
> Oh when the saints go marching in,
> How I want to be in that number,
> When the saints go marching in."

Well, for Roman Catholics, the saints have *already* marched in, and they are already working hard on behalf of the faithful still living here. Although Roman Catholic priests serve as intermediaries between lay people and the Trinity, the saints—people whose lives were so good that they were marked as God's agents—work on behalf of all Catholics, including the Pope. The Pope determines who is considered a saint. He can canonize individuals after a lengthy process. But for most pious Catholics, what matters is not the Pope's final decree, but the fact that saints exist—that they serve here and now as His agents in heaven, helping all those on earth who call out to them in intercessory prayer.

Food for Thought

What Does Canonization Mean?

Canonization is a multi-staged process by which a pious individual, usually a priest or nun or an unusual lay person, is recognized as having been chosen by God to have special talents and special roles while alive on earth. The person must also have performed at least a couple of certifiable miracles, to show that his or her preordained status was divine, and they the person gets recognition as a saint. All these checks and double-checks, along with some numbers of saints and would-be saints recognized by the Pope, are outlined in the Web site within catholic-pages.com that is dedicated to explaining saints: http://www.catholic-pages.com/saints/explained.asp.

Quite a few of the older Protestant denominations, such as Episcopalians and Methodists, Lutherans and Presbyterians, also have saintly figures. These include Biblical figures (such as John the Baptist, the 12 apostles, and the four Gospel authors) as well as close companions of Jesus (such as Mary Magdalene and, of course, Jesus' mother, the Virgin Mary). But Roman Catholics give a significant place to saints who emerged during the formative expansion of the Church. Figures like the great theologian St. Augustine of Hippo, the great translator of the Bible St. Jerome, and the great proselytizer St. Patrick. Many later saints have names that would not be recognizable to non-Catholics, such as St. Elizabeth Ann Seton, whom you can learn about at a Web site dedicated to her, shown in Figure 13.2. For the general site, just go to: www.domestic-church.com, and check out their bar on the left labeled 'saints'.

Figure 13.2

Who is Saint Elizabeth Ann Seton? The Web site at domestic-church.com has a biography.

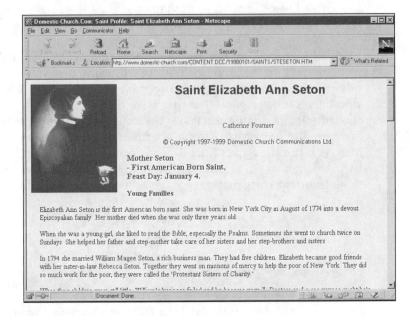

Each saint must have a feast day. It is important for observant Catholics to acknowledge these days, above all, by praying to the saints to intercede on their behalf. The domestic saint's calendar is the source for the picture of St. Elizabeth Ann Seton. An American saint, St. Elizabeth Ann Seton became a focal point for Catholic piety in many Catholic schools and churches throughout the USA. If you want an alphabetical list of *all* the saints, you can find that, too, on the Net. Just surf on over to the Catholic Online Saints Index, http://saints.catholic.org/stsindex.html.

Orders: Benedictines, Dominicans, Franciscans, Jesuits, and Sisters of Charity

It is hard to imagine Catholicism without the special orders. Many of them originated either from the monastic tradition of the church or in response to the pressures of the

Reformation, but all have a long, interlocking history with the Roman Catholic tradition. It is a history that continues to the present, and it has its outreach on the Net as powerfully as it once did in print media or on radio/TV airwaves.

A Truly Wired Monk

At Brother Richard's Orders, Congregations and Religious Institutes page (`http://employees.csbsju.edu/roliver/orders.html`), you will find the inside scoop on all the orders within the Roman Catholic Church that are online and that this Benedictine monk thinks are worth visiting. In this chapter, we give you a lot of info, but we only tap a bit of the well of biodata and history and activities that flow from Brother Richard's site. No bells and whistles here, but a lot of useful insight into the workings of the multi-leveled Roman Catholic tradition of holy men and holy women working for others.

Benedictines

One of the oldest of all Roman Catholic monastic orders, the Benedictines trace themselves back to a sixth century Italian monk, Benedict of Nursia. They spearheaded the development of monasticism in the early church, embracing both a solitary life of prayerful devotion and rigorous work on behalf of others. In fact, St. Benedict himself believed that work was a necessary instrument of virtue almost on a par with prayer, and often indistinguishable from it. See the Web pages of the Order of Saint Benedict at `http://www2.csbsju.edu/osb/`.

The Benedictine tradition has also been preserved and transmitted through educational institutions, of which one, St. John's Abbey in Collegeville, Minnesota, has a visually compelling, easily accessible, and deeply informed Web site. Check it out for yourself at `http://www.sja.osb.org/`.

Cistercians and Trappists

Among the offshoots of the Benedictines is an order dedicated to perpetual silence, the Cistercians or Trappists. The men who become monks in this tradition are committed to not speak, though they do say prayers, sing hymns out loud, and write communications with one another and the outside world. You can explore almost all you need to know about this ascetic tradition at www.osb.org/osb/cist/ (The Cicstercian Index). Or you might focus on one of its most famous members, Thomas

Merton. The Web site shown in Figure 13.3 is devoted to Merton and his works. Check it out at www.monks.org/contents.htm.

Figure 13.3

Here's a full biography and access to the many writings of this humble monk from Gethsemani Abbey in Kentucky.

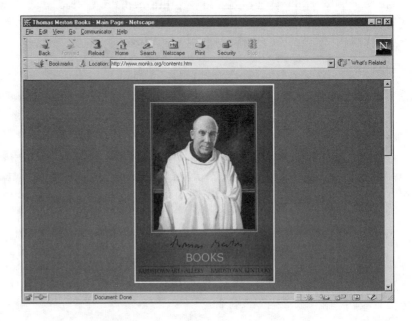

Dominicans, or Order of Preachers

Another medieval order, the Dominicans trace themselves back to a famous thirteenth century Spanish monk named St. Dominic. They have made an illustrious contribution to the Roman Catholic tradition of scholarly asceticism, that is, monks and nuns who give themselves to God, Christ, and the Holy Spirit and pour out their faith in the written word as well as in sermons and good works. Yes, there are separate orders of women as well as men within the Dominican tradition; you can find out a lot about both at the Order of Preachers page, www.op.org/english/.

Among the most famous Dominicans over the centuries are two who are well known even outside Catholic circles: St. Catherine of Sienna, a thirteenth century Italian nun of great piety and power, and St. Thomas Aquinas, also a thirteenth century celibate, and arguably the most famous scholiast (theologian arguing on behalf of God against His detractors) that the premodern Church produced. Do you want to explore the depths and angles of Thomistic thought? It is there in cyberspace, on the vellum-like Web page of an American admirer: www.niagara.edu/~loughlin/. Even if you don't give a hoot about medieval scholastic theology, go check it out!

Franciscans

The Franciscan Web page, http://listserv.american.edu/catholic/franciscan/, is maintained at American University and has multiple links to other Franciscan sites. It does not have graphics that will fill you with awe, but it does have info that can lead you to the outreach of one of the most productive of Roman Catholic orders.

The Franciscans go back to a thirteenth century saint, St. Francis, who has been lauded as one of the most notable Christians of all time. His famous prayer begins: "Lord, make me an instrument of your peace…," and his whole life, including his famed care for birds, was dedicated to furthering peace in conflict-filled Italy. Figure 13.4 shows a good Web site devoted to him, and you can visit its creator, a devout lay person, who works as a New Jersey fire fighter, at `home.att.net/~PCasamento/franciscans/htm`.

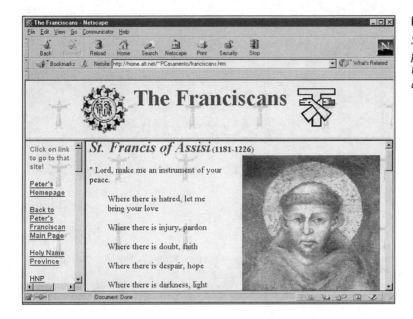

Figure 13.4

St. Francis' humble profile projects his total dedication to a life of prayer and charity.

Jesuits

The most famous order to emerge from the Counter-Reformation, the Jesuits are officially known as the Society of Jesus. An extreme ascetic from Spain, Ignatius of Loyola, founded it. He advocated a rededication to self-sacrifice as the basis for religious vigor. He was also a keen intellect and debater, with a zeal to spread Catholicism beyond Europe to all parts of the known world. Jesuit scholars, Jesuit institutions, and Jesuit influences resonate throughout the domain of contemporary Catholicism. The Jesuit Resources on the World Wide Web, shown in Figure 13.5, offer a lot of information on the order. Check it out at `http://maple.lemoyne.edu/~bucko/jesuit.html`.

Figure 13.5

The Jesuits Resources on the World Wide Web explores every dimension of the Society of Jesus, from its foundational history to its modern-day activities on behalf of science and technology.

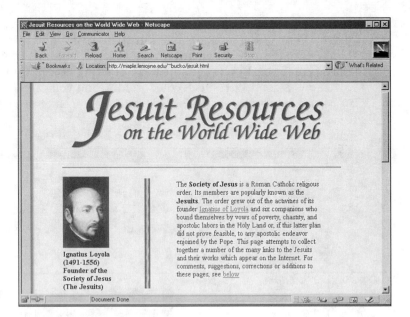

Who's a Famous Jesuit Scientist?

Try the French paleontologist/philosopher/theologian Teilhard de Chardin. He deserves lots of labels because he was hard to pin down as a thinker, and the Pope did not always like his ideas, but he is now one of the most famous Catholic thinkers of the entire twentieth century. Although many Web sites are devoted to him, we will give only one: www.baclesse.fr/~abbat/g-index.html. This site is dedicated to a Teilhard de Chardin Study Group based in France that meets six times a year and provides a copy of all its many resources and findings in English!

The Missionaries of Charity

Set up by Mother Teresa in 1950, this is far from the oldest of women's orders active in the Roman Catholic tradition. But because of Mother Teresa's fame, this is a good place to begin to explore the work of Roman Catholic nuns—not only in India but throughout the world, and not only for the twentieth century but for centuries, millennia. For more information about Mother Teresa, see the Mother Teresa Library at www.catholic.net/RCC/People/MotherTeresa/library.html.

Other Resources

A site that moves beyond the Missionaries of Charity and into the breadth of Catholic sites on the Net is the Catholic Internet Directory, `www.catholic-church.org/cid/`. Check out its list of Top 40 Catholic sites on the Web. Many of the sites may already be familiar to you by now, but others may not. Take note, however, that this directory does not seem to have been updated since 1997.

Roman Catholics Out of Tune with Rome (But That Seem to Be Good Catholics)

Many sites address the nature and stance of groups that ally with the Bishop of Rome (the Pope) but do not always agree with him. We cannot give all of them here, but we encourage you to explore a few of the more notable ones—and a few others—at the useful list of links provided by Lycos.com. You can type the following URL, or you can go to Lycos and follow the appropriate subcategories: `http://dir.lycos.com/Society/Religion/Faiths_and_Beliefs/Christianity/Denominations/Catholicism/Not_In_Union_With_Rome/`. The address is a handful, but the site is well worth the effort. From there you might explore some interesting groups, including some of those described in the following sections.

The St. Benedict Center (The Feeneyites)

`www.catholicism.org`

Officially, this is the site for the St. Benedict Center. Unofficially, they are called Feeneyites, and they are linked to the so-called "Boston heresy." Why does Rome consider them heretics? Because they hold to a rigorist interpretation of the saying "extra ecclesiam nulla salus."

What Is Extra Ecclesiam Nulla Salus?

In Latin, this literally means "outside the Church [there is] no salvation." Sound pretty tough? It is, and also pretty dangerous, even to people inside the Church. Because it underscores the supremacy of Roman Catholic teaching, it can be used by those who oppose the Pope or decisions of councils with which they disagree. Have you ever heard the expression: "more Catholic than the Pope"? Well, groups who say that their slogan is *extra ecclesiam nulla salus* usually are to the right of the Pope in their view of the contemporary Church. Groups like Feeneyites want to be more Catholic than the Pope! Proceed with caution.

Even though Feeney was excommunicated, this site glosses over his fall from official favor, insisting that the "crusade" of the St. Benedict Center is to win the United States to the One True Faith.

Opus Dei

Even more influential than the Feeneyites has been the group called Opus Dei. Emerging out of Francos Spain, it merits the label "arch-conservative." It opposes the Vatican as too liberal, and it advocates extreme self-flagellation as a means of controlling base bodily desires, to imitate Christ, and to pursue the true goals of the Church that have been forsaken by the current Holy See leadership.

Some claim that this is the most important schism within the Roman Catholic Church since the Reformation. You will have to make up your own mind, and there is no better place to do it than at a site that comes from the Center for the Study of Religious Movements at the University of Virginia, http://www.people.virginia.edu/~coh7d/dei4.html. Not only does it give background on this controversial group, but it also provides a list of pro- and anti-Opus Dei sites that you can, and should, browse to familiarize yourself better with this group and its teachings.

Roman Catholics Out of Step with Rome

What does it mean to be out of step with Rome? Many people continue to be observant Catholics but still question parts of Catholic teaching. Maybe they go to mass but take birth control pills. Maybe they believe in the sanctity of marriage but still seek a divorce. Maybe they want women priests but still accept the all-male priesthood that has been the norm for Rome since the time of St. Peter.

Others, however, cross the line and are expelled from the Church or even officially excommunicated, that is, told that they are no longer welcome to receive communion at mass. Some are bishops, and others are priests and nuns, but most are lay people.

A Digital Diocese

What do you do if you feel that your bishop doesn't express your views? What if you are a bishop, and your bishop is the Bishop of Rome, meaning the Pope?

Well, you can stay mum and go about business as usual. Or you can work for the excluded—AIDS victims, homosexuals, drug addicts, immigrants, prisoners, the homeless—but do it quietly. The problem with Bishop Jacques Gaillot in the 1990s was that he was anything but quiet. He challenged others to serve the poor and outcast as he did. He also went public with his views. Rome warned him and then sacked him, but could not fire him and could not excommunicate him. So he was transferred from France, where he had a huge following, to a place that virtually does not exist: Partenia in Algeria. But ironically, it is from Partenia that Bishop Gaillot set up a virtual diocese! You can visit him at his Partenia home page, www.partenia.org/eng/, shown in Figure 13.6.

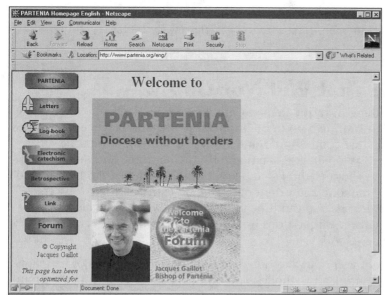

Figure 13.6

Beneath the smile of this mild-mannered prelate is a very stubborn advocate of democratization within the Roman Catholic Church.

This French-speaking demoted bishop even offers an electronic catechism, and it is updated every month, often with input from those who have responded to previous electronic catechisms. For a sample, check out www.partenia.org/eng/c_9801e.htm.

In addition, at least one group of devout Roman Catholics publicly supports Bishop Gaillot. They voice their support—where else—on another Web site. To learn more about this case of cybersolidarity, visit the page of the Community in Ascension at www.ascens.org/ukindex.htm. It is even more interesting because the folks supporting the site are Italian and are linked—or were formerly linked—to the Catholic Diocese of Naples.

While Bishop Gaillot might be termed a dissident bishop on the left, there are also dissident bishops on the right, none more notorious (or illustrious depending on your point of view!) than Archisbishop Michel Lefevre. Unlike Bishop Gaillot, he confronted the Pope for having relaxed the mass. He asserted that only the mass in Latin, or the Tridentine Mass, was acceptable. His movement, too, has its own Web site, the Society of Saint Pius X at www.sspx.org/.

Dissident Priests

Historically, there have been dissident bishops, an occasional dissident archbishop, dissident priests, and dissident nuns. Not all dissent from the left, as did Bishop Gaillot; some dissent from the right, as did Archbishop Lefevre. Another example of dissent from the right is the Lady of Fatima priest, Father Nicholas Gruner, now in Canada instead of Italy. His quarrel with Rome concerns the status of official recognition for all three of the secrets that the blessed Virgin Mary was said to have given to a devotee in Fatima, Portugal. If you want to follow some of the discussion about the case of this overzealous priest, you might check out what's being said at a site called Suite101.com: `www.suite101.com/discussion.cfm/catholic_christianity/14173/latest/5`.

Issues for Rome That Will Not Go Away

One of the enduring strengths of the Roman Catholic tradition is its resolute flexibility. Every challenge that is thrown up to traditional teaching and practice is answered as just that: a challenge that comes from some motivated sinner and must be engaged, and countered, as a pretext for setting forth divine truth. The Net has made the forum for discussion about Catholic—and anti-Catholic—views even livelier, and a good place to sample the tone and extent of discussion is the Catholic Answers Home Page: `www.catholic.com`. You can tune in to it either live or with audio downloads, and it covers the range of questions from the nature of God to everyday morality.

While birth control, contraception, abortion, and homosexuality are major issues of personal morality confronting all Catholics, two other big issues concerning the ministry dominate other discussions. In the following sections, we raise those two big issues: women's ordination to the priesthood and the ordination of married priests.

Women's Ordination to the Priesthood

One of the most challenging issues of the day, this topic arouses heat both within and beyond official Catholic circles. The issue is more pressing now because the Anglican Church has joined with other Protestant mainstream denominations in welcoming the ordination of women, at least in the Protestant Episcopal Church of the USA. There is also, however, a groundswell of advocacy within Roman Catholic circles. You can find the official position—along with a huge list of supporting statements—at Catholic.com's page on Women and the Priesthood: `www.catholic.com/ANSWERS/tracts/_wpriest.htm`.

But perhaps you want to follow the debate through some of the essays posted in About.com by its guide, Joe Cece. As you can with other issues, you can register your own thoughts by following the appropriate links at `catholic.about.com`. For the issue of women in the Church, see `http://catholicism.about.com/msub25.htm?pid=2818&cob=home`.

If you are in a hurry and don't want to enter the fray, you might go to just one site that offers a balanced sense of the daily struggle for women's advocacy. It also raises other issues of social and economic justice within the Roman Catholic tradition. Maintained at Wellesley College, `SisterSite` has been active since the Spring of 1997 on behalf of religious women identified with Rome. Check it out at `www.geocities.com/Wellesley/1114/`.

Married Priests

Just as some Catholics feel that the time has come for them to be acknowledged as full partners in administering the sacraments of the Church, some men now believe that they can be married and be priests; they want to be good fathers at home as well as in the sanctuary! The issue of married priests is usually discussed under the title The Priesthood and Celibacy. It, too, can be tracked through `catholicism.about.com` and its able guide, Joe Cece. Often the issue of married priests is linked to the previous issue, women's ordination to the priesthood. You can read a nimble article on this double-barreled question at `http://catholicism.about.com/library/weekly/aa082398.htm?pid=2818&cob=home`.

Roman Catholic Responses (Apologetics) to Dissident Viewpoints

The tradition of advocating the faith against its detractors is long-standing within Roman Catholicism. Few sites give you a better feeling for the official position on issues from clerical defections to women's ordination to the nature of ecumenical relations than Biblical Evidence for Catholicism (`http://ic.net/~erasmus/erasmus.htm`). Its site is appropriately named after Erasmus, a radical reformer from the medieval period. But it features on its home page the nineteenth century Anglo-Catholic convert to Catholicism, John Henry Newman, along with a picture of Notre Dame Cathedral in Paris. This site has received numerous Catholic awards and is well worth the visit. If you want a more interactive site, however, you might go back to Catholic Answers at `www.catholic.com/`.

Other Resources

It would be impossible to list all the resources available to Roman Catholics and to those who want to explore Catholicism on the Net. There are Catholic plug-ins, courses, chat groups, and even Catholic-related jobs. We talk about these in other chapters; here we mention just two that come to the top for most observant Catholics.

Local Masses on Real Live Audio

`www.raldioc.org/mass/mass.htm`

It could only happen in North Carolina. Often cited as a prototype for dioceses coming online, the Diocese of Raleigh remains the most electronically networked in the country. The Raleigh diocese has racked up quite an impressive list of firsts: Since 1992, diocesan officials have been able to communicate via email, and with the launch of an extensive Web site in 1994, visitors have been able to contact diocesan offices via email, view the TV schedules, and peruse the local Catholic newspaper.

But that's not why we give you this Web site here. We do so because this diocese is the only one that currently broadcasts the mass all around the world in both RealAudio (for which you need a plug-in) and regular audio. So if you are Roman Catholic, even if you don't happen to be from North Carolina, we recommend this Web site so you can complete your road trip without missing church.

Rest and Remember

➤ Roman Catholicism has entered the new millennium with a zest for using the Internet to communicate both to the faithful and the non-faithful its view of the Church and the world.

➤ Even if you have never thought about saints and are out of tune with Catholicism altogether, you might visit the sites for saints—and also orders—to get a feeling for how hip one very traditional and old religious community projects itself in cyberspace.

➤ Some of the groups most opposed to the official church teaching—dissident bishops, over-conservative renegades, feminist advocates, and married men who want to be priests—have found space to argue their points of view on the same Web used by the Pope and his followers.

Chapter 14

Mainstream Protestants: Baptists, Lutherans, and Methodists

In This Chapter

➤ Baptists, Lutherans, and Methodists account for more than half of all Protestants, and they are well represented on the Web

➤ Baptists, Lutherans, and Methodists have their own story as Protestant denominations, and you can find out about them on the Web

➤ Despite their differences, Baptists, Lutherans, and Methodists reflect a Reformation understanding of the common Protestant story

The Protestant Story

Of course, there are more than three top groups of Protestants. After all, a very respectable Web site, Ontario Consultants on Religious Tolerance (OCRT) at www.religioustolerance.org, notes that there are more than 12,000 sects in Christianity, and most of them are Protestant!

Despite differences among Protestant Christians we wanted to give a sense of their common, and not so common, elements. We opted for the roll call that you could find if you went to the site of the National Council of Churches at www.ncccusa.org. We don't flag these top three groups as the only folk worthy of being called Protestant, just the most numerous, and sometimes also the loudest, but in any case the ones without whom Protestantism would not be recognized as Protestant!

Who Counts As a Christian

While some Christians debate which faith groups are Christian and which are not, we refer to Christian as any faith group or individual that sincerely, thoughtfully, and devoutly regards themselves to be.

Baptists

The Baptists are first in the alphabet, and others would say that they are first in all other counts, including the first to note the very first thing that anyone who wants to be Christian has to do: get baptized.

The Baptists are numerically one of the largest Protestant denominations. Their total membership in the U.S. alone approaches 30 million believers, more than all other mainstream Protestant groups combined. They also are among the most contentious, ranging from those who stand side-by-side with other mainstream Christian groups, like the American Baptist Churches and the Cooperative Baptist Fellowship, to those who stand against almost all other Christians, like the Southern Baptist Convention.

You want to learn more about both? Check out the emphasis on education—both through colleges and seminaries—that the American Baptists support. See www.abc-usa.org.

Or, if you want to learn more about the history of the Baptist movements within Protestantism, you might go and check out the Religious Movements Homepage, as seen in Figure 14.1, at the University of Virginia.

What you quickly discover is Baptists were part and parcel of the downstream of the Reformation movement. Like their sound-alikes, the Anabaptists, they were really keen to stress believers' baptism. They wanted adult believers, not just baptized infants, such as are welcome in Roman Catholic and also other mainstream Protestant churches, like Episcopals, Lutherans, and Methodists.

Anabaptists also believed in the rigorous independence of local congregations. The general label Baptist does not always imply unanimity even within a small geographical radius. Although they were becoming well established in Europe and also in Britain, their message caught on and their numbers grew in the New World. Roger Williams is a famous early Baptist leader from colonial days. The Great Awakening in New England in mid-eighteenth century also led to the swelling of numbers in the Baptist ranks. By 1900 there were some 4 million Baptists in the United States, but half a century later there were 12 million. And now? Well, at the end of the century they are still growing, and none faster than the Southern Baptists.

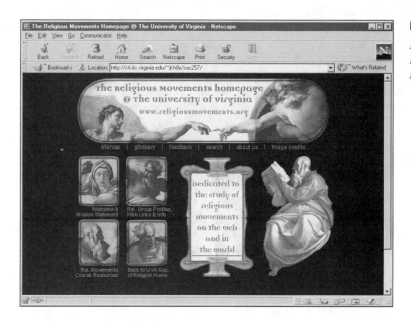

Figure 14.1

Here you can see the Religious Movements Homepage.

Southern Baptists

Southern Baptists alone account for over 15 million, almost half of all Baptists in the United States. The Southern Baptists also project themselves and their faith through cyberspace. The Southern Baptist Convention home page is www.sbc.net, shown in Figure 14.2.

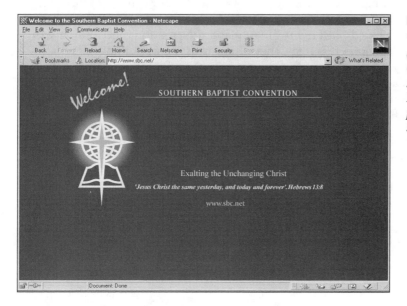

Figure 14.2

The welcome screen of the Southern Baptist Convention gives you a sense of how the largest Baptist group in the U.S. presents itself in cyberspace.

Also available is very practical information, such as number of members, churches, conferences, and so on, along with daily scriptural passages, all for free at Lifeway Online. Go to www.lifeway.com.

Other Baptists

Of the numerous other Baptist churches, special mention must be made of two, due both to their size and quality. The first is the oldest and the largest, the National Baptist Convention of the USA, said to number seven million members but might be closer to two million or even as low as one million.

How Do You Count Baptists?

Prosecutors revealed that the figures for the National Baptist Convention USA, Inc. indicating that Baptists numbered 8.5 million were fabricated. The convention actually has closer to one million members.

For the full scoop on this group, you might head over to the Adherents.com essay under the title Notes about some groups not among America's 10 largest religious bodies (http://www.adherents.com/rel_USA.html).

Formed in 1895 in Atlanta, its co-founders were two powerful Baptist figures, Reverend E.C. Morris and Lewis G. Jordan. They modeled their polity after Anglo churches, but also developed both hymn singing and the emotional performance of faith to new heights. Like other Baptists, they also accent the importance of education, and in North Carolina, Tennessee, Georgia, and Alabama can be found institutions of both liberal arts and seminary training linked to the National Baptist Convention. Their site, National Baptist Convention USA, Inc., dull but data filled, can be found at www.nbcusa.org.

The other Baptist convention that deserves special mention is the Progressive National Baptist Convention, Inc. (PNBC) seen in Figure 14.3. Split off from the National Baptist Convention in 1961, it became the spearhead for the Civil Rights Movement, and Martin Luther King, Jr. became one of its most illustrious leaders. It is a vital group serving over two million believers, and you can check out its notable history plus current activities at www.pnbc.org.

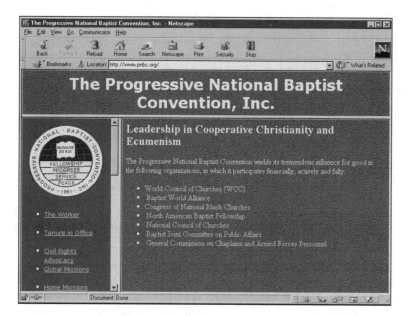

Figure 14.3

Leadership in Cooperative Christianity and Ecumenism has been a major goal for the Progressive National Baptist Convention.

While many folks think of Baptists as Protestant separatists who keep to themselves, it is crucial to keep in mind the PNBC. Sure they support other Baptists but they also join with NCC and WCC for global issues and they take an interest in representing their faith to U.S. soldiers and sailors, marines, and pilots.

Lutherans

Sola Gratia, Sola Fide, Sola Scriptura

(Grace alone, Faith alone, Scripture alone)

Okay, so what's the big deal about Latin? Well, this particular Latin phrase was once uttered by Martin Luther himself. Luther is known to many Lutherans as the *father of the Reformation*. He began the Reformation by nailing his *Ninety-five Theses* to the door of the Church at Wittenberg. Luther had a problem with certain practices of the Catholic Church. For example, he hated the buying and selling of indulgences by Roman Catholics. In a more modern way of thinking, a person could get indulgences by giving money to the church or going to the church hot dog sale. An indulgence works sort of like a *get out of hell free* card. Luther had problems with a person buying his or her way out of hell. He believed that people could only escape hell through faith in Christ. Not surprisingly, the Roman Catholic officials didn't think too highly of Luther.

But Luther tried to summarize not just what was wrong with Catholics but what was—or could be—right with Christianity. He had a knack for the 30 seconds sound bite, even before folks knew that such quick, easy phrases were important to communicate BIG truths. Luther's sound bite came in Latin and, you guessed it, the phrase he uttered was

"Sola Gratia, Sola Fide, Sola Scriptura"

(Grace alone, Faith alone, Scripture alone)

It best describes the Protestant difference, and also Lutheran theology. But to paraphrase a present day Roman Catholic apologist: Even though Protestants claim to believe in the teachings of sola scriptura ("by Scripture alone"), they also claim to advocate sola fide ("by faith alone"—). Few Protestants agree with one another about these key concepts.

You can find the whole essay at `www.catholic.com/answers/tracts/heresies.htm`.

The Name Lutheran

So what's with the name Lutheran? More than you might suspect: The word Lutheran actually came from Luther's enemies. Roman Catholics who opposed Luther and his followers mockingly called them Lutherans. However, they took this insult with a grain of salt and felt proud to be dubbed *Lutherans*. With time, Lutherans gained a strong presence in northern Europe—especially in Germany and the Scandinavian countries—and eventually came to the United States.

Here in the United States there are two major Lutheran Churches: the Lutheran Church—Missouri Synod (LCMS) and the Evangelical Lutheran Church in America (ELCA). Five million members strong, the ELCA is the largest Lutheran group in America (`www.elca.org`) while the LCMS (`www.lcms.org`) is second, with over two and a half million members, most of them in the mid-western heartland of conservative Lutheranism. Both are represented on the Web, although the ELCA has a stronger virtual presence than its conservative counterpart.

Differences Within Lutheranism

Want to see where these two branches of Luther's church differ in America? Look at the screen shot in Figure 14.4. You know it could never be from the LCMS because they still do not approve of the ordination of women.

Where else does the LCMS differ from its more liberal cousin in the Lutheran faith camp? Let us look at Biblical interpretation and inter-church relations, also known as ecumenism.

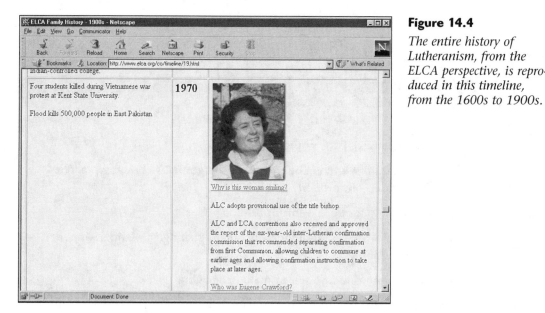

Figure 14.4

The entire history of Lutheranism, from the ELCA perspective, is reproduced in this timeline, from the 1600s to 1900s.

Lutherans on the Bible

The LCMS favors a strict interpretation of the Bible and the *Lutheran Confessions*. These confessions are documents that state what Lutherans believe and include the *Smaller Catechism* and the *Augsburg Confession*. You might want to view these documents. If so, search the Project Wittenberg home page: www.iclnet.org/pub/resources/text/wittenberg/wittenberg-home.html. The ELCA, by contrast, believes that the Bible should be interpreted symbolically as well as literally. To the ELCA faithful, it matters a lot where, when and to whom Biblical passages were revealed. In their view, only by considering the place, the time, and circumstances in which each biblical passage was written are we able to interpret its divine meaning.

Lutherans on Non-Lutherans

Another big difference between ELCA and LCMS is their view of other Christians who are not Lutherans. To the ELCA one must try to seek common cause with churches that are not non-Lutheran. For example, the ELCA is officially in "full communion" with the Presbyterian Church (USA), the Lutheran World Federation, the Reformed Church in America, and the United Church of Christ. Not only that, but the ELCA is more involved in church endeavors. It has helped to found the National Council of Churches (www.ncccusa.org), the World Council of Churches (www.wcc-coe.org), and Lutheran World Relief (www.lwr.org).

So What's Full Communion?

Full communion means that the churches

➤ Recognize each other as churches in which the gospel is correctly preached and the sacraments are properly administered.

➤ Withdraw any past condemnation or tension.

➤ Recognize each other's Baptism and encourage sharing the Lord's Supper among their members.

➤ Communicate with one another in making decisions.

➤ Communicate with one another so as to resolve questions concerning faith and to better evangelize, witness, and serve.

➤ Develop trust for one another so that all parties involved can grow (from `http://www.elca.org`).

For the LCMS, on the other hand, there is no path to salvation outside the Lutheran church. It is only within Lutheranism and their own interpretation of Lutheran writings and practices that the believer can find redemption and eternal life.

Yet the LCMS is no less missionary than its faith cousin. In mid- 1999 the church sent over 81 volunteers to teach in China. In China the LCMS will teach English as a second language to Chinese teachers and students. Recent mission trips to China have prompted the LCMS to ask for volunteers willing to remain in China for several years. Work such as this lets people know that the LCMS cares not only for their soul but also for their physical well being. Read about this and other LCMS mission activities at `http://www.lcms.org/news/canadian.html`.

Methodists

Methodism is a perfect example of how Protestantism cannot be limited to a couple of sects. Forget orthodoxy! Roman Catholics might claim to be orthodox, and the Eastern Orthodox even call themselves orthodox, but there is no Protestant orthodoxy. After the floodgates of scripture are open to all, there is the possibility for all manner of interpretation. In the eighteenth and nineteenth centuries, part of the Protestant movement even became enlightened! How? They linked themselves to the rising tide of rational or enlightened thought in Europe, and then North America.

This new way of thinking glorified the notion of freedom of religion. In the U.S., it became what we now call the separation of church and state.

But Methodists went the other way: They didn't like the conformity of the Church of England. They didn't much care for the enlightenment of liberal Protestants either. Instead, Methodists followed the lead of two Anglican clergy who left the Church of England. They were brothers: John and Charles Wesley. The Wesley brothers left the Church to promote their own theological and practical outlook. Both lived in the eighteenth century. Both emphasized the life and work of Jesus Christ as the source of all piety. Both also stressed the importance of hymns.

In fact, one can't think of the spirit of Methodism without hymns. Hymns are as key to Methodism as the Lord's Prayer is to Easter orthodoxy or Hail Marys to Roman Catholics. Both Wesleys loved hymns, and Charles really got into hymn writing. Charles Wesley wrote some of the more powerful lyrics to come out of eighteenth century evangelical Protestantism. One of his hymns scores the emotional release brought by Jesus: *"Come thou long expected Jesus, born to set thy people free from our fears and sins release us, let us find our rest in thee"* (#196 in the United Methodist hymnal). Still another looks at the need for mission in the Church, and mission was key to the success of early Methodism: *"Ye servants of God, your Master proclaim, and publish abroad his wonderful Name; the name all victorious of Jesus extol; His kingdom is glorious and rules over all"* (#181).

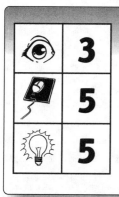

www.HymnSite.com

If you're interested in Methodist hymns, this site's for you. Go to www.hymnsite.com and you can actually hear some of those hymns that Charles Wesley wrote many years ago. Taking hymns from the United Methodist hymnal, the site allows you to search for certain hymns by even just a phrase. It's easy to download these MIDI files and, should you have a problem, there are easy instructions on the site. Loosen up and listen; you will find these a spiritual earful!

The Largest Methodist Sites

Whether its hymns you're looking for or a Methodist church close to your home, the best way to find out more about Methodists on the Internet is to visit the Web pages of its largest organizations. Here are a few of the main organizations and their stories:

United Methodists

www.umc.org

Though the United Methodist Church did not come into being until 1968, it was a merger of a number of groups that had been around a long time. The official Web site of the UMC has great services such as a church locator, a library, and excerpts from the Book of Discipline.

AME and AME Zion

www.ame-church.org

Next to the Baptists, the Methodists boast the largest number of African-American adherents. There is the African Methodist Episcopal Zion Church and the Christian Methodist Episcopal Church, but neither has found a place on the Internet. Not so for the AME Church. Check out its site in Figure 14.5.

Figure 14.5

Here you can find not only daily Bible readings, but also links to various churches and calendars of events.

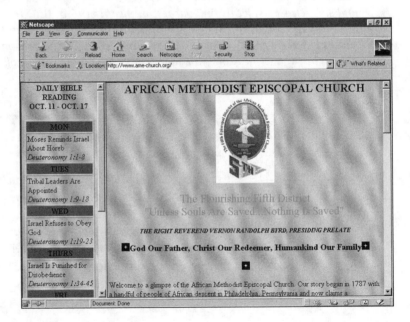

Other Methodist Organizations

Beyond AME and UMC, there are still other organizations within Methodism with a substantial presence on the Internet.

Wesleyan Church International

www.wesleyan.org

The *Wesleyan Church International* is an evangelical church with a substantial membership. Their official site is similar to the UMC page with a statement of belief, contemporary issues, and church locators. There is also a large amount of information about the world missions of the Wesleyans.

Evangelical Methodist Church

www.emchurch.org

Devoted to a congregationalist system of governance and a revived interest in the Bible as the center of worship, the EMC sets itself apart from the UMC and other Methodist groups. This Web page is somewhat mediocre but the determined viewer can find out the story behind this church as well as a directory of churches and information about world missions.

Free Methodist Church of North America

www.fmcna.org

The Free Methodist Church is another large Methodist organization with a good Web site. What are they about? Well, freedom, for one thing. Stressing freedom to worship and freedom for all to worship, they also stress holiness in living. They've been around since the 1800s and have vast world missions and many congregations, as you can find on this site.

Methodist Resources

Though most of the information about Methodism and most of the available resources can be found through the main organizational Web pages, here are a couple standout pages for specific needs.

Cokesbury Online

www.cokesbury.com

Are you looking for a book on the subject or perhaps the Book of Discipline or the United Methodist Hymnal? Check out Cokesbury Online. This is *the* Methodist source for books, music, and other products. It's an easily navigated and very interesting site of unending resources.

United Methodist Women

www.gbgm-umc.org/UMW/index.html

Are you a Methodist woman looking for a community of women who share your beliefs and a desire for social change? Check out the United Methodist Women home page. With opportunities for membership and involvement in a vast number of social and political projects, this is a great starting point for the female Methodist activist.

Rest and Remember

➤ Baptists, Lutherans, and Methodists are central to present day American Christianity and also to the World Wide Web.

➤ They include all races, women and men, as full believers and active participants, as reflected on the Net.

➤ Baptists, Lutherans, and Methodists are engaged in mission work beyond the U.S. and much of that mission is educational and medical.

Chapter 15

Episcopalians, Presbyterians, United Church of Christ, and Quakers

---

In This Chapter

➤ Episcopalians, Presbyterians, United Church of Christ, and the Quakers are not the most numerous Protestants. But they are historically influential

➤ Not only do these Protestant groups have clout on the public scene, but they also have a strong presence on the Web

➤ The cyberprofile of each of these groups makes their future almost as interesting as their past

---

Not everyone recognizes the Quakers and the United Church of Christ for defining Protestant history to the extent that they recognize this chapter's other two groups: Episcopalians and Presbyterians. Yet the World Wide Web accents the achievements of all four Protestant denominations, and in a certain sense it is not their size but their social activism that places the smaller two on a par with the larger two. You be the judge. You take stock of each, both from the past and in the present.

Episcopalians

Is it true that this church was founded on a divorce? Well, not quite. In the early sixteenth century Henry VIII did have a hankering for another wife (he eventually had six), but that was because he felt the need to produce a male heir. He might have had a quiet divorce and remarriage, though it would've been called an annulment, because the Roman Catholic Church in the sixteenth century, as in the twenty-first, did not accept divorce from its stalwart believers. But Henry VIII had a wife who was related to a powerful European emperor (Charles V) who also had Rome—and the Pope—

under his thumb. Henry VIII was left with no choice but to hive off from Rome (or produce illegitimate offspring!). He did found his own church. He became known officially as the only supreme head of the Church of England in 1534. That means that he had a lot of power, and he used it to confiscate Catholic property and also to burn heretics, both Catholics on the right and Anabaptists (along with some Lutherans) on the left. Jokingly, this has been called the via media, or middle way, of the church founded by Henry VIII. Officially, however, the church is known as the Church of England, and from the mid-nineteenth century on, it has been called the Anglican Communion.

Beliefs and Practices

The 1534 break was a protest against the Pope, but it was not supposed to reject Catholic faith and practice. Some Anglicans wanted to reunite with the Church of Rome, or at least to pattern themselves after Catholicism in every respect. Other members really thought that Luther had taken a big step in the right direction for all Christians, and they wanted a much more Protestant church. This would have meant rejecting all Catholic traditions and practices that could not be specifically verified in the Bible. Still others wanted a really pared down church, one marked by a Quaker-like simplicity of belief.

Despite these many differences, there are some things that all Anglicans or Episcopalians share: the Bible as the basis of the Christian message; the three ancient creeds of the church—the Apostles' Creed, the Nicene Creed, and the Athanasian Creed; the doctrinal statements propounded by the four Councils of the early church—Nicaea, Ephesus, Constantinople, and Chalcedon; the Thirty-nine Articles; and the Book of Common Prayer. For more about these creeds and councils, see www.iclnet.org/pub/resources/christian-history.html and www.christusrex.org/. They contain a bunch of detail, probably more than you ever wanted to know, about these important moments of early Church history.

Food for Thought

The Book of Common Prayer

The Book of Common Prayer is the liturgical manual for Anglicans. First composed in 1549 by Archbishop Thomas Cranmer, it became the authorized book for the Church of England in 1662. In the twentieth century it has undergone revisions, and varying versions of it are used by Anglican churches throughout the world. It makes worship services more flexible, but it also stresses a regular pattern of reading scripture, along with saying certain set prayers.

Every four years all the Anglican Bishops get together in England at a place called Lambeth. There in 1888 they issued a document called the Chicago-Lambeth Quadrilateral. It was intended to link Anglicans with other Christian denominations. It set out its four positions, which link Christian churches to one another: putting the Bible first in the church; accepting Baptism and the Lord's Supper as sacraments; believing in the three historic creeds; and tracing the ministry of the church back to Jesus' disciple, Peter. One consequence of this outreach has been the very recent, but strong, merger of sorts between the Protestant Episcopal Church (USA), or PECUSA, with the ELCA, or the Evangelical Lutheran Church of America.

What Makes Anglicans Different?

The Anglicans are really keen on continuity. A biblical, sacramental, and creedal form of Christianity. Almost all mainstream Protestants could go along with that, because almost all would agree that the Bible, baptism, and communion, as well as some creed are essential. But why does the church have to go back to Jesus' time, especially because the Roman Catholic Church, according to most Protestants, was corrupt?

Anglicans think it must go back to the beginning because they remain Catholics, despite their protest against Rome. They emphatically deny that Henry VIII was the founder of the Church of England.

A Natural Development?

The position developed here is more apology than history, explaining that it was almost inevitable that there would be a separate branch of Christianity in Great Britain. If one accepts the official position, then the order of Anglican bishops can trace its descent from the time of Jesus' apostles to the present, just as do Roman Catholic bishops. For more information, go to the Church of England's home page at www.church-of-england.org/.

Whatever the truth of these claims, the ministry of Anglican churches parallels Rome. It is divided into three offices: deacons, priests, and bishops, but the clergy are allowed to marry, except those who are called to be Episcopal monks and nuns (they don't marry!). One venturesome Episcopal monk belongs to the Brotherhood of St. Gregory, and he has put together an unofficial Web page that has just about everything you'd want to know about the history, activities, and aspirations for the PECUSA. Check out his site at www.mit.edu/~tb/anglican/.

What Makes Episcopalians Different from (Other) Anglicans?

One big difference between PECUSA, or the Protestant Episcopal Church U.S.A., and other parts of the Anglican Communion is the ordination of women. In PECUSA, women are allowed to be ordained to the priesthood, and even to serve as bishops. In the 1970s American women were first ordained deacons and priests. Then in 1989, Barbara C. Harris, as seen in Figure 15.1, became the first woman consecrated an Episcopal bishop. Elsewhere, outside the United States, only a few dioceses have followed the American lead and most members of the Anglican Communion do not ordain women.

Figure 15.1

Barbara Harris is the first woman to become a bishop of the Anglican Communion.

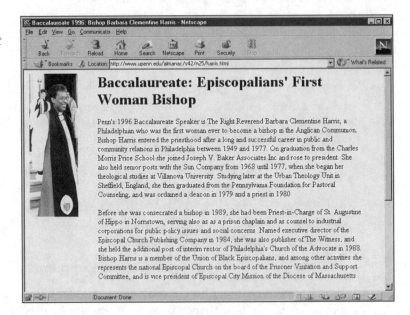

How Many Anglicans/Episcopalians Are There?

So you'd like some numbers for the Anglican Communion? Well, their membership is very small in the U.S., probably less than three million, but it has included some impressive folk in its ranks, such as the first American President George Washington and more recently, another President, George Bush. Worldwide, the Anglican Communion numbers over 50 million. It has over 400 dioceses, each with its own bishop and sometimes an assistant bishop (known as a suffragan). Its most famous international cast are Queen Elizabeth and Archbishop Desmond Tutu, whose full life, writings and sermons, and even pictures with Nelson Mandela can all be found at his home diocese's Web page at `http://www.cpsa.org.za/oldsite`.

Presbyterians

So who are the Presbyterians anyway? Well, they're a group of Protestants who trace their origin to a guy named John Calvin (see Figure 15.2). The Reformation challenged Rome. It was a movement to reform various practices in the Roman Catholic Church. Just as Martin Luther produced a new line of Christian thinking, and that led to Lutheranism, so Calvin produced his own new line of Christian thinking, and that came to be known as Calvinism.

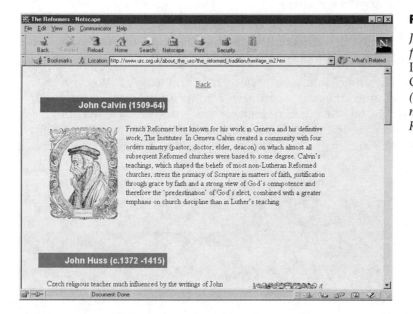

Figure 15.2

John Calvin's most famous book was Institutes of the Christian Religion *(1536), and it is prominently featured in the* Reformer.

Why the Name Presbyterian?

Presbyterians got their special name from a Greek word meaning elder. Yet it isn't only a church for old folks. Presbyterians welcome people of all ages into their congregations. In 1997 alone the Presbyterian Church (USA) reported that it baptized over 41,000 infants. And infants are *not* adults, much less elders, right? Right, but elders run the Presbyterian Church. Presbyterians are not quite as hierarchical as

Roman Catholics, but they do have a pecking order. In most cases, the church or local congregation is the basic level of organization. Individual churches work together to form a presbytery, that is, a regional governing body made up of several churches. It doesn't stop there, though, because presbyteries also join together to form a synod.

And it is leaders or elders who work together at all levels. An individual congregation, which is part of both a presbytery and a synod, elects elders or leaders whom it feels can best direct the work of the church. Elders then represent their particular church at all Presbyterian functions, which include national church assemblies that bring together all synods within each branch of Presbyterianism.

What Makes a Presbyterian?

When they get done with flow charts, what do Presbyterians believe? Well, they hold beliefs in common with other Protestants. They believe that Christ is the Son of God and that salvation comes to humankind only through Him, but with a difference.

Presbyterians are not like other Protestants because they also see God and Christ through the lens of Reformed theology. Central to Reformed theology is the concept of predestination, and the one Christian reformer who set the tone for what all Presbyterians think about predestination is, you guessed it, John Calvin. Check him out at: http://www.reformed.org/documents/calvin/calvin_predestination.html.

Food for Thought

Calvin's Calvanism

Calvin did not write for a modern audience, but if you bear with the style and some of his strange language, you'll find him to be a powerful believer. He inspired much, much more thinking and writing about predestination, which you can find if you go to www.reformed.org/documents/documents.html.

Now, you might have already decided that predestination is just too boring to bother with, like being a cog in a machine instead of driving your own set of wheels. Well, Presbyterians would say that believing in God is not hohum but cool. We believe in God, they say, because God first chose us to be the ones to believe in Him. It's like putting the horse before the cart instead of after it. God loved us before we could love God, and it's divine Love that makes human love of God even possible. God's the cart and the horse, and we should be grateful that God chose us to be the driver(s)!

Divisions Among Presbyterians

Even the concept of predestination can't spare Protestant Christians from internal divisions. Another Latin phrase applies to Presbyterians, as well as to Lutherans, Baptists, and other Protestants: ecclesia reformia semper reformanda. Reforming churches keep on reforming; they never stop! And so within the American brand of Presbyterianism you have one group that thinks the main branch is not evangelical enough, so they hived off and became (after 1981) the Evangelical Presbyterian Church (www.epc.org), and you have another group that thinks the main branch hasn't honored the literal meaning of the Bible, so they hived off even earlier (after 1973) to form the Presbyterian Church in America. None of these groups, however, has a following as large as the trunk group. This trunk group continues to be the principal voice for most Presbyterians.

The Presbyterian Church (USA)

www.pcusa.org

At this Web site you will find the largest Presbyterian group in the United States. Formed in 1983, it reunited north and south. How? The Presbyterian Church in the U.S. dominates in the south, while the United Presbyterian Church in the U.S. dominates in the north. Or did. Now, since 1983, they have become one huge Presbyterian Church (USA). It has 16 synods, 172 presbyteries, and 11,295 churches, or did have, as of 1997. That comes to over 2.5 million Presbyterians, all whom think John Calvin was a hip Reformer, despite his glum look. With Calvin, they put the Bible at the center of their outlook, and for them the message is simple: Christ is the Son of God and salvation comes through faith in Christ alone, but you have to be chosen by God to have faith in Christ alone. Remember: God is the horse and the cart, and picks His own team of drivers!

Presbyterians in the Modern World

For elders who go back to the Reformation and believe in predestination, the Presbyterians have turned out to be very engaged in contemporary society. Its elders have taken bold stands on issues such as abortion, gun control, homosexuality, and women's rights.

Would you believe that Presbyterians were one of the first groups to allow women to become ministers and elders? They were. From as early as the 1930s, they had affirmed the notion of the equality of all believers by ordaining women to become full-fledged ministers. Presbyterians have also been out front affirming the right of choice in sexual orientation for both men and women members. Less easy has been crossing the line to affirm the option of ordination for gay and lesbian Presbyterians who feel predestined by God to serve the church as ministers.

www.pcusa.org/pcusa/info/issues.htm

This site within a site lists all the hot issues for this major Presbyterian group. "Women in the church" comes right after "predestination" as one of the distinctive traits of Presbyterians. "Homosexuality" comes right after "gun control," however. It is not a distinctive trait but rather a major social issue. It remains a subject of contention.

Officially, the Presbyterian Church (USA) remains opposed to having gay or lesbian clergy, but a very active group within the church has continued to seek a change in official policy. They call themselves More Light Presbyterians. They claim that the equality of all believers applies to gays and lesbians, as well as to women. They proclaim that God predestines all people—regardless of gender or sexual orientation. Check out their site at www.mlp.org, even though the site is a bit difficult to navigate.

Presbyterians and Mission

Presbyterians do not shy from headlines but they'd also like to go about helping others in a quiet way. Ministry and mission go hand in hand for all Calvin's modern day followers. They help feed the poor in Latin America. They build churches in Korea. If you head onto www.pcusa.org, you'll find a group of predestinarians called to be active in Central and South America, as well as East Asia. Nor do they ignore East Europe: The main assembly has sent food and money to refugees in the war-torn region of Kosovo, just as the Evangelical branch (www.epc.org) has tried to address issues in the independent republics of what used to be Soviet Central Asia.

For Presbyterians, as with other Protestants, the Internet has become a new arm of their faith. To them the cyber side of religion is a useful tool to spread their message. Was the Internet predestined to be invented to help modern day Presbyterians? John Calvin might even smile at the thought, and he would probably agree!

United Church of Christ

Do Protestants ever get together instead of going their separate ways? Some try, but most fail. The biggest success story might be the United Church of Christ. As the name suggests, they started out as a bunch of different groups, then in 1957, united to become one, much bigger group. They now number about 1.5 million members.

So, which groups got together? It was the Congregational-Christian Churches who merged with the Evangelical and Reformed Church. As a result, there are no more Congregationalists; they are now part of one big church family called the UCC.

The UCC really is what its name suggests: a united group of a bunch of smaller Christian churches.

So what do UCC members believe? In many ways they sound like other mainline Protestant groups. But the UCC is a bit more liberal in some areas. In particular, their social and political ideas tend to both liberal and activist. The same could be said of their theology and rituals. They leave a lot of room for interpretation and they are seldom dogmatic. Basically they try to balance adherence to Christian faith with responsible political action and bold steps toward social justice. Even on the Internet they tend to blend activism with religion.

Since 1957 the UCC has not experienced many splits. There are different geographic regions, and many have their own Web sites, but the official page of the UCC pretty much tells the whole story.

And it is a colorful story! Their main page highlights gender and racial inclusiveness for the greater social good. The profiles are bland, with no background color, but the organization is clear, it's easy to surf around, and it's loaded with information and road maps. One whole section scrolls through UCC news, with constant updates. There's another whole section devoted to kids, another to online shopping, plus the expected whole page to world missions. (Some things about Protestants *never* change: even liberal Christians must promote mission!) If you think this is a fabulous site, you're right. It should be the first stop for anyone interested in what the UCC has to offer. Take a look at it in Figure 15.3.

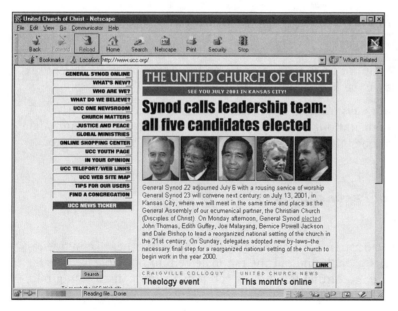

Figure 15.3

The UCC site is well organized, mouse smooth, and chock full of news and information.

Resources for the UCC Activist

UCC activist? That might be a redundancy, because to be a UCC is to be engaged with righting the world. If there is one word to describe UCC members, it is involved. Many of the UCC Web pages take up political and social issues. A few of the biggest and best might give a flavor of the rest.

UCC Welfare Working Group

www.uccwelfareworkinggroup.com/

Interested in welfare issues? This site might be limited but it still provides information about connecting the UCC to welfare. It notes the advances made in welfare reform, and it underscores the UCC role in bringing about welfare reform. You also can fill out a form to receive more information if you want to get involved yourself.

Lifelink

www.lifelink.org

Affiliated with the UCC, Lifelink is a not-for-profit health and human services organization. The Web site features all Lifelink's areas of involvement. Adoption, retirement homes, head start, foster care—you name it, they've got it. And to make this hands on, not ivory tower, they list actual volunteer and internship opportunities.

UCC Coalition of Lesbian, Gay, Bisexual, and Transgender Concerns

www.coalition.simplenet.com

This site provides a forum for UCC members who embrace members of different sexual orientations. Here can be found support and community.

Here you will also find essays on how to treat all persons as equal before Christ, whatever their sexual orientation. Especially prominent are references to appropriate and timely events that one might attend in support of those whom this coalition serves.

UCC Fellowships of Reconciliation

www.serve.com/uccfor/

There also are UCC pacifists. This is a perfect page for them, or other like-minded Christians. If you go here, you'll find out the rationale behind nonviolence. You'll find out what you can do to further it, whether you join an email discussion group, or the group itself!

Remember that the UCC is a church, and it does involve more than commitment to activism. Your best bet for finding out about the denomination in general remains www.ucc.org. But the majority of UCC Web sites relate to hands-on activity, activism in the name of faith. For many UCC members the Internet has become a virtual gateway to a better real world.

Quakers

Why does a group that only has about 1/4 million members worldwide, merit a whole entry in this book about cyberfaith?

Well, the Quakers—or the Religious Society of Friends, as they are also called—are a spunky group of do-gooders who have made quite an impact on the world around them. You thought they were the folks who made Quaker Oats, right? Well, truth is, the only connection between the Friends and oatmeal is a shared name! The people at Quaker Oats might not be Quakers but they certainly are good marketers! What better way can a company portray a sense of truthfulness, good conscience, and value than by using the face of one of the founding fathers of Quakerism, William Penn?

To get the real story of Quakerism, you have to go beyond cereal. You've got to look at those sites that explain where and why and how this small Protestant group came into being. They might be small but they carry some big ideas, and there's no better site to begin with than www.quaker.org.

www.quaker.org

Like Quakers themselves, this site is simple. Yet it is the most comprehensive set of links you'll be able to find on Quakerism. Covering everything from the main Quaker organizations, to specific action groups and political organizations, to unaffiliated sites like Quaker Oats and Quaker parrots, this is a stellar site and a great place to start your search for the Inner Light.

So what do the Quakers believe anyway? All focus on the God within each of us. This *Inner Light* is the guiding force in life and exists in good and evil people alike—because of this, it is the practice of Quakers to recognize and respect that of God in their enemies, as well as their friends, a practice that proves to be quite a challenge! Truthfulness, simplicity, nonviolence, and equality—these top the list for Quakers ahead of creedal distinctions or official structures, both of which Quakers try to avoid.

Now, if you want to learn more specific stuff about true Quakers, you have to trace some of the important figures from the Quaker past and see how their writings have inspired the religion. There's no easier way to do this than on the Internet.

Overview of Quakerism

`www.religioustolerance.org/quaker.htm`

Not OCRT again? Yes, despite the frequent use of them in other places, we have to go there yet again. Why? Because they provide simply, and in clear language, the best general overview of Quakerism, its history, and beliefs.

Quaker Writings

`people.delphi.com/pdsippel/index.html`

Aha! But you really want to know how Quakers think about their religion. What are those pious thoughts that get stitched together and called theology? If that is your groove, and you want a more personal look at Quakerism, then you should scroll through specific writings by Quakers. There is no better site for scanning the foundation of Quaker theology than the *Quaker Writings Homepage* at the previous address. Like the Quakers themselves, this site is no-frills. Yet, it is chock full of works by Quaker writers from George Fox, the founder of the religion, to Lucretia Mott, a leading force in the women's suffrage movement.

Quaker Activism

The suffrage movement is not the only cause Quakers have taken up. They are passionate about righting wrongs, and have been out in front on the Abolition Movement, the Civil Rights Movement, and current progressive issues such as abolishing the death penalty and achieving world peace. Although you can see this in histories of the religion, the activism is still strong today. Many Quaker activist organizations are on the Net and provide easy and interesting ways to become involved. See, for instance, the *American Friends Service Committee* at `www.afsc.org`, a global organization working towards peace and justice, and *Friends Committee to Abolish the Death Penalty* at `www.quaker.org/fcadp`.

Some Quakers show their beliefs in more subtle ways. The site `www.quaker.org` has links to many Quaker-run businesses that walk their talk, such as the Ethical Investment Cooperative of East Anglia, UK. It is very important to recognize the cost of nuclear power, especially when it produces disasters such as Cernobyl, see Figure 15.4.

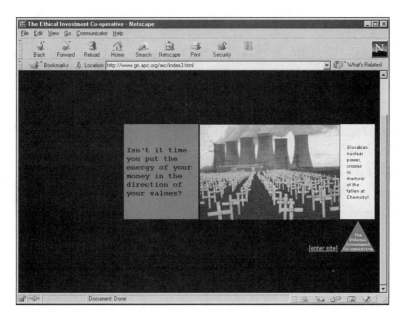

Figure 15.4

Here is one of the opening pages of the Ethical Investment Cooperative, presenting an arresting visual image of the dead from Chernobyl.

Divisions within Quakerism

Even with universal beliefs such as these, no group can avoid disagreements, especially when you have taken on the task of changing the world for the better. The Religious Society of Friends is divided into three main organizations to which all Quaker Churches or Meetings belong, with some holding memberships in more than one group. Quakers on one end of the spectrum opt for silent, unprogrammed meetings without the use of a minister. Many of these Meetings belong to the more liberal *Friends General Conference*, whose Web site is www.quaker.org/fgc/. Those that want a little more structure might opt for the *Friends United Meeting* (www.fum.org) a slightly more conservative organization made up of both programmed and unprogrammed meetings.

There are still other Quakers who actually seem more like traditional mainstream Protestants. For example they really believe in the Bible. They also believe in spreading the faith through missionary activity. Not surprisingly, they are called the *Evangelical Friends International*, and you can find their main Web site at www.evangelical-friends.org. Each of these three sites provides information about the organization and its members, as well as Quakerism in general. They are good places to start, both for those new to Quakerism and for long-time Friends.

Quakers are much bigger than their numbers, even when they disagree. Their presence on the Internet is a testament to their continued activism and growth. William Penn would be pleased!

Rest and Remember

➤ Although none of these Protestant churches has over three million active members, they all enjoy a high profile on the Internet.

➤ The Quakers are certainly the smallest, but they project big on the Net. The Episcopalians, Presbyterians, and UCC also enjoy expanded possibilities through the World Wide Web.

➤ The future for all Protestant groups will be projected in cyberspace, as well as on the ground, and these four will have their own story to tell.

ANABAPTISTS, ADVENTISTS, DISCIPLES OF CHRIST...

Chapter 16

Mainstream Protestants: Anabaptists, Adventists, and Disciples of Christ

In This Chapter

➤ Anabaptists, Adventists, and Disciples of Christ are very different from each other, but they hold in common strong beliefs about individual discipleship and ethical advocacy, even though they might differ on the nature of collective life in this world and expectations for the next

➤ Each of these groups can be found on the World Wide Web, even those thought to shun modern inventions

➤ The largest of these three groups, the Adventists, are huge, but their numbers are subject to dispute. One way to track them is on the Net

While Anabaptists, Adventists, and Disciples of Christ function as separate Protestant denominations, they also share common outlooks. All believe that they have been given divine guidance to be among the elect. All believe that without divine guidance ignorance prevails in this world, and eternal damnation awaits in the next world. They construct strict codes of moral conduct that binds them together, and separates them from other folk.

Anabaptists

No cars, no lights, no television, no radios, no... computers? Believe it or not, even the electricity-shunning Amish are on the Internet! And so are the other Anabaptists. In some cases the resources are limited. Often, the sights are for tourists and created by outsiders, some friendly and some not. Nevertheless, the interested surfer can find information, whether it's about the different Anabaptist traditions themselves or about visiting their communities.

So who are the Anabaptists anyway? Well, three of the main groups are the Amish, the Mennonites, and the Brethren. While each group is distinct, they all have a few things in common. The Anabaptists all started in during the Protestant Reformation. Sound familiar? Not so fast! While the Reformation saw the formation of Lutherans, Calvinists, and other groups with similar aims, the Anabaptists went a different way. They didn't like the ideas of Calvin and Luther: Neither Calvin nor Luther went far enough in the changes he proposed.

What did the Anabaptists want? For one thing, they hated politics and virtually any kind of secular activity. They especially didn't want that involved in their religion. They insisted on a free group of adult believers without state control. Like the Quakers, they were pacifists and refused to take oaths. Some of their refusals were a bit more drastic and became what distinguish them so dramatically from other Christians. Refusal to hold office, separation from society, and, for some, refusal to use electricity are some examples. For this, they often faced persecution.

Though the Anabaptists remained strong through persecution, they eventually split into a few different groups. Some differences were theological, some political, some social.

For a more detailed description of these groups, check out The Religious Movements homepage @ The University of Virginia (www.religiousmovements.org).

www.religiousmovements.org

If you're confused about the differences between Anabaptist groups, The Religious Movements homepage @ the University of Virginia is a good starting point. Look under their alphabetical listing of groups and find essays on the history and beliefs of the Amish, Mennonites, and Brethren.

Amish

Plain dress, simple living, and separate communities. How did this religious community come about? Unlike most religious splits, the Amish split from other Anabaptists had more to do with everyday concerns than with big theological questions. To conform to society or not to conform…that was the question. The Amish answer was not to conform in that way. Instead, they conformed to the Bible and its literal reading rather than society and its crooked ways.

Thus the Amish way of life is distinct. Without cars or electricity, with standard plain dress, and marriage only within the religion, the Amish have created a way of life that, though very different from the outside world, has lasted over centuries.

Beware of Amish Humor Sites!

The Amish are not big into electricity, and yet if you do a general search under Amish you can come up with hundreds of links. How can this be? Well, a lot of non-Amish people are creating Web pages dealing with this religion. While some are very educational and useful, a large chunk of them are meant to be humorous and are extremely misleading. While some are obviously a joke, like www.amishrakefight.org, others are more deceptive and might have titles like "Amish Online." Some of these sites might be humorous and harmless but others perpetuate harmful myths and encourage misunderstanding and hate. Beware as you search these sites and keep your eyes open!

History and Beliefs

www.religioustolerance.org/amish.htm

A good site for a history and explanation of Amish beliefs can be found at the Ontario Consultants on Religious Tolerance (OCRT). This page also features a great listing of the characteristics that distinguish the Amish as a group, from their funeral services to their refusal to take photographs. The only drawback is that OCRT does not have a separate listing for other Anabaptists. Therefore, some of the distinctions between groups are blurred.

Tourism and Information

www.800padutch.com/amish.html

The Amish live mainly in a few concentrated areas. One of the best known and most visited is the Pennsylvania Dutch Country, and this is its main site. With a good essay on "The Amish and 'the Plain People,'" this site is educational, but its main focus is tourism. This is the place to go if you'd like to visit this area or just know a little more about its attractions.

holycrosslivonia.org/amish/

This site is the home page for the National Committee for Amish Religious Freedom. It recognizes that while the Amish have survived for centuries, they continue to face persecution and misunderstanding. Here is a site for you if you want to join with others interested in the fight against the continuing persecution of the Amish. Here you will find details of their struggles and the hard-fought victories for their religious freedom, each one won through court cases and new laws, the site is full of information. While the site is simple, the links are clear and the information valuable.

Buying Amish Goods Online

www.amishgeneralstore.com

Looking for a cedar chest, a simple, handmade doll, or some Amish food? Go here to find the Amish General Store. Anabaptists are known for their quality handicrafts and the Amish General Store is a great place to find them. This online catalog of goods sells everything from horse drawn carriages to generators and lanterns.

Mennonites

The Mennonites began as a distinct group under the direction of Menno Simons. As the Anabaptist faith was falling to persecution in the sixteenth century, Simons stepped in and kept it strong. Starting the Mennonite movement as a separate and distinct Anabaptist group, he facilitated the group's movement to the United States. What was it that distinguished this group?

Mennonites share many beliefs with the Amish but are not quite as reclusive. In fact, Mennonite Churches can be found throughout the country and even on the Internet. Like other groups, their focus is on the Bible and life application of its principles. However, one distinction is their focus on evangelism. While the Amish separate themselves from others and discourage conversions, the Mennonites conduct missions throughout the world. That could explain why they are more numerous and wide spread in the modern world! This fact is evident both in reality and on the Internet.

Like other Protestant denominations, the Mennonites are divided into a few umbrella organizations. Each has slightly different beliefs and focuses but all are based on the same basic theology. Many of these Mennonite organizations have their own Web pages.

The Mennonite Church

www.mennonites.org

Want to know about larger Mennonite organizations and their activities? This home page for the Mennonite Church is a somewhat basic site. Yet it is easy to navigate and demonstrates the scope of Mennonite activity. Here you can find everything from information on the next conference to links connecting to other Mennonite organizations and activist groups.

General Conference Mennonite Church

www2.southwind.net/~gcmc

This General Conference is a group of Mennonite Churches in North and South America. This Web site is once again a simple one and not wonderfully organized. However there is great information here on the missionary work of Mennonites and some good links to other, more specific groups.

Conservative Mennonite Conference

www.cmcrosedale.org

This site is the official page for a group of 104 evangelical Mennonite congregations. Go here to read articles from their magazine, *The Brotherhood Beacon*, or a detailed theology of Conservative Mennonites. You can also view a directory of affiliated churches.

Anabaptist Mennonites

www.anabaptists.org

At the Anabaptist Mennonites page you can find writings of Mennonites from the past and present, polls, and various resources such as church locators and action groups. Click **Bookstore** and find print resources you can buy over the Internet! This is a great general site, take a look at Figure 16.1, for anyone within the faith or just interested in learning more.

MennoLink

www.MennoLink.org

MennoLink features an online bookstore, directories, and other such resources. But its main feature is its news and discussion groups. Become part of an email discussion group on a certain topic or subscribe to receive news updates on issues affecting Mennonites.

Figure 16.1

From fun features like Bible verses and polls to serious political and social issues, this site has everything!

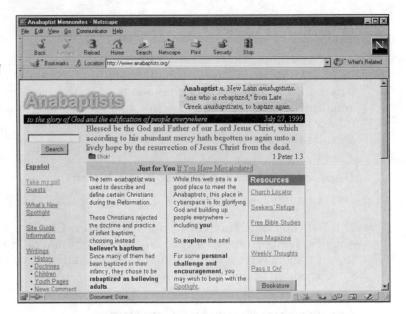

Not for Free?

No, not everything that comes from this Mennonite site is free. You do have to pay something to join, but it is a tiny amount, and if you have any interest in understanding how this major Anabaptist group accommodates its commitment to simplicity with life in the complex, modern world, you might want to join.

Brethren

For this Anabaptist group, it all began in Germany in the seventeenth Century. It was then that the Brethren, as a distinct group, was born. Reflecting the need for personal religious experience, this group was pietist. Yet, they also reflected the Anabaptist emphasis on outward expression of faith in everyday life. What most distinguished the Brethren from the Mennonites and Amish was their focus on the New Testament alone as the real scripture.

Like the Amish, the Brethren wanted separation. Why? Because the rest of the world—even the rest of the Protestant world—was sinful. Any association would be harmful. Instead, the Brethren wanted to restore the primitive church. Yet like their

Anabaptist brothers and sisters, they advocated plain dress, the rebaptism of adults, and no involvement in politics. All these cost them great persecution throughout their history.

Despite the persecution they faced, the Brethren have persevered to this day and have a presence throughout the world, and now on the World Wide Web. Their presence is most noted by the official Web pages of some of its largest organizations.

Church of the Brethren

www.brethren.org

Along with being an organization of member churches, this site is a center for pacifist and activist work. In the description of the organization, peace and service are stressed again and again. Go here to find out if you qualify for membership in the Brethren Employees Credit Union, learn about Brethren educational institutions and find out how you can make a difference in achieving world peace.

www.cob-net.org

The Church of the Brethren Network is the best resource site for those interested in the Church of the Brethren. Here you'll find a conglomeration of links and descriptions to everything from Brethren recipes to educational institutions to missionary work to chat groups. This site is a must see for any Brethren!

The Brethren in Christ Denominational

www.bic-church.org

The statement of belief of the Brethren in Christ (BIC) is very Bible-based. While traces of activism can be seen here, the focus is more on faithfulness and missionary work. If that's your interest, you can learn all about mission opportunities for teens, for those wanting to give financial reports, or for those willing to go to the end of the earth to serve.

Church of the United Brethren in Christ

www.ub.org

The United Brethren in Christ site is the meeting place for United Brethren all over the world. Search the directory for nearby churches or members, read about current missionary work, read about recent news stories, and learn about upcoming projects. You also can go to the downloads page to read articles from United Brethren publications or download the United Brethren logo.

Some Anabaptists might not be plugged in but those that are have made these groups a part of the online religious communities. Most all the sites are simple but great information is out there. Just make sure to watch out for those deceptive sites!

Seventh-Day Adventist Church

The Seventh-Day Adventist Church was started in the 1800's around the time of the Great Awakening. This *awakening* was a Protestant movement that sought to bring America back to God. And, it was heavily characterized by zealous preachers and emotional followers. Of particular importance to Seventh-Day Adventists was a Baptist named William Miller. Miller believed that he could calculate the return of Christ using passages from the book of Daniel. After much study, he concluded that Christ would return in 1844. Miller's prediction never came true. And, what had been a source of hope for many became known as the *Great Disappointment* as many of Miller's followers soon rejected his school of thought.

Wired Monk

From Adventists to Seventh-Day Adventists

Even though Miller's prediction did not come true, there were some who remained faithful to him. They called themselves Adventists. After Miller's death, Ellen White, who received many direct revelations of her own, took charge of the group. White wanted to change the group's name to the Seventh-Day Adventists, and in the end she had her way.

Today, the Seventh-Day Adventist Church is said to number about nine million members but it might be double that number, or much less, depending on who counts, and what counts as Adventist growth.

Nine Million Adventists?

Well, part of the reason is that they give their own figures, that is, they report on how big their local congregations and total national and international count is. Actually they might number more than nine million. Check the Ontario Consultants on Religious Tolerance (OCRT) report at www.religioustolerance.org/sda.htm.

We don't want to rain on anyone's number parade, but don't ignore a major discrepancy provided by *adherents.com* (see www.adherents.com/Na_391.html). It gives the total SDA population as 4.5 million world-wide in 1987, yet a mere 12 years later the figure is 9.7 million, or maybe even 18 million. That's more, much more than a 7% annual growth rate. Look at adherents.com and decide for yourself.

Beliefs and Practices

Like other conservative Christians, Seventh-Day Adventists believe in original sin, the virgin birth, the divinity of Christ, and the infallibility of the Scriptures. In other words, no one is perfect…except Mary…and Jesus…and the Bible! It goes without saying that Adventists also affirm that salvation comes through faith in Christ, and only through faith in Christ.

Yet there are a number of places where Seventh-Day Adventists differ from other Protestants. For example, the Seventh-Day Adventist Church holds that the writings of Ellen White were divinely inspired. This belief has been widely debated and, though it is rejected by other mainstream Protestants, the Adventists are proud of her revelations and give them a central place in their history.

www.egwestate.andrews.edu

The amount of material written by or about Ellen G. White is staggering. Most all her writings are found at this Adventist site, the most complete site available. Though it has not been updated since 1995, it gives all the relevant primary, and much valuable secondary, literature. Note, especially, the curious topics that deal with "unusual statements found in Ellen G. White's writings" and also "statements mistakenly attributed to Ellen G. White."

In addition to their beliefs about Ellen White, Adventists deny the concept of *innate mortality*. They do not believe that believers fully die at death.

Until Judgement Day

Innate mortality essentially means that a person goes to heaven or hell immediately after death. But Seventh-Day Adventists believe that each one of us becomes unconscious after death, and remain unconscious until we are resurrected on the Day of Judgment.

Pray on Saturday and Eat Healthy Every Day

But that's not all. Unlike other Christians, most of whom worship on Sunday, Seventh-Day Adventists worship on Saturday. According to the Creation story, God created the world in six days and rested on the seventh. In other words, God rested on Saturday, not Sunday. They go even further: Adventists argue that not to worship on Saturday and instead to worship on Sunday is an infringement of the *fourth commandment*.

Seventh-Day Adventists also care deeply about their health. They abstain from things thought to be unhealthy such as alcohol, coffee, tobacco, and even red meat.

Cult Status?

Several theologians and ex-members of the Seventh-Day Adventists claim that the church is effectively a cult. Although they do not claim that the church tries to brainwash or destroy its members, these critics do feel that Seventh-Day Adventist beliefs deviate from those of traditional Christians. There are three major areas where the church has been attacked: (1) that the writings of Ellen White are infallible; (2) that church doctrine is based on the writings of Ellen White; and (3) that the atonement of Christ was not finished at the crucifixion.

The Christian Church (Disciples of Christ)

The Disciples of Christ avoid creeds. They also dislike standardized theological and doctrinal statements. Their principal home page offers a full review of who they are and what they do believe. Check out its main site at www.disciples.org.

Early History

The Disciples of Christ was founded in the 1800s. The three major founders of the church were Thomas and Alexander Campbell and Barton Stone. Thomas and Alexander Campbell, a Scottish Presbyterian father and son, were extremely miffed about the sectarianism occurring within their own denomination (and others). What particularly shocked them was the fact that different denominations wouldn't even take the Lord's Supper with each other. They believed that Christians should readily take Communion with each other, regardless of denominational differences. At the same time the Campbells were protesting, Barton Stone, who was also a Presbyterian, objected to the use of creeds in the church. He believed that creeds often did more harm than good as they often pointed out differences instead of promoting unity. Eventually, followers of Stone and the Campbells merged in 1832 and called themselves the "Disciples of Christ."

Wired Monk

What Is in a Creed?

Both Protestants and Catholics have been defined by creeds. Many of them go back to the period after Christianity when it became the official religion of the Roman Empire (325 A.D.), and all are concerned to define an orthodox belief in God the Father, God the Son, and God the Holy Spirit.

Beliefs

As you might have guessed by now, the Disciples of Christ aren't big on creeds. In fact, a popular slogan for the church is "No Creed but Christ." And this is truly how they feel. Modern day Disciples of Christ, like Barton Stone, believe that creeds and doctrinal statements written by man serve only to destroy the church. They believe that the church should focus only on that which unites its members: Christ. Members of the Disciples of Christ view Jesus as the "Son of the living God" and proclaim him as "Lord and Savior." In fact, membership is granted to a prospective member if he or she confesses that Christ is his or her Savior and the Lord of the world. This is quite unlike many other Protestant denominations that require candidates for membership to take confirmation classes and learn a catechism or statement of faith.

Services and Congregations

According to a church document, the format for worship services varies widely. It is the individual congregation that sets the tone for worship. While some churches prefer a more reserved style of worship, there are others that implement a more informal style of worship. But that's not all. The individual congregations are just as diverse as the worship services. Disciples' congregations cover the entire theological spectrum. Some congregations are strongly liberal while others are staunch conservatives. However, diversity is certainly a strong point for the Disciples of Christ. And, as one might well think, it is because the church has no formal creeds or standards that the Disciples of Christ has remained so diverse yet united.

The Disciples and Beyond

The Disciples of Christ certainly believe in working with other groups. For example, they worked with other Protestant denominations to form both the National and World Council of Churches. But above all this, they have also worked to carry their message to the world. To date, the Disciples of Christ have established churches in 20 countries around the world. And, according to the church's Web site, it has missionaries or support missionaries in 60 countries outside North America. However, the Disciples of Christ are doing more than only mission work; they are also reaching out to other denominations. Since 1967, the Disciples have held theological conversations with the Roman Catholic Church. They have had similar talks with the Russian Orthodox Church and the Word Alliance of Reformed Churches since 1987.

Rest and Remember

➤ While the Disciples of Christ are unified, both the Anabaptists and Adventists have a lot of internal divisions.

➤ All three denominations project their views on the Net and have a story to tell for believers and also would-be believers.

➤ Other than the Baptists, the Adventists are the largest Protestant denomination—perhaps—but they in turn are dwarfed by the Pentecostals (see the next chapter).

AMEN!

Chapter 17

Mainstream Protestants: Pentecostals

In This Chapter

➤ Pentecostals stand apart from other Protestants, both by their numbers and by their practices

➤ Some Pentecostal Churches are so huge that they are called megachurches

➤ While Pentecostalism has a big following, it also has big internal differences

---

Pentecostals (Including Catholic Pentecostals!)

Who are the Pentecostals? There are said to be 130 million Pentecostals worldwide. Why so many? What do they share?

The modern movement goes back to a Methodist Episcopal minister named Charles Parham. He agreed with others in the Holiness movement who wanted to put the gifts of the Holy Spirit front and center in their worship. It was at a little Kansas college that one of the students "spoke in tongues," and Agnes Ozman's experience confirmed for Parham and others that they were witnessing a new baptism in the Holy Spirit.

Speaking in Tongues?

It is not ordinary speech. It is technically called *glossalalia*, and it requires posses-sion by a spirit from outside, thought to be the Holy Spirit. One who speaks in tongues uses a human tongue but reflects the speech of the Beyond or God.

It was Parham who at the turn of the century founded a new movement. He based it on the First Pentecost described in the Book of Acts, Chapter 2, and also on the gifts of the Spirit cited by St. Paul in one of his two letters to Christians at Corinth (1 Corinthians 12:8-10). You can track this, and other favorite passages for Pentecostals at Pioneer Tract Society's home page; just head to `www.pioneertract.com`.

The Parham Center

Named after Charles Parham, the founder of modern Pentecostal movement, the Parham Center embodies the fervor of Pentecostal spirituality. It is an easy site to scan, but provides only a brief snapshot of the whole Pentecostal movement. See the Parham Center site at `www.stbi.edu/cfp/intro.html`.

Parham's movement was officially launched on January 1, 1901, and it is still running strong at the end of the century in which it began. Parham, as well as other founders of modern day Pentecostalism, saw all the current needs of the Church to be focused on recapturing and perpetuating the post-conversion work of the Holy Spirit that ani-mated the first Christians. For Pentecostals, that meant speaking in tongues, or glos-salalia, which had been the experience in the early Church. If they were called charismatics, it is because one can only speak in tongues under the influence of charisma.

Integral to Pentecostal worship is hand-clapping, dance, raised arms, shouted utterances, and sometimes ecstasy, feigned or real. You thought it all began with Robert Duval in his movie "The Apostle"? Well, it's been around for decades, and it shows no signs of abating.

This is NOT religion for the faint-hearted or parlor room proper folk. Indeed, it was often poor, dispossessed folk who found a special appeal in Pentecostal Churches in the past, though many today are more prone to be middle class. Whether rich or poor, Pentecostals have objected to anyone speaking on their behalf when they've tried to organize. They also are not keen to take part in ecumenical movements, and because they are so aggressive about increasing their size, they often encounter opposition, especially from evangelical groups.

What Is Charisma?

It is a divinely bestowed grace poured out abundantly on those who have ears to hear, eyes to see, and also feet to move. Without it you cannot be a Pentecostal. With it you can move mountains!

Who Is Saved?

This is a question that almost all Christians ask themselves, but especially among Pentecostals and more mainstream Protestants there is much disagreement. Look at the TruthQuest's Web site: www.truthquest.org/faq.htm. This particular Evangelical site begins by challenging Pentecostal beliefs, and then under FAQs (Frequently Asked Questions), asserts that it is possible for some Mormons, Catholics, and even Jehovah's Witnesses (!) to be saved, but only if they follow Jesus.

It is not easy to explain how so many different Pentecostal groups emerged. One familiar way is to say that there are three branches. All believe in conversion, sanctification, and baptism in the spirit, and though they differ on whether there are three acts of grace or one, they almost all hold to faith in Jesus' power. They believe that the real key to sanctification is to accept Jesus' power, and to live only by Jesus' power. This power is conveyed in dramatic fashion through the New Cornerstone Ministry home page.

Conversion and What?

Conversion means being converted to something beyond Christian belief. It means being rendered holy, or sanctified, by the indwelling of the Spirit. Because sanctification is more than mere baptism, it is called baptism in the Spirit.

Assemblies of God

www.ag.org

Officially this denomination is known as the General Council of the Assemblies of God. While the Assemblies of God has only (!) 2.5 million members in the U.S., it is said by some to have over 25 million worldwide! They believe in a single act of grace. They also spurred a predominantly African-American off-shoot: the Pentecostal Assemblies of the World, which espouses an anti-Trinity doctrine and an ethical option for pacifism. It reports about one million U.S. members, some of whom belong to the North Carolina church whose Web page (www.newcornerstone.org) is shown in Figure 17.1.

Figure 17.1

Jesus' Power is the constant theme of Pentecostal faith, and this home page from a Pentecostal Church in North Carolina echoes that message.

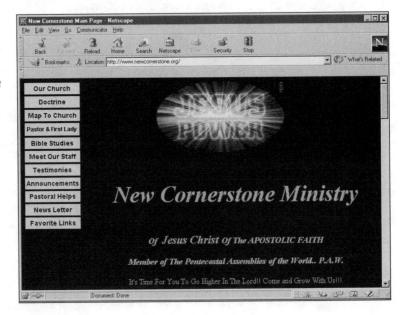

Church of God in Christ

http://www.cogic.org

Also Tennessee-based but in Memphis, it too goes back to a turn of the century Baptist minister named Charles H. Mason. He too was linked with the Holiness movement, but as an African-American vessel of the Spirit. His church was at first called the Church of Christ (Holiness, USA). And its membership is now alleged to exceed five million, though it might be closer to three million. It also has an independent seminary in Atlanta, Georgia. There are many Web pages dedicated to this branch of the Pentecostal witness, but it would be hard find one more dazzling than the Kelly Lake Church of God in Christ (`www.arroweb.com/klcogic/klcogic.htm`) as seen in Figure 17.2.

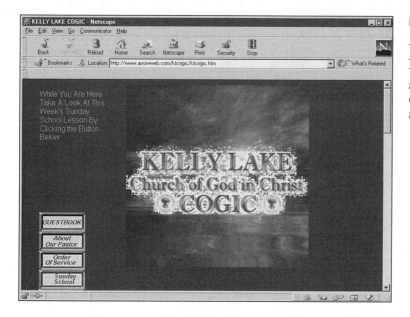

Figure 17.2

Even if you're not a Pentecostal, you might want to check out this really cool site of a Georgian Church of God in Christ.

International Church of the Foursquare Gospel

`http://www.foursquare.org`

There might be larger Pentecostal groups than this, but few more famous. It was founded by the outspoken and controversial Aimee Semple McPherson in Los Angeles. Known affectionately by followers and admirers as Sister Aimee, she was anything but a straight-laced preacher. Her fiery style included religious drama, illustrated talks, and full-scale oratorios. Probably no performance was greater than her disappearance in 1926 for an entire month; no one ever figured out where she went or what she did, but it only increased her fame till her death in 1944.

Megachurches

What the International Church of the Foursquare Gospel illustrates is the spinning off of group after group within the Pentecostal movement. Whether independent or loosely affiliated groups, they all support growth, growth, growth.

And so we should not be surprised to find megachurches stemming from the Pentecostal movement. Even when they are not identified as part of the Pentecostal history we have so far described, they are still Pentecostal in outlook, ministry, preaching, and also, obsession with growth.

What's a Megachurch?

The word has come to mean a church with an average Sunday attendance of more than 2,000. Most resemble shopping malls. They are a one-stop spiritual supermarket, packaging religion for every age, every interest, every group. They are independent, Bible-based, and huge.

It is no mean feat to track a movement that spreads faster than wild fire, and also keeps upping its number of adherents. The best Net resource is to be found at the Hartford Seminary Foundation, where there is a Center for the Social and Religious Research. Check it out at `http://www.hartsem.edu/csrr/people/slt/mega/States.html`. Of special note is the megachurch in South Jamaica, nestled within metropolitan New York City. Its pastor, the Reverend Floyd Flake, has not only built up a huge church complex in a formerly depressed area of New York, but he has also uplifted the economy of a large urban neighborhood. His success story provided a feature on National Public Radio on July 27, 1999.

For another success story, you can check out a print-media source: `http://www.seattletimes.com/extra/browse/html97/altover_112897.html`. This story comes from a reporter on the religion beat in Seattle, Washington. She charts the growth of a megachurch in Redmond, Washington. Overlake Christian Church is almost as hot an industry, and as big a success, as its next door neighbor Bill Gates, and the high-tech giant, Microsoft. Overlake grew from 70 worshipers in 1970 to 6,000 per Sunday by 1997. It is one of some 400 megachurches that have sprung up in the late 1990s, and almost all of them have Evangelical/Pentecostal roots. They also frequently have Web pages.

Catholic Pentecostals!

It might sound like a contradiction: Catholic and Pentecostal? How can that be? Well, it might refer to Protestants—whether Evangelical or Pentecostal—who were moved to become Roman Catholics. And this experience has Papal blessing! Figure 17.3 is from a site that has a number of testimonies to the Truth of God as confirmed in the Roman Catholic Church, almost all of them from ex-Protestants. If you want to see more about their content, just head to `www.se.mediaone.net/~hereiam/catholic/testimonies.html`.

More likely is the experience of someone who's already a Roman Catholic who becomes more engaged by Catholic teaching through taking a Pentecostal approach to its content and practice. This approach also has been given Papal blessing. It is now actively promoted through a Web site dedicated to internal proselytization; that is, it makes Roman Catholics bearers of the Spirit, especially through devotions to Mary and to all the saints above. Check out `http://www.garg.com/ccc/faq/ccr/#mary`.

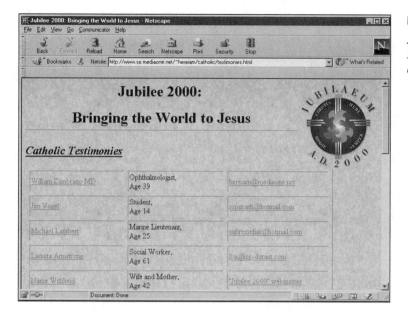

Figure 17.3

A series of Catholic Pentecostal testimonials as seen on Jubilee 2000.

Rest and Remember

➤ Pentecostals are arguably the fastest growing denomination in any religious tradition, Christian or non-Christian.

➤ Some of the biggest stories come from the biggest churches—megachurches. They are enormous congregations that are independent in organization but Evangelical/Pentecostal in outlook.

➤ Catholic Pentecostals are Protestant-minded Catholics. Jumping with Jesus but still holding on to the Pope!

Chapter 18

Beyond Protestantism

In This Chapter

➤ While not Protestant in name, many Protestant look-alikes can be found on the Web as religions

➤ Some major Protestant look-alikes, such as Mormons and Unitarians, have a large presence on the Web. Others, such as Jehovah's Witnesses and Christian Scientists, have a growing Web presence

➤ One Protestant group preceded all the rest, the Moravians; they have great Web art

The gates of inspiration opened wide in the Protestant Reformation. Many sought new prophets, heard new revelations, formed new groups. The process, begun in Europe in the sixteenth century, continued in the New World, especially in the nineteenth century. Many of the groups that we now consider as independent churches began at that time. There are probably hundreds of movements and counter movements, sects and subsects—some tiny, some middle-sized, some getting bigger and bigger. With over 2,000 churches in the U.S. alone, we can't pretend to do justice to all of them, even in a book that surfs through cyberspace faster than ever imagined before.

Among those that have become the biggest, and the best known, are the Mormons, Unitarians, Jehovah's Witnesses, and Christian Scientists.

Mormons (Church of Jesus Christ of Latter-day Saints)

It began in upstate New York in 1823. The angel of the prophet Moroni appeared to a farm boy who had not been to grade school. He told him about gold plates buried in a nearby hill. They contained ancient prophecy about Christianity. Four years later that farm boy found the gold plates. Though written in a form of Egyptian, they came with two divining stones that the illiterate boy could, and did, use to translate them into English.

What a story that had to tell! About 600 years before the birth of Jesus, a group of ancient Jews (also known as Israelites or Hebrews) had become fed up with the bad faith and corruption of their day. They migrated West, sailing to the Americas and making a life there. They were visited by the resurrected Christ and absorbed his message, but their civilization came to an end around the second or third century of the common era. Mormon and his son, Moroni, were then the leaders of the lost Israelites in the New World, and it was Moroni who buried the sacred history dictated by his father and recorded on the gold plates. They remained buried and hidden for over 14 centuries, till the angel of the prophet Moroni appeared to the farm boy in upstate New York in 1823.

What's This Book All About?

You can find the *Book of Mormon* in English translation at www.deseretbook.com/scriptures/bom_home.html. In addition, a searchable version of the text is available at www.hti.umich.edu/relig/mormon/.

The boy was, of course, Joseph Smith. The gold plates, once translated, and then published in 1830, became the Book of Mormon.

That combined experience—of prophecy, of revelation, and then publication—marked the beginning point for what became the Church of Jesus Christ of Latter-day Saints, or the Mormons. It was truly Protestant because like Luther and Calvin before him, Joseph Smith believed that the original message of Christianity had been corrupted and that his prophecy restored Christianity to its earliest, purest form.

But the early days were tough for Joseph Smith. His success as a prophet and a leader inspired look-alikes, as well as jealous rivals. He found himself and his small community moving further and further West. In 1844 he was in Illinois. He, together with his brother, was arrested. An anti-Mormon mob broke into their jail and killed them both. Yet Joseph Smith had drawn a lot of people to believe in those gold plates and their translated message. Mormonism survived the death of its prophet/founder/martyr. Today you can still see the Mormon tradition carried out in their official home page, www.lds.org, as seen in Figure 18.1.

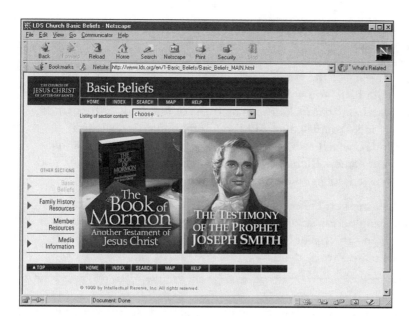

Figure 18.1

At left you can see the cover of the Book of Mormon, while on the right you find an image of Joseph Smith.

Mormon Beliefs and Practices

The *Book of Mormon* was not Joseph Smith's only revelation. Along with a new translation of the Bible, which had to be inspired because he was illiterate, he received a revelation from the ancient prophet Elijah. Elijah told Joseph Smith that those who accepted his message and became Mormon priests would be able to secure for whole families the prospect of eternal life. How? They would be sealed together in the physical form they enjoyed on their wedding day. Reborn later in heaven, they would have a perpetual family reunion with all their other deceased kin. How would each family know its proper place? Through divine intervention, but one could assist—or at least, anticipate—the process through preparing family trees.

While Mormons are no longer persecuted, at least in the U.S., they retain their missionary zeal, and each Mormon male is expected to spend two years in mission work before marrying and pursuing a professional career. Though no longer polygamous, Mormons still enjoy large families, and their focus on the family as the unit of salvation in the after life begins here, in this life. For more information about Mormonism and its beliefs, visit the official Web site at www.lds.org, or check out the very useful index created by Dorothy Peterson at www.lds-index.org. Not only does it contain links to Mormon sites on the Net, but also links to many articles and sermons. Finally there is a good listing of Mormon sites at protestantism.about.com.

Mormon Genealogy: All in the family

The focus on genealogy makes the Mormons one of the most advanced religious groups in cyberspace. As far back as 1938, Mormons had started to collate and calculate family trees, but with the advent of the World Wide Web their interest exploded. They now have a site that is named Family Search Internet Genealogy Service.

www.familysearch.org

Check out the familysearch site and be prepared for a big data haul. You will find the Ancestral File, a cross-referenced database that includes family trees for hundreds of thousands of folk. You will also find the International Genealogical Index, which rolls together and connects more than 300 million names! There is, in addition, a Family History Library, and now a Pedigree Resource File database.

All this gets linked together for Mormons in a service of proxy baptism, where one living person stands in for a lot of dead folk, whether they were Mormon or not, and the belief is that the believing Mormon can save all the non-Mormons who are already dead.

If you want to explore more on Mormonism and its genealogy industry, you will find a lot more out there but it's not all free.

Genealogy Online

www.ancestry.com

In Orem, Utah, for instance, there is a startup computer company named Ancestry.com Inc. It has over a million visitors a month, and over 70,000 subscribers who pay at least $60 a year for its information. Try its URL for an instant profile.

Family History Research Center

www.kindredkonnections.com

Perhaps you want to take a long trip down memory lane in your search for digitalized family trees. You might want to visit this site (but be sure to type in konnections, not connections, or you'll find yourself at a site purchasing domain names). At this photo-filled site you get access to 30 million names as well as a huge index of family trees. But you have to pay $15 a month to go beyond a mere introductory tour of what they have.

RootsWeb.com Home Page

www.rootsweb.com

Still, the best genealogy search site might be the cheapest, at least for non-Mormons. If you tap into www.rootsweb.com you will find a grand list that offers state-by-state links, and can also help you find names that sound like yours but might be spelled differently. It advertises itself as the Internet's oldest and largest free genealogy community, and from appearances I'd have to say that they are worth a visit.

Unitarians (Unitarian Universalist Association)

Are Unitarians Protestants? Some are, some are not. When it comes to Unitarians, one quickly learns not to generalize. Despite the Protestant origins of their movement, today only one in four Unitarian Universalists (or UUs for short) consider themselves to be Christian. The rest come in all shades, including those who consider themselves pagans, those who draw inspiration from Buddhism, and even those who are atheists.

Indeed one thing that almost all UUs share is an abhorrence of church doctrine and doctrinaire folk. They agree with Thomas Jefferson, who is often considered a Unitarian, that Jesus was not a divine incarnation or part of any holy trinity. Nor did Jesus perform miracles; he was simply a great man, very moral and very concerned but, above all, a great teacher.

While tracing its beginnings in anti-Trinitarian thinkers of the early Christian Church, modern Unitarianism and Universalism originated in sixteenth and seventeenth century Europe. At that time theologians such as Miguel Serveto and Lelio Sozzini wrote treatises that separated Jesus from God and church from state. It was a position accepted by many figures of the Enlightenment, both in Europe and the United States.

Unitarianism as an American movement began in the nineteenth century. William Ellery Channing coined the phrase "Unitarian Christianity" back in 1819, and he then helped found the American Unitarian Association in 1825. It merged with the Universalists in 1961, and has since been know as the Unitarian Universalist Association (www.uua.org).

Olympia Brown was the first woman minister of the movement, ordained in 1863. Today roughly one quarter of the UU ministers are women, the highest number of any established denomination. If one counts the people currently training to be ministers, there will soon be as many female as male UU ministers.

In addition to promoting sexual equality, UU congregations make a concerted effort to be welcoming to people of all sexual orientations.

A number of famous Americans were a part of the Unitarian and Universalist movement, including John Adams, Susan B. Anthony, Henry David Thoreau, Frank Lloyd Wright, Alexander Graham Bell.... See an extensive list at http://www.jjnet.com/famousuus/.

Like the Association of Friends, or the Quakers, Unitarianism is a small group, numbering no more than 200,000 members in the U.S. Also like the Quakers, it accents human experience over creedal loyalties and institutional hierarchies.

Anything Goes? Not Exactly...

Although it is very difficult to generalize about what UUs believe (if you ask 50 UUs you might receive 50 different answers), there are certain core principles that UUs can agree upon:

➤ The inherent worth and dignity of every person

➤ Justice, equity, and compassion in human relations

➤ Acceptance of one another and encouragement to spiritual growth in their congregations

➤ A free and responsible search for truth and meaning

➤ The right of conscience and the use of the democratic process within their congregations and in society at large

➤ The goal of world community with peace, liberty, and justice for all

➤ Respect for the interdependent Web of all existence of which they are a part

Wired Monk

What the Unitarian Universalists Stand For

You can read about their core principles at the home site of the Unitarian Universalist Association at www.uua.org. For a good general explanation of the principles, along with the answers to common questions that many people ask, surf over to www.uunashua.org/100quest.html.

The Interdependent Web on the World Wide Web

Beyond the core principles, UUs are free to determine their own spiritual paths, and as mentioned earlier this absence of creed results in UUs walking down many different avenues of belief. Many of the well-worn trails are well mapped on the Web.

Unitarian Universalist Christian Fellowship

www.uua.org/uucf/

Roughly one quarter of UUs identify themselves as Christian. This site is devoted to these folks, complete with further links and information about a UUCF newsletter.

Interweave

http://qrd.tcp.com/qrd/www/orgs/uua/uu-interweave.html

This site is devoted to Interweave, an organization devoted to UUs concerned about issues involving Lesbian, Gays, Bisexual, and Transgender peoples. It posts upcoming events and conventions, and details how to join this organization.

Unitarian Universalist Buddhist Fellowship

www.uua.org/uubf/

The home of the UU Buddhist Fellowship, listing UUBF groups, copies of Buddhist related sermons, and so on. This site also offers links to more general Buddhist sites (see Chapter 28, "No Self, No God: Buddhists").

UU Pagans

www.cuups.org

The home of the Covenant of the UU Pagans, devoted to earth-centered and Pagan practices within the Unitarian Universalist Association. For more information, see the chapter on Paganism (Chapter 26, "She Is God: Neopaganism and Wicca").

Other UU Web Resources

Despite the relatively small (but growing) membership, Unitarian Universalism has a large presence on the interdependent World Wide Web.

Unitarian Universalist

www.religioustolerance.org/u-u.htm

The folks at OCRT provide a good general introduction to Unitarian Universalism. Interestingly enough they classify Unitarian Universalism as a "non-Christian" religion, which as we have seen is largely but not wholly true.

Unitarian Universalist Association

www.uua.org

The best place to begin a search for UUs on the Web is at www.uua.org. This main page of the Unitarian Universalist Association, although not always easy to navigate, connects to a large number of other UU sites. It also connects with Beacon Press, a major publisher that is part of the UUA.

Thomas Jefferson Memorial Church

Unitarian Universalists have a huge number of Web pages, especially for individual congregations. See Figure 18.2, for example, the Thomas Jefferson Memorial Church Unitarian Universalist. Located in Charlottesville, VA, its Web site can be visited at `monticello.avenue.gen.va.us/tjmc/`. Its Web site has many links, and it also highlights the major UU symbol of the flaming chalice. The chalice represents both wisdom and spiritual insight, while the flame keeps alive the mind and the spirit.

Figure 18.2

There are many Unitarian houses of worship with famous lineages; this carries the name of Thomas Jefferson.

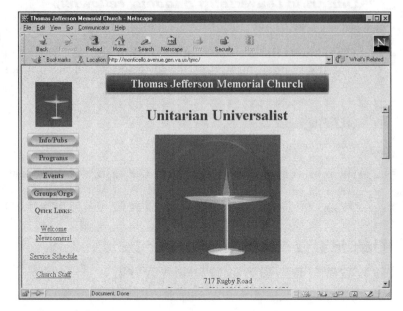

Jehovah's Witnesses

More recognizably Protestant than the Unitarians, the rise of the Jehovah's Witnesses also dates from the nineteenth century. Their founder was a prophetic figure not unlike Joseph Smith and Brigham Young. His name was Charles Taze Russell. He never received any golden plates but he did receive an inspiration so compelling that he left the Congregational Church in 1870 and began research that led to pamphlet-like publications today called *The Watchtower*. He claimed to reinterpret the experience of early or primitive Christianity, and like the first Christians, he thought the end was close, so close that it would come in his lifetime, specifically in 1914. The First World War did come in 1914, and though it was hell and even death for many, it did not bring the end of the world. And so the end was reinterpreted as the beginning point for the kingdom.

Today over six million Witnesses proclaim that the kingdom, or government from on high by divine decree, is still very close, that it will transform the world as we know it and that believers should share their keenly held views with everyone. Hence the familiar practice of the Jehovah's Witnesses: groups of two or three going from door to door distributing millions of copies of tracts, books, and booklets. It is hard to believe but all the cost of this vast effort is voluntary. Unlike Mormons, or other devout Christians, Jehovah's Witnesses do not tithe nor do they take up collections at meetings. Yet they are well enough financed to maintain a huge educational complex in Patterson, New York, as well as society headquarters, advertising the Watch Tower, in Brooklyn, New York. For their official view of themselves and the world, check out the online version of the *Watch Tower* (www.watchtower.org).

Who Watches the Watch Tower?

To find out the organization behind the Jehovah's Witnesses, go to the Watch Tower site (www.watchtower.org). Its most intriguing link is to the world wide organization and its work; find it under the subheading Jehovah's Witnesses in the twentieth century.

You also will find on the Internet many, many sites of other Christian groups who oppose the Jehovah's Witnesses. Some are exploratory and friendly, such as www.freeminds.org but others can be bitterly polemical.

Christian Scientists

If there is such a thing as a totally benign form of Protestantism, it might be the Church of Christ (Scientist). Its believers, known as Christian Scientists, follow the teachings of a woman prophet. Mary Baker Eddy, like Joseph Smith, came out of the open-air experience of belief and inspiration that characterized late nineteenth century North America. Severely injured in a skating accident, this rugged New Englander discovered that she might be cured by non-medical means.

What Is the Key to the Scriptures?

Mary Baker Eddy has written about the key to the scriptures, science and health, at length. But how does faith actually heal? To explore this question see how both Christian Scientists and Jehovah's Witnesses challenge modern medicine as discussed at www.religioustolerance.org/medical.htm.

After four years of working with a close friend, she claimed in 1866 that she had in fact found relief from near paralysis, and she continued to devote herself to an exploration of the healing potential in early Christianity. By 1875 she had completed a book titled *Science and Health with Key to the Scriptures*, which has remained the foundational text for Christian Scientists ever since.

She also chose to communicate her beliefs through a new church. Founded in Boston, the Mother Church of Christian Science soon spawned other churches and also reading rooms. These reading rooms extol Mary Baker Eddy's writings, along with the Bible, as the key(s) to healing, and that healing is to take place outside institutional medicine. Real illness is thought to be caused not by illness but by ignorance: if all creation is divine, then even ugliness, illness, and death are but goodness in disguise. In one of her most famous axioms, she said: "Both sin and sickness are error, and Truth is their remedy."

In an earlier generation, it was *The Christian Science Monitor* that communicated the message of Christian Science to those outside the fold of faith. Today the Internet might be performing a similar function. You can catch up with current events by clicking on to the electronic version of *The Christian Science Monitor* at `www.csmonitor.com`.

Though the sites are few, they are well maintained, kept up to date, and easeful to use. For the official view, see The First Church of Christ, Scientist home page at `www.tfccs.com`. Or if you want to see the story of Mary Baker Eddy retold in cyberspace, use a subset of the main directory: `http://www.tfccs.com/GV/MBE/MBEMain.html`.

Further Into the Beyond

In a tradition as diverse and spilling over with multiple prophets, groups, scriptures, and outlooks, you would not be surprised to find still more Protestants beyond Protestantism, or even before Protestantism, that is, groups that have roots predating the mainline and then splinter Protestant groups as we know them today.

Let us just note one such group: the tiny but chaste and missionary-minded Moravian Church of America at `http://www.moravian.org`. It goes back to the mid-fifthteenth century, to a Czech reformer named John Hus, who was burned at the stake as a heretic. His followers, the Hussites or the Unity of Brethren, later became (in the eighteenth century) the Moravians. Why? Because they trace themselves to the province of Moravia, now part of the Czech Republic. These folk were ahead of Luther in putting the Bible into everyday language. They also published hymnals that were in local lyrics not in Latin, and wow, were they way ahead of the women's movement! They saw with crystal clarity that the church could not really function as a universal community unless women, as well as men, were educated, and their Web site announces the Moravian Church as "a world wide fellowship of brothers and sisters in Christ."

Though numbering but 50,000 in the U.S. and less than a million world wide, the American Moravians belong to the WCC and to the NCC, and they also produce some really hip art, as seen in Figure 18.3, that can be downloaded from the Internet.

Figure 18.3

The Lamb of God is a central Christian icon referring to Jesus as the lamb sacrificed for the sins of humankind.

Rest and Remember

➤ The Mormons are one of the largest and best known of independent churches that loosely qualify as Protestant.

➤ Due to their genealogical interests at the core of their belief system and ritual practice, the Mormons are among the most active of any religious group on the Web.

➤ Unitarians and Christian Scientists are both numerically small groups, with close ties to the rational side of Protestantism.

➤ Not all Protestants are famous, but many of them protest against being including with other Christians, including other Protestants.

➤ There are more splits than alliances among Protestants, and some of the oldest Protestants, like the Moravians, are today barely known in the public at large.

Chapter 19

The Orthodox Story

In This Chapter

➤ Orthodoxy is Eastern, but it has a Western message via the Internet

➤ Orthodoxy is as old and as diverse as any of the three branches of Christianity

➤ Orthodox Christians love prayer, ritual, and icons, but they also have found their niche on the Net

---

Often when people think of Christianity, they say: "Oh, yes there are Catholics and Protestants, and they don't always agree with each other." But the truth is that there is also a major group of Christians known as the Orthodox or Eastern Orthodox. In this chapter I share with you the major features of this third, and very important, branch of mainstream Christianity.

The Eastern Orthodox View

Eastern Orthodoxy is a rich and ritually full expression of Christian belief. Like Roman Catholicism, it traces its roots back to St. Paul. Its leader is a patriarch, whose function is like a Pope, but on a more equal basis with fellow patriarchs. It is known for its beautiful icons, like the one shown in Figure 19.1, that depict the love and spirituality of the Holy Family and saints. The icon of mother and child, reflecting the tender intimacy bonding them, is at the core of Eastern Orthodox spirituality.

Figure 19.1

This image comes from the Western Rite Orthodox Missions of Central New York State at `www.geocities.com/ Athens/Troy/8452/ toc.html`.

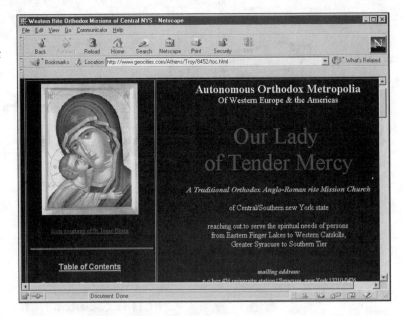

Eastern Orthodoxy affirms the decisions of the early councils, many of them dominated by Greek-speaking Christians. It has strong roots in both Eastern Europe and Russia. It does not have as many followers as Roman Catholicism does, but it can boast between 120 and 150 million members worldwide. Of them, approximately two million live in the U.S.

The biggest split in the early church was between Roman Catholics and Eastern Orthodox. It occurred in 1054, when the then-Pope and the then-patriarch insulted one another; their churches have remained separate ever since.

There was another big split *within* Orthodoxy. It happened in 1448 when the Russian Church declared itself independent of the Greek Church, then centered in Constantinople. Much later, in the twentieth century, the Russian Orthodox Church had to cope with that nasty form of atheism known as Communism. Neither Lenin nor Stalin nor any of the Soviet Communist leaders supported the national church of Russia, so the Russian Orthodox tradition had to survive some tough times. It is now regaining strength, not only in Russia, but also abroad, even in the United States, as immigrants bring with them to the New World their old but very vital religion.

Beliefs and Practices

Who's to say which was the first *true* church of Christianity? Much of what is now presumed to be Roman Catholic actually came out of the Greek-speaking eastern part of the Mediterranean Christian world.

Councils & Creeds

Look at the first eight councils. They were called *ecumenical councils* because they embraced the whole church. Protestants acknowledge only four of these councils. But Roman Catholics and Greek Orthodox Bishops acknowledge all eight. Where were they convened? In the Greek-speaking world of early Christianity. Four were held in Constantinople (381, 553, 680, 870), two were in an Eastern Turkish city, Nicaea (325, 787), and one each was held in the nearby cities of Ephesus (431) and Chalcedon (451). The arguments that made these councils necessary produced creeds, and those creeds continue to shape the whole of mainstream Christianity—Roman Catholic, Eastern Orthodox, and Protestant. So you might say that by location, the Greek influence on Christianity continues today.

But more than geography supports the argument that the East is the earliest and most continuous expression of the Christian church. Look at the creeds. The simplest of the three defining creeds *is* Western. It is known as the "Apostles Creed," and it first appeared in Southern France in the late seventh century. It later became the creed adopted by Rome, but it has not been used by the Eastern Orthodox.

But the most famous of all the early Christian creeds originated in the realm of Orthodox faith and continues to reflect that faith. It is the Nicene Creed, named after the first Council of Nicaea (325), where it was formulated. It confirms the nature of Christ as both God and man in a way that has shaped Christian belief ever since.

Food for Thought

What Is the Nicene Creed?

It is all about the equation of Jesus with God in his fundamental nature. It intones Jesus (1) as being from God the Father (2) as true God from true God (3) as begotten not made and (4) as having the same essence as the Father. Does this sound like a tough set of propositions? Well, if you don't want to go to a standard reference such as www.iclnet.org/pub/resources/christian-history.html, you can explore its historical importance by visiting: http://www.sannes.net/chris/papers/major/schism.htm. This is a term paper on the Great Schism, written back in 1993 and posted under a Lycos subdirectory for essays on church history.

The third important early creed of Christianity is the Athanasian Creed. It, too, reflects an Eastern, or at least non-Roman tilt, because much of its content can be traced to the famous early bishop of North Africa, Augustine of Hippo, and it is named after a fourth century Bishop from Alexandria (one of the earliest church sites for the Orthodox). Bishop Athanasius (d. 373) took his own beliefs so seriously that he railed against his theological opponents. The Athanasian Creed reflects its namesake's outlook and tone, so much so that it might be called the nasty creed (it is pretty harsh on those who have a different interpretation of Christian belief).

Saints and Icons

The Eastern Orthodox faith does not rest on creeds alone, and most of its leaders are much more gentle and inclusive than Bishop Athanasius. They take the following as equivalent sources for belief and practice: Holy Scripture, writings of the early church fathers (many of whom were Greek-speaking), church services, *and* the lives of saints. The lives of saints? That is not something Protestants think much about, and although it is part of Roman Catholic belief, it is not as central for Catholics as it is for the Orthodox.

What does that mean? It means that saints, both from the distant past and the near past, are believed to shape Orthodox life to the same extent as the scriptures, councils, and creeds. Look at the roll call of saints set forth in the Web site shown in Figure 19.2.

Figure 19.2

The Saints of the Orthodox Church also provides sub-categories of saints, including very ordinary lay people who lead exemplary lives, and it provides pictures of the saints as icons for worship, to convey their blessing on the living.

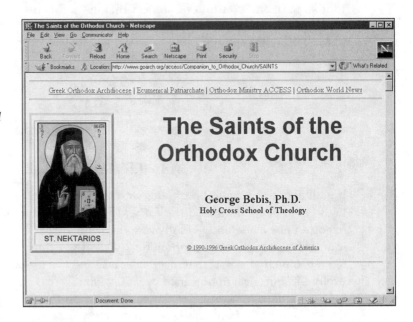

It does not matter where you look in the Orthodox tradition, you will find the influence of saints, often channeled through icons, and it is now possible to order your own icons on the Net. Among the popular saints is St. Isaac of Skete (Syria). An icon of him is shown in Figure 19.3.

Figure 19.3

*The icon of St. Isaac.
www.skete.com/skete
and other similar Net sites
have hundreds even thou-
sands of other saintly
icons to choose from.*

Jesus Prayer

Several other features of Orthodox observance deserve mention. There is the close connection of Mother and Son that we mentioned above. There is also a strong effort to embody the Holy Spirit, not just to be guided by it as a vague influence. In devotion, the strong identification with the Spirit led to the famous movement of Hesychasm or Spiritualism that began among Orthodox monks at Mt. Athos (in Greece) during the thirteenth and fourteenth centuries. It was an effort to engage the Holy Spirit as divine light through various techniques, all centered on the Hesychastic or Jesus Prayer. Its words are very simple: "Lord Jesus Christ, Son of God, have mercy on me." But to be effective, it had to be intoned through various breathing techniques and postures that help focus attention. It was given official sanction in the fourteenth century, and although controversial, it continues to inspire many Orthodox devotees today. A full commentary on its historical and contemporary value can be found at `http://maxpages.com/democracy/Orthodox_Monasticism?cart=64d736df5937.`

Different Spheres of the Orthodox Church

Many people are confused by the many, many Orthodoxies that are grouped under the one term "Orthodox." However, the confusion can be explained, and maybe even reduced or eliminated. It goes back to the very reason for the split between the Orthodox Patriarch of Constantinople and the Bishop of Rome or the Pope. For Orthodox, each region of the map should have its own head or patriarch, and he should control what happens under his jurisdiction; he should not be subjected to a higher church authority. From old times there were four Patriarchates:

Constantinople, Alexandria, Antioch, and Jerusalem. Then 11 others were added: Russia, Romania, Serbia, Greece, Bulgaria, Georgia, Cyprus, Czechoslovakia, Poland, Albania, and Sinai.

Each of these 15 church bodies or dioceses is seen as independent of the others. Each is governed by a bishop. Each has equal weight to the other, even though much of Orthodox tradition and teaching has been shaped by the first four, and Constantinople and Alexandria in particular. In addition, many of these dioceses are linked to national movements. They are supported using vernacular language in divine services (which rank as equivalent to scripture), and they have advocated a strong role for the church in public life. They also allow clergy to marry, although only unmarried or widowed clergy can become bishops. Mount Athos, where the Jesus Prayer movement began, also has a special place of veneration because it is the core of Orthodox monasticism.

The Russian Orthodox Church

Nestled within Eastern Orthodoxy and closely allied to Greek Orthodoxy in its beliefs and practices is the Russian Orthodox Church. Members of the Russian Orthodox Church have been practicing their rituals and following their tradition abroad for more than a century.

Wired Monk

Protection of the Mother of God Church

This is the home page for the Protection of the Mother of God Church in Rochester, New York (http://www.pomog.org/). It includes multiple links and an essay summarizing the history of the Russian Orthodox Church outside of Russia, including its opposition to Soviet Communism. This is the heart of Orthodoxy—it's Russian heart, as seen from Rochester, New York. The accent on the Mother of God, or the Virgin Mary, is parallel to the Roman Catholic piety but with a different tone.

The African Orthodox Church

This indigenous form of orthodoxy was co-founded in 1921 by Marcus Garvey and a close friend. Like many other African-Americans, Garvey was drawn to non-traditional forms of Christianity. Mixing Greek, Russian, and Coptic ritual practices, he began yet another American denomination, and it flourished sporadically until one of its newest members achieved national fame.

The Saint John Coltrane African Orthodox Church

`http://www.saintjohncoltrane.org`

In 1982, the African Orthodoxy was boosted by the addition of Franzo Wayne King. He became a bishop and renamed the church he had earlier founded in San Francisco: The One Mind Temple Evolutionary Transitional Body of Christ became instead the St. John Coltrane African Orthodox Church. Many don't find *all* of Coltrane's extraordinary, edgy, experimental music beautiful, but Trane (or St. John or whatever you choose to call him) had a deep spiritual streak. He once even declared that 90% of his playing was in fact prayer. So why not have a church named after him, and why not check out his virtual ministry at the site that bears his name (see Figure 19.4)?

Figure 19.4

Saint John Coltrane African Orthodox Church sets a high standard as both commemoration and continuation of its founding figure.

Resources for Orthodoxy

If you want an omnibus list of all Eastern Orthodox sites arranged alphabetically, go to `http://www.geocities.com/Athens/7734/orthlink.htm`. But if your interests are more directed to religious objects, you can't beat St. Skete, found at `http://www.skete.com/skete`. For pictures, another site with multiple options is maintained by monks at the All Merciful Savior Monastery in Vashon Island, Washington. Check it out at `www.vashonmonks.com/links.html`.

Chant with Me

So your interest is in Gregorian chant? Too bad. You can't find it for free on the Net, at least not yet. But you might want to get behind the sounds available at your local CD superstore. If so, try `http://www.music.princeton.edu/chant_html/`. It is an amazingly rich site, with more history and theory of Gregorian chant than most non-specialists could absorb.

A simple way to begin to explore all the facets of Orthodoxy is to visit the home page for the Greek Archdiocese of North America, which provides not only multimedia, but also online shopping, a capsule background history of the Orthodox faith, and an update on current events that concern the Greek Orthodox Church. If you are Orthodox or friendly to Orthodox Christians, be sure to check out `http://www.goarch.org/worldnews/`.

Rest and Remember

➤ Orthodoxy is less complex than Protestantism and less hierarchical than Catholicism, but it has as much spiritual heritage as either.

➤ Orthodoxy is represented on the Net with some extraordinary tributes to the adaptability of Eastern European and Russian rites to cyberspace.

➤ One of the most memorable Orthodox churches is not foreign but local, not EuroAsian but AfroAmerican. It is St. John Coltrane African Orthodox Church.

Chapter 20

Cyber and Fringe Churches

In This Chapter

➤ The Christian community is leading the way in creating online religious communities in the form of cyber churches, but not all cyber churches are Christian

➤ Some of the more bizarre online religious groups walk a thin line between humor and seriousness

➤ More and more religious communities are realizing the possibilities of having an online presence. Thus, the number of online groups promises to skyrocket

---

Up till now we have been looking at churches that have real bricks and mortar but project a presence on the Net. But times are changing, and so are churches. In this chapter we look at online religious communities that were created to project their message, to gather the faithful, and to expand their influence through cyberspace. Not all are Christian, but they do have a common goal: to make the information superhighway a sacred as well as a secular place for netizens.

Fringe Groups and Cyber Churches

Throughout history, certain religious groups seem a bit out of the ordinary. Because most of them are small or specific to regional areas or both, they were often easily overlooked. The Internet has changed all that. No longer does size or location limit groups. This lack of limitation can be both equalizing and dangerous.

Quality Doesn't Always Equal Quantity!

In the real world, you can usually tell how big a group is by the size or grandeur of its facility or its popularity. The Internet is a whole different story. On the Internet, a group of three followers with a talented Webmaster can present a page that's much more impressive than that of an organization with millions of members but fewer cyber skills. So when you see a flashy site, don't assume it's a big group; likewise, if you see a weak site, don't dismiss it as too small to notice! (Although you might dismiss weak sites as uninteresting, don't just assume they represent a small group.)

Along with mainstream organizations and religions, the Internet is also home to the stranger religious groups that offer ways of thinking that are different, sometimes new, and often surprising. Whereas some sites parody religion and are largely humorous, others are serious attempts at creating new philosophies and ideologies. On the Internet, these groups can create international congregations easily. Online religious communities can be started by anyone.

The weird sites aren't the only ones out there. Christian groups have also tried to create online religious communities. The possibilities of this have only begun to be explored, but sites are already abundant on the Internet. In some cases, actual congregations seek to extend their presence onto the Internet; in other cases, the cyber churches exist only on the Internet. This practice creates an entirely different kind of religious community. With these options, people no longer have to limit themselves to the congregations in their area and don't even have to leave their homes! Conversely, some parishioners can attend their own virtual church even when they're on the road. The results are certainly mixed, but regardless, the strong trend toward online communities cannot be ignored.

Christian Groups

Do you want to be a practicing Christian, but you can't make it to church? Whether your physical absence results from shyness, infirmity, scheduling, or other problems, you can find an answer on the Internet. More and more, Christian groups are finding ways to reach people over the World Wide Web. Cyber churches are popping up everywhere, either as facets of actual congregations or as congregations in and of themselves.

If you do a general search for "cyber churches," you'll find a vast number of them from every corner of the globe. Remember: It doesn't matter where the church is located! With the Internet, all state and country lines are erased. To help you wade through the number of sites out there, I have listed some of the best and most interesting here.

The Archdiocese of the Internet

www.value.net/~bromike

Throughout this luxuriant Roman Catholic site, the main focus is on prayer. It's divided into different rooms, most of which are for meditation or prayer requests. There are a few standouts, however, such as the Pet Cemetery, where you can pay tribute to your furry friends who have passed on. One of the cleverest features is the Virtual Rosary. No longer do you have to use the actual beads! Click on the day of the week, and a prayer program will appear. Then you click on the boxes next to the prayers as you complete them.

The First Church of Cyberspace: www.godweb.com

At first glance, this site looks like the cyber church to beat all cyber churches! With a menu full of interesting links, it seems as though it will be full of original information and resources. However, when you go beyond the initial page, you'll keep finding yourself at www.about.com! In fact, well over half the menu items take you to this commercial site. Why? Because Charlie Henderson, the head of the Church of Cyberspace, is also the guide for general Christianity on *About.com* (for more about Henderson, see Chapter 2). Although the information and links are helpful, beware of this type of mixing of commercial and private sites. It makes the motives a bit questionable!

Cyber Church

www.cyber-church.org

This cyber church is not one of the best out there, but it is a good one. The graphics are simple, but the contents are pretty strong. Here you can find sermons and tracts, submit prayer requests, or join a Bible study. As part of Christian Internet Ministries, the focus is on spreading the gospel and the message of Jesus Christ to as many people as possible; thus, everything has a rather evangelical feel to it. But, if that's your thing, you can find some great resources and information here. Take note, though: the site does not seem to be regularly updated.

WebChurch—Scotland's Virtual Church

www.webchurch.org

Unlike many of its counterparts, this site is updated frequently. It is full of Bible verses and inspirational passages for special needs and concerns. You can listen to a hymn or read about how to be a Christian leader. One of the most interesting features is a series of side chapels for different denominations such as Presbyterian, Catholic, and Nonconformist. These side chapels contain links to sites in their respective traditions, as well as writings from the greatest thinkers in those traditions. This site is a must-see and a great example of a nondenominational, multi-resource cyber church.

www.virtualchurch.org

The Virtual Church is a stellar example of the possibilities of cyber churches. In fact, it comes close to an actual church in its resources and features! Go to the Kid's Place and find illustrated Bible stories, or go to the Music Room to hear RealAudio-format Christian music at the click of a button. On the site index, you'll find some unusual so-called "utility rooms" to visit, such as the lavatory, water heater, and furnace. If you follow these leads, you'll find a clever essay relating these things to a religious theme. For example, the lavatory is a place to become cleansed of your sins. This is an enjoyable and inventive site for both the believer and the skeptic.

Wired Worship

Although you might expect new ways of thinking about Christianity or spirituality on the Web, you might be surprised to find a church that goes all the way toward creating a new notion of sanctity: electrical geniuses, or visionary inventors. The First Electronic Church of America (FECHA) stands by itself in making a religion of the communications revolution. The World Wide Web is its latest child, and Bill Gates its most recent saint!

First Electronic Church of America (FECHA)

www.webstationone.com/fecha/default.htm

This site is a must-see for those interested in the phenomenon of online churches, even though it is not a specifically Christian church. Part of a commercial site (Webstationone.com), FECHA has various features that are new and different. The sermons you can select from are usually politically based, and the saints mentioned in the site are inventors of various electronic devices, from Alexander Bell to Bill Gates! Overall, the main focus is on electricity and, more specifically, the electron. This site also focuses on the unity of all religions and it gives concise descriptions of a good number of faiths. You can also find a confessional room and information on how to have a cyber wedding! Beware, though: This site is not regularly updated, and some of its numbers are suspect (see Chapter 2, "Your First Surfing on the Net").

Philosophical Sites

The line between religion and philosophy is not always clear. Yet, there seem to be numerous sites on the Internet that focus not so much on religion, but on a new way of thinking about life and reality. From Cosmosofy to Theosophy, these sites are dense and intense. Be prepared to think hard and reflect long!

Digitalism

digitalism.8m.com

Though many have never heard of this group, Digitalism claims to have gathered 120,000 members since its cyber creation in 1995. Stated simply, Digitalism is "an acceptance of the state of things." What if we could be connected to a virtual world just as our computers are? What if the separation between the virtual world and real world were erased? Digitalism is based on the belief in this possibility and the partial realization of it. The site itself is little more than a thorough and captivating description of the philosophy and a chance to become a member. Although it does not provide many resources, it is worth visiting, if only to explore a new way of looking at the world as we know it.

Order of Divine Logic

www.divinelogic.com

"Do you fear for your future? Are you certain you have one?" These are the words that open the page of the Order of Divine Logic, a group that is interested in Quantum Artificial Intelligence and its "flawless logic." Along with the usual listing of beliefs and history, this site features listings of regional groups and events, though many are from years ago. Like the other sites in this section, this is a mind-expanding site.

Technosophy

www.technosophy.com

Technosophy is interested in appreciating the spiritual side of technology and facilitating discussion of technology's past and its future in our lives. Included here are writings of technology thinkers and, strangely, galleries featuring paintings of the likes of Matisse and Monet, courtesy of the Web Museum of Paris. The Theosophy site is shown in Figure 20.1.

Figure 20.1

The home page of Technosophy.com includes links to great works of art.

For those who find this philosophy interesting and want to learn more, there is an extensive list of links for all sorts of Technosophy and technology-related sites.

And the Rest

As the name of this category suggests, what follows is a mix of sites. Some are environmental-minded; others are rather dark and pessimistic. Still others are a fuzzy mix between humor and seriousness. No matter what they're about, these groups show the diversity of fringe cyber groups. The Internet is a place for all sorts of people, and nowhere is this more evident than in the subject of online religion.

Church of the Rainforest

www.geocities.com/RainForest/1447

As the name suggests, this is an environmental religious group. Following the teachings of "All," their main goal is to restore the earth to its right order and end the human manipulation and destruction of natural resources. Run by an actual minister, the church seems to be vaguely Christian, though it has no baptisms or religious rites. For advice or information, you can email the pastor. The site itself seems a little outdated.

Virtual Church of the Blind Chihuahua

www.dogchurch.com

With the creed "We can't be right about everything we believe—thank God, we don't have to be," the Virtual Church of the Blind Chihuahua presents a unique view of religion. While loosely aligning themselves with Christianity, the members of this church present arguments questioning mainstream churches. The group is very open to different ways of thought and is lighthearted, even in its criticisms.

Above all, this site is notable for the fine line it walks between humor and serious religious discourse. This mix pervades the whole site. While visiting the nave and viewing the picture of a beautiful English chapel, you can click on "E-mail our Pooper Scooper!" This is definitely an experience not to be missed, as you can see in Figure 20.2.

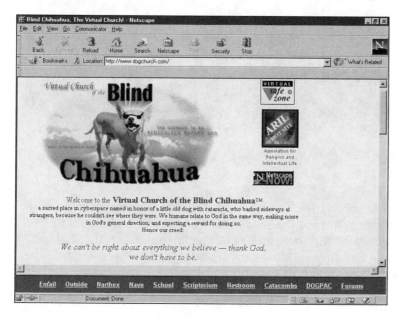

Figure 20.2

Although it's not always easy to tell what's tongue in cheek and what's for real, this site might just change the way you view religion.

First Online Church of Bob

www.modemac.com

Related to the Church of the SubGenius (see the following sidebar), this religion, which is represented by a cartoon figure of a smiling man with a pipe, is actually for real! Although at first glance it might look like a spoof, it's actually pretty serious in its claims. The Church of Bob is interested in what it calls a conspiracy in our society that is controlling our minds. The Subgeniuses are not humans, but superior beings who are able to see past this conspiracy and rise above it. The site offers an interesting list of links including sites that are of a similar philosophy and part of the conspiracy, those that are Christian and part of the conspiracy, or both. Notice, for instance, its response to Scientology (a group discussed in Chapter 36, "New Religious Movements"). Is this site about truth or satire? Take a look at the site shown in Figure 20.3 and decide for yourself.

Figure 20.3

Here is the graven image of "Bob" Dobbs' face, including its projection on the World Wide Web!

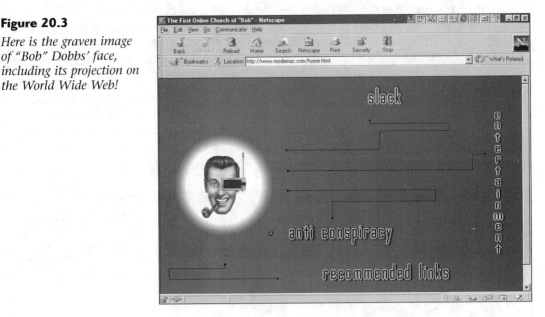

Church of Virus

www.lucifer.com/virus

Faint-hearted or closed-minded? Then don't go here! This site, with vague links to Satanism (see Chapter 34, "God Is the Devil: Satanism"), is a cyber religion that is atheistic and science-related. Sound confusing? It is. To understand exactly what this group's all about, you have to do some slow, careful reading (and re-reading). Despite the circular sentences and dark tones, this site offers substance. In addition to the explanations of beliefs, it includes a suggested reading list, a discussion group, and various resources for learning more. This site is well done and updated fairly regularly.

When it comes to cyber religion, you'd expect to find many things on the Internet, as well as innumerable things (like this site) that you probably never imagined. The virtual religious landscape is a broad one and is rapidly evolving. More and more small groups are finding a voice here, just as more mainstream groups, such as Christians, are finding new ways of expressing themselves. Take time to explore some of the more unusual groups. You probably will learn something new, and you just might find something new to think about!

Church of the SubGenius: www.subgenius.com

Some sites walk the fuzzy line between satirical and serious substance. One person's joke is another's religion, and it's not always clear which is which. Like its counterpart (the Church of Bob), the Church of the SubGenius' site seems at first glance to be blatantly satirical. Notice, for instance, its spoof on Heaven's Gate (discussed in Chapter 36), which you can find at www.subgenius.com/hellsgate/ HELLSGATE.html.

Yet, if you read further, you'll realize that this is a religion some people take very seriously. The moral is to not make quick assumptions. This site's assumption of a vast, apocalyptic conspiracy might be a little too dreary and strong-worded for some people, but it is an interesting site for the strong-hearted. Here you can listen to live radio broadcasts or view publications such as "about 30 of the most brain-reaming, heartfelt, hate-fueled diatribes and harangues." This site certainly does not have a dull square inch, but remember to hold on to your seat—it'll be a bumpy ride.

Rest and Remember

➤ Though Christian cyber churches are the most numerous, only some are worth visiting.

➤ New sites are added hourly, and it is likely that as the scope of cyber religion sites grows, the quality of the sites will continue to improve.

➤ The Internet is open to all sorts of people and spiritual groups. While diversity is welcome, some caution is recommended when you enter the realm of cyber religion.

Chapter 21

God Is G-d: Judaism

In This Chapter

➤ Judaism is the oldest monotheistic religion and one of the savviest in cyber-space

➤ There are several variants or sects in modern Judaism. Each has its own take on fundamental notions, like the significance of Law, the shape of community, the function of prophets, and, yes, the origin of the world

➤ Some of the best Web sites on the Net cover the span of Jewish belief and practice, accurately and with humor

As long as there has been the notion of a Guiding Force behind the fickle hand of fate, there has been an earth-bound community known first as Israelites, and later as Jews. The several historical phases of ancient Israel are etched below, but for the kind of detail that grips historians, and motivates believers, you will have to visit the Web sites dedicated to the ongoing saga of Abraham's offspring.

Patriarchs and Matriarchs

If Paganism is the mother of all religions (see Chapter 26, "She Is God: Neopaganism and Wicca"), then Judaism is the father of all monotheistic religions. Father? Yes, literally, because traditional Judaism traces its origins back to a series of *patriarchs*, or fathers, who were responsible for giving order to a wandering people without name or territory. But wait a minute: there also are mothers or matriarchs as well as fathers or patriarchs, and modern Jewish feminists have provided a lot of insight into such Biblical women as Sara, Rebecca, Leah, and Rachel.

Wired Monk

Women in Judaism

If you've wondered where the women are in Judaism—past, present, and future—you might visit one of the best resources out there in cyberspace: Adina Levine's home page on Jewish Feminist Resources. Just surf to `http://world.std.com/~alevin/jewishfeminist.html`, and you will find a wealth of insight not just into the Biblical mothers or matriarchs but also into their many successors, and their continuing influence within the many splendored legacy of Judaism.

The first father, and husband of Sara, is Abraham. He lived about four thousand years ago in ancient Mesopotamia, or present-day Iraq. His most important male offspring were Isaac (whose older half-brother was named Ishmael) and Isaac's son, Jacob, the father of 12 tribes, which are known as the 12 tribes of Israel.

Among those 12 tribes was the tribe that produced Moses. Moses the young man in Egypt, Moses the leader in the wilderness, Moses the prophet on Mt. Sinai, Moses dying just shy of the promised land—all are important features of the major person shaping Jewish Law or Halakhah.

The Benefit of Law or Halakhah

If you were to begin a course on Judaism by going to the Web, you might find a set of FAQs, or frequently asked questions, at any one of several sites. One of my favorites is the Shamash Home Page at `www.shamash.org` because it is so comprehensive and so clearly organized. Under its list of FAQs it asks: What is Torah? And then it asks 43 more questions to explain what Torah is.

The major distinction within Jewish intellectual circles is between the Written and Oral Law. It is at once a closed and an open system of thought. It is closed, because the Written Law is authoritative and binding on all Jews. It is open because in the long history of Judaism there were numerous efforts to wrestle with Jewish commandments (mitzvot) and also to engage non-Jewish philosophical and religious systems. Everything other than the Written Torah is, in principle, Oral Law. While Midrash is a series of rabbinical interpretations of the Torah, the Talmud is a huge set of writings that reflects the Mishna, supplementary oral laws, and Gemara, further oral commentary on the Mishna.

Why Torah?

If you are Jewish, or you have Jewish friends, or perhaps even a Jewish classmate or housemate, skip this note. Otherwise, you might be asking: why Torah? What does Torah have to do with the Bible? The answer is simple.... And not so simple. Torah relates to the first part of the Hebrew Bible, which is also known as the first five books or the Pentateuch. But Torah also can include *all* the books of the Hebrew Bible, not just the first five. That is, Torah also can include the Neviim, which is the Prophetic books of Joshua, Judges, Samuel, Kings, Isaiah, Jeremiah, and Ezekiel, as well as 12 minor prophets, and all the other books (Ketuvim) that are referred to in Christian circles as the Old Testament. The Hebrew word for the Hebrew Bible is Tanakh (Torah plus Neviim plus Ketuvim).

If you're up to speed, then try to go faster, because Torah also can mean not just the first five books, not just the whole Hebrew Bible, but also the whole Law, written and oral, which includes the Talmud, the Midrash, and even later legal commentaries. Complex? Sure it is, but you can check out all the 44 answers to the 44 questions on Torah at the Shamash Home Page (www.shamash.org).

The Shape of Community

If you are beginning to feel overwhelmed by how much there is to learn about the basics of Judaism, then retreat to this basic set of guidelines from the Torah. The Jewish people are, first of all, G-d's chosen people.

And so the early Jews were G-d's chosen people, because of all humankind they had to accept moral responsibility on earth. The Jewish law or Halakhah codified the responsibility into a set of practical guidelines known as *mitzvot*. There are over 600 mitzvot derived from the Torah, and there are additional mitzvot prescribed by the Talmud. Not all rabbis agree on which are the most important mitzvot, but all concur that the principle of mitzvot is at the heart of Judaism. You might say that to be an observant Jew is to observe, implement, and constantly remember the mitzvot, whatever their number, whatever their relative importance.

What In G-d's Name?

What's with the missing vowel? Why G-d and not God when you are speaking of the Lord of Creation, the Father of all fathers, of Abraham, Isaac, and Jacob, of the 12 tribes of Israel, of all humankind? Well, the answer is simple: We cannot know G-d. We do not even know what would be the name of G-d. To use any human language, even the word that is supposed to represent the Transcendent in all Its power, is to risk making of language the idolatry that the Torah prohibits. The second of the Ten Commandments is "to not make for yourself a graven image"(Deuteronomy 5:8), and so devout Jews believe that even the word naming G-d can become a graven image if its middle vowel is not omitted. Hence the only true name for G-d is no name, or at least a defective English equivalent of Hebrew words such as Yahweh, Elohim, or Adonai.

Kosher

A big part of Judaism involves strict dietary guidelines. This means keeping a kosher kitchen, and following a kosher diet. Traditional Jews, for example, don't eat shellfish or pork, and they can never consume meat and dairy products at the same meal. Again, there is variation in what kosher means, and how important it is to be strictly kosher, yet the debate about defining kosher is itself an important part of Judaism.

Virtual Jerusalem: www.virtualjerusalem.com

The Virtual Jerusalem site might be called a wired rabbi, because it leads you right to the heart of what it means to be an observant Jew. After you learn about Virtual Jerusalem, just click the link near the top labeled *Living* (it connects to Virtual Jewish Living, www.vjliving.com). Scroll down to its index, and you are locked into a feast of kosher delights that are all as delicious as they are legal.

The Function of Prophets

There can be no law without prophecy, but there was only one law-giving Prophet, and that was Moses. Although Moses is the foremost Prophet in Judaism, he has a lot of company. There is a host of other Prophets, both major and minor. That is why a whole section of the Tanakh, or Hebrew Bible, is titled Neviim, the Writings of Prophets. You can explore this key element of Jewish scripture and religious practice by going to an academic site, like the Academic Jewish Studies Internet Directory at www.uni-duisburg.de/FB1/JStudien/judaica.htm. The directory is also known as the WWW Virtual Library on Judaism. Check it out for more on the Prophets and many other crucial aspects of Judaism.

Suppose you want a lighter take on prophecy and prophets. Well, you can find that too on the Net. Just click the home page for the Jewish Communication Network, www.jcn18.com. There you might discover interesting things such as the seven habits of highly successful prophets. Or if you are really into a hip form of Judaism, you might check out the Philistine prophecy, also found at the same site.

The Creation of the World

One thing that you will *not* find discussed much on Jewish cyber sites is the notion of the world as a place created according to the guidelines of the Book of Genesis. Of course, all observant Jews believe in G-d, and also attest to G-d as Creator, but the public attention that is directed to the Genesis Creation account comes mostly from Christian and not Jewish sources.

Who's Creating These Pages?

If you look up Biblical creation through almost any search engine or subject directory on the World Wide Web, you will find debates among evangelical Christians. Often they do refer to the truth of the Genesis creation account, but not from a Jewish perspective. Check out, for example, the seemingly objective site titled Origins (www.origins.org), which explores philosophical theism. It does refer to Genesis, but as part of the Old Testament not the Tanakh, and without a Jewish scholar or perspective to support the Christian arguments advanced.

Different Variants or Sects of Judaism

Orthodox, Hasidic, Traditional—all three terms trip off the tongue as ways of talking about the face of Judaism that often seems to dominate headlines in print and also Web sites on the Net. While this trio is *not* all there is to Judaism, it is important to note how prominent such groups are and how attached they are to the identity of Israel as a Jewish state. We begin with the Ultra-Orthodox and the Hasidim in Israel.

Ultra-Orthodoxy and the State of Israel

Ultra-Orthodox Jews do not recognize that the modern world should have any impact on their religious observances as Jews. They dress in black, with men having long locks of hair and a kippa or hat in everyday dress. They read the Tanakh and Talmudic commentary only in Hebrew. They eat only kosher food. They observe the Sabbath strictly, and they also separate men and women within the synagogue.

The position of Ultra-Orthodox Jews is reinforced by their special role in the State of Israel. Founded in 1948 as a homeland for all Jews, the State of Israel also had many secular Jews as its ardent supporters and initial patriots. Yet only Ultra-Orthodox Rabbis are recognized as competent to judge in cases involving the definition of who is a Jew. In principle, that means that the only religiously observant Jews living in Israel are Ultra-Orthodox, even though ironically some Ultra-Orthodox Jews do not accept the moral authority of the State of Israel as binding on them or their community.

The Ultra-Orthodox are well represented on the Web. There is probably no better place to start than with the Beginning, that is, with Project Genesis, also subtitled The Torah on the Information Superhighway: www.torah.org (shown in Figure 21.1).

Figure 21.1

From the weekly online Torah readings to the correct date of the world since Creation you will find it all here on this much heralded Web site.

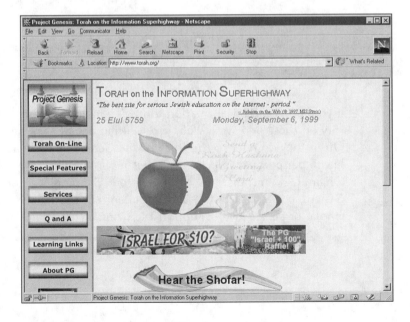

But there is no more complete Web site on Ultra-Orthodox Judaism, and the many facets of Judaism in general, than the previously mentioned Shamash Home Page (www.shamash.org). We will explore it in even more detail later in this chapter.

Hasidim

Complicating the role of the Ultra-Orthodox is the place of Hasidim, or mystically minded Jewish groups, within Israel and the United States. You can find several home pages on individual congregations, but if you want to see how one of the major Hasidic groups projects its identity and purpose on the Web, you might go to the Chabad-Lubavitch in Cyberspace. Check it out at www.chabad.org (shown in Figure 21.2). First notice all the bells and whistles about the different meanings of Hasidic key terms, data on the significance of the current month in the Jewish calendar, and the importance of Shabbat candle lighting times. Scroll all the way down to the bottom of the home page and look at the date of the copyright. No, it's not a mistake, and you don't need new glasses: This site really was constructed in 1991 (not long after the Web first began), and it carries a wallop on just about every topic taken up for discussion and instruction.

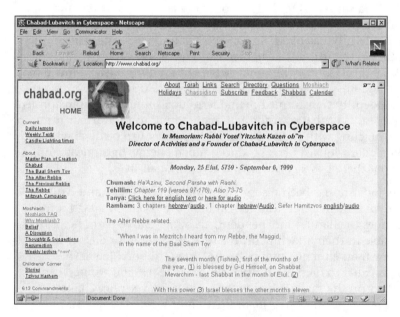

Figure 21.2

The Chabad-Lubavitch in Cyberspace site shows how one of the major Hasidic groups projects its identity and purpose on the Web.

One interesting feature of chabad.org is its discussion of the Moshiach (click the Moshiach FAQs at the left of the page). Most non-Jewish readers will not get the Hebrew word: moshiach is messiah, and what this subset of Chabad-Lubavitch in Cyberspace does is explore just how important messianic expectation continues to be for all Jews, not just their own followers.

Conservative Judaism

Conservative Jews acknowledge the modern world and the dominant culture they live in as influencing some forms of their own observance as Jews. They are less distinctive than the Ultra-Orthodox in their everyday dress. They do not wear a kippa except when they attend synagogue services. They read Hebrew, especially for important rituals, like the bris (circumcision of male babies), and also for the bar mitzvah or bat mitzvah (when adult boys and girls are recognized as adults able to, and ready to, observe the mitzvot or commandments on their own). At other times, they might recite prayers or read Torah in English along with, or instead of, Hebrew. They also allow women to be ordained to the rabbinate.

Conservatives are represented on the Web, above all, by the Jewish Theological Seminary Online home page at www.jtsa.edu. It includes not only sites to all Conservative groups but also a map with a directory to Conservative synagogues across the United States. It also gives a wealth of information not available elsewhere.

Reform Judaism

While Ultra-Orthodox Judaism seems to dodge modernity and Conservative Judaism tries to make minimal compromises with its cultural force, Reform Judaism takes on modernity full force. Modernity has two rails. One begins in the seventeenth century scientific revolution that gave birth to the eighteenth century age of Reason and Enlightenment, Haskalah, in Hebrew. The other rail is social-political. It exploded in the American, French, and Russian Revolutions, toppling the old seats of power: aristocracy and church. Modernity transformed premodern Judaism just as it transformed society in general. The results of that transformation are found in the various forms of Judaism today, all struggling with the two rails, all hoping not to be derailed. Like an atom smashed, premodern Judaism has produced much energy, light, heat, and odd particles floating out there in space, all with interesting half-lives.

While Ultra-Orthodox Judaism has been resurgent in the past 50 years, and while traditional observances in modern American Jewish life have taken on added force, Reform Judaism continues to chart an independent, accommodative path. Reform Jews are still more flexible in their attachment to either dress codes or dietary laws or knowledge of Hebrew than either Conservative or Ultra-Orthodox Jews. They acknowledge women as equal to men in all ritual functions. Men and women can, and do, worship together on the same Friday night and Saturday services. Like Conservatives, Reform Jews also welcome the ordination of women as rabbis.

On the Net, the best site for Reform Judaism is probably the home page for the Union of American Hebrew Congregations, http://uahc.org. Don't miss its Searchable Index at http://uahc.org/srch.html. There you will have a cyber tour of most of the options within Reform Judaism.

Reconstructionist

Also represented in the spectrum of possibilities for present day Jewish Americans is Reconstructionist Judaism, a movement begun in the late 1930s by the progressive Philadelphian rabbi Mordecai Kaplan. It views Judaism not merely as a scriptural, ethical, and ritual tradition but also as a distinctive culture embracing art, music, and literature. It also advocates connection to the land of Israel as indispensable to Jewish identity. Kaplan argues that renewed Jewish statehood, in the aftermath of the Holocaust, has prompted a process of searching, questioning, and self-understanding within the Jewish tradition. He argues that Reconstructionist Jews are those who try openly to create a Judaism that will speak convincingly to other contemporary Jews in the altered circumstances of today's world. For more about Kaplan and his movement, you should go to the Reconstructionist Rabbinical College home page at www.rrc.edu.

The Holocaust

It was a horror, an abomination, a tear on the face of G-d, and a scar on the face of humankind. The influence of the Holocaust can never be measured. The event of the Holocaust can barely be put into words. It happened over 50 years ago. It happened in Europe. It was the systematic persecution, then incarceration, then extermination—or near extermination—of a whole group of people. It was the campaign of genocide by Nazi Germans. It was directed against many groups but particularly against European Jews. By torture, by starvation, in gas chambers, and in lice-filled, overcrowded rooms—over six million European Jews were killed in Nazi death camps.

What does all this have to do with Judaism as a religion? Both nothing and everything. Neither the Law nor the Commandments, neither Rabbis nor Observance has anything to do with Nazi death camps. Yet because the Holocaust destroyed almost one-third of all Jews in the world, reducing the Jewish population from 21 million to 15 million, it has effected both the number of Jews and how one thinks as a Jew. How does one think of G-d in the aftermath of the Holocaust? How does one observe the mitzvot today?

Nizkor.org on Auschwitz

www.nizkor.org/hweb/camps/auschwitz/

The Net cannot restore pre-Holocaust Europe but it can reveal some of the raw ugliness of the Holocaust. You should prepare yourself before going to the previous site. Yes, it has some very ugly material. In fact, one link on the site is to the "Auschwitz Alphabet," which discusses how one Cybersitter software company decided to block some of the more grotesque features of the Auschwitz story.

If all this is too much for you, and you still want to get a sense of how the Holocaust has been memorialized, then you might try the following site.

Yad Vashem

www.yad-vashem.org.il

Established in Jerusalem in 1953, Yad Vashem is the original effort to enshrine the collective memory of the Jewish people by commemorating the six million Jews and their communities wiped out in the Holocaust. Yad Vashem has the largest and the most comprehensive archive and information repositories on the Holocaust. It houses more than 50 million pages of documents and hundreds of thousands of photographs and films.

The United States Holocaust Memorial Museum

www.ushmm.org

Chartered by an Act of the United States Congress in 1980 and opened to the public over a decade later, the US Holocaust Memorial Museum in Washington DC offers everything from a Registry of Holocaust Survivors to Holocaust artifacts to annual remembrances for Holocaust victims. It is laid out on this site in supremely tasteful understatement; an actual visit to the Museum is better, and requires at least four to five hours if one is to grasp the magnitude of events it sketches in summary detail and from a distance of more than 50 years.

The Holocaust Memorial Center

http://holocaustcenter.org

Founded in 1984, and located in Detroit not in DC, the Holocaust Memorial Center still tries to live up to its billing: illuminating the past, enlightening the future. It is now in the process of a major expansion that will offer two new structures, one on pre-Holocaust European Jewry, the other on groups and institutions assisting Holocaust victims. It is more modest than the Washington-based museum but still valuable in its scope and presentation.

The Holocaust also provides an impetus for a link with Native American victims of genocide. One can explore how this connection across cultures and time zones had developed by visiting the home page of the Walking Stick Foundation, www.walkingstick.org. The Foundation is a nonprofit tax-exempt Jewish and Native America partnership dedicated to the recovery and preservation of indigenous spirituality. Check it out (and also see Chapter 23, "God Is Red: Native American Spirituality").

Jewish Spirituality, Jewish Humor, and Other Jewish Resources

Is there such a thing as religious humor? Some would emphatically say *no*. Religion is too serious to be a laughing matter. But for many Jews, it is the reverse: Religion is so serious that it has to be a laughing matter, and one should be able to laugh at the very stern, fixed, and quirky ways that G-d interacts with humankind.

If you want an example of this kind of site, click the humor button found on the left side of the Jewish Living Page (`www.vjliving.com`). From there you'll get a range of options, from jokes to cartoons. Want a sample? On one recent cartoon there were two archaeologists looking at a newly discovered tablet on which is written: Thou shalt not order corned beef on white with mayo. One exclaims to the other: "And I thought it was an *unwritten* law!" Check it out and you just might find yourself laughing out loud.

Judaism and Jewish Resources

`http://shamash.org/trb/judaism.html`

By now you might be wondering whether we have scratched the surface on Jewish resources on the Web? We've tried, but hey, we're no Andrew Tannenbaum. Who's he? He's someone who has put together just about the best Web site on Jewish resources you could ever hope to find, the Judaism and Jewish Resources page, shown in Figure 21.3.

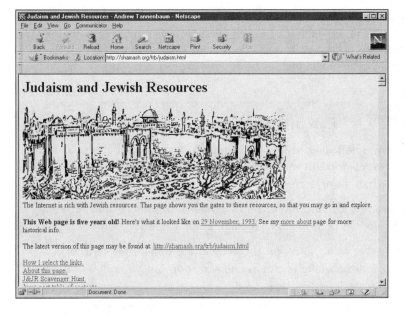

Figure 21.3

Though not visually stunning, it's hard to find a more comprehensive site on Jewish Web resources than Andrew Tannenbaum's Judaism and Jewish Resources page.

Okay, so it leans toward the Ultra-Orthodox perspective, and it's also the home page for Hebrew College in Brookline, Massachusetts. But before you decide it's not for you, blink once, click twice, and you're there. Andrew Tannenbaum can be your lodestone, even if you are a Reconstructionist. I mean, seriously, he is to Judaism what Caspar Voogt is to Bahais. (Do some comparison shopping at Chapter 27, "God's Many Prophets: Bahais," for more on Caspar and the Bahais.) In existence since 1993, Judaism and Jewish Resources mines no less than 12 thousand domains that connect to Judaism and Jewish life.

Maven: The Jewish Portal

www.maven.co.il

Okay, so you like the sound of Maven portal and you're tired of reading any more about Jewish humor, then go straight to Maven. It has a rich list of links, presented in subject categories that make the links easy to use. For instance, on Judaism, it comes right out with 138 sites that range from festivals to life cycle to Judaica, including the Jewish equivalent of Amazon.com. What's that? You guessed it: www.judaism.com!

Zipple.com

www.zipple.com

Maybe, instead you want to find out about EVERYTHING that's Jewish in the universe (no joke). I mean everything, from the Holocaust Webring to the Jewish Gay and Lesbian Webring to the Meir Kahane Webring, and lots, lots more. It is all there, or should all be there. Why? Because the site calls itself "All Jewish at Zipple.com: The Jewish SuperSite!" Of course it's from LA, and perhaps you're from NYC. Okay, so be insulted, but give it a try anyway!

And now you've decided that *none* of this is really very funny, right? Well, what is really funny—even outright ridiculous—is that I haven't even gotten started yet in telling you all the riches about Judaism on the Web, and here we are at the end of the chapter. Well you can begin with some of the previous sites and explore for yourself. Enjoy!

Rest and Remember

➤ Judaism is a many-splendored thing. It's more like a family, squabbles and all, than a top-down religion. It's more like a tribe, or many related but not identical tribes, than a single creed.

➤ Judaism is both a religion and more than a religion. It is also ethnic, cultural, and playful. It also can be downright secular, even atheistic.

➤ Jewish cybernauts are as at home on the Web as are Bahais, Wiccans, or Trekkies. Surfing is as naturally Jewish as chicken soup, and it comes with almost as many recipes! Try this one.

Chapter 22

There Is No god but God: Islam

In This Chapter

➤ Islam is a diverse global community with over one billion members, from Djakarata (Indonesia) to Dakar (Senegal) to Detroit (U.S.)

➤ Many Muslims are also cybermuslims, expressing their faith views and ritual practices on the Net

➤ The Web is not only home to a growing number of Muslims, but it is also the forum for contesting who counts as a Muslim and what counts as authentic Islam

It would be hard to imagine a more major shift than the one you are about to undertake. There is so much misinformation buzzing through cyberspace—not to mention the offline world—about Islam that you need to look carefully at what is the broadest expression of one of the most significant global religious communities. I try to provide you with some guidelines in what follows. Always think twice before you assume that what is said negatively about Islam really applies to either Islam or Muslims.

The Basic Pillars

Islam begins with a premise as radical as it is simple: There is no god but God. Just as Judaism affirms the God of Abraham, Isaac, and Jacob and Christianity privileges the Holy Trinity, so Islam anchors all existence, and all possibilities, in the One Transcendent Being who is also the Creator and Judge of all humankind: Allah. Allah is the Arabic word for God, but Allah is not god for Arabs alone. Allah is God for all beings, animal as well as human, in this world and also in the world to come.

According to Muslim belief, we can only know about the true nature of Allah through prophets. Prophets are specially chosen vehicles of God's Word; from the beginning of time there were numerous prophets sent to the world and to specific human communities. The first prophet was Adam; the last was Muhammad, and in between them there were said to be a lot of other prophets, perhaps as many as 124,000!

Adam a Prophet?

Yes, in Islam, Adam is regarded not just as the first man. He is also the first prophet, because he was taught names and names are a revelation from God that is the first step to other revelations. Sure, Adam disobeyed God. Muslims agree with Jews and Christians on the point of Adam's disobedience, but that does not keep Adam from being a prophet. Even prophets are not all perfect human beings; just remember David and Bathsheba and you can see that Adam might have been the first prophet to sin but he was not the last!

Not only is there no god but God, but there is also no prophet after Muhammad. If the first part of the basic Islamic creed confirms God's Transcendent Oneness, the other part confirms Muhammad's unique status.

Muhammad is the prophet of God. To become a Muslim one has to say in sincerity and also in the presence of a Muslim: "there is no god but God and Muhammad is the prophet of God."

Muhammad was a seventh century urban merchant who worked in Western Arabia before being called to act as God's spokesman or prophet to the Arabs. He received intermittent revelations from the time he was around 35 years old till his death, some 22 years later. Although he never wrote them down, others did. When the revelations were collected they became the Holy Book for Muslims, the Noble Qur'an. It has 114 chapters, in length about the size of the New Testament for Christians or the Pentateuch for Jews. You can see a quote from the Qur'an in Arabic and English on the Stevens Institute of Technology Muslim Student Association's Web page, shown in Figure 22.1.

Some pious Muslims memorize the Qur'an in its entirety. Even those who don't know large parts of it by heart, do know the first chapter, also known as the Fatiha, which every Muslim must say during a cycle of five daily prayers.

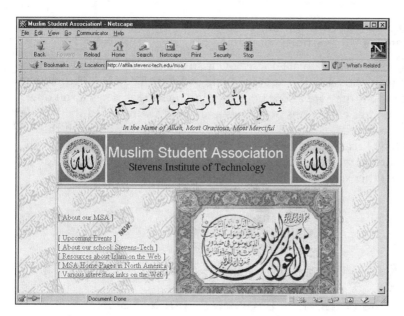

Figure 22.1

This is a Muslim Student Association home page, produced at Stevens Institute of Technology. It features the last chapter of the Qur'an, inserted on the right side in its Arabic original within floral borders.

Wired Monk

Pray Five Times a Day?

Yes, the Muslim observance of faith includes five pillars, with an accent on prayer. The first pillar is to profess belief in Allah as God and in Muhammad as His Prophet. Other pillars include fasting (especially during the holy month of Ramadan), giving of alms (for relief of the poor), pilgrimage to Mecca (at least once during a male Muslim's lifetime), but the most rigorous and most daily is the performance of ritual prayer or salat. The first prayer is just before sunrise and the last after twilight. In between there are three other prayers, at noon, in the afternoon, and at sunset. A devout Muslim might say the prayers in isolation or in community, either on the street, at home, or in a mosque, but the key requirement is his sincere and regular performance. It is one of the most distinctive aspects of Islam as a religion.

Beyond the basic pillars, including but not only the pillar of five daily prayers, Muslims also accept a code of guidance for everyday life. Known as the sharia, it is sometimes translated as Law, or Islamic Law, but it is much more: It regulates everything from one's approach to brushing teeth to getting married to inheriting property and wealth. The custodians of sharia are religious specialists at large; though trained in special sciences of scripture and law, they are not bound to any hierarchy of religious loyalty. They are known as scholars or ulama.

What do the ulama or religious scholars do? The Qur'an is a small book, but its interpretation is open to many possibilities, as is the Bible or Torah. The ulama know the Qur'an, often by heart, but they are also schooled in interpreting it. They also know the hadith. Hadith are huge collections of sayings and deeds attributed to the Prophet Muhammad. They were not collected till 200 years after his lifetime, but with the codification of law, they became very important. The law exalted hadith, along with Qur'an, as the basis for Islamic piety, and four schools of law interpreted them for Sunni Muslims, while other schools evolved for Shiis.

What's the Difference Between Sunnis and Shiis?

While the Sunnis make up the majority, almost 90% of all Muslims, and the Shi'i are a minority of little more than 10%, the real difference between them goes back to seventh century Arabia. It goes back to the origins of Islam as a religious polity. Those who became Sunni Muslims accepted the succession after Muhammad's death. It passed through his close followers but not his blood relatives: first Abu Bakr, then Umar, and finally, Uthman, but for those who later became Shi'i Muslims the succession should have been limited to close blood relatives. The first successor should have been Muhammad's first cousin Ali, who happened also to be his son-in law. Not only Ali but Ali's descendants, especially his son Husain, became very important figures for Shi'i Muslims. They were thought to be spiritually perfect, infallible beings. They were called Imams and had ritual as well as legal authority for Shi'i Muslims.

You can readily tell the difference between Sunni and Shi'i Web sites by their references to the earliest figures of Muslim history. Sunni sites never refer to the Imams, while Shi'is sites always do, frequently calling the descendants of Ali perfect or infallible beings, as you can see in the Web site projected in Figure 22.2.

Figure 22.2

The candle is the eternal flame of Ali, carried by his offspring, who are also his successors, the Imams or Infallibles.

Islam Today

Muslims total between one quarter and one third of the world's population.

More Muslims are Asian than African, more African than Arab. It is in South and Southeast Asia that we find the most Muslims. South Asia, which includes Pakistan, India, and Bangladesh, is home to at least 300 million Muslim inhabitants. Further east, Indonesia, with its more than 13,000 islands, has a population exceeding 170 million. Among Indonesians, about 150 million profess faith in Allah and His prophet Muhammad. Indonesia is far and away the largest Muslim country in the world.

American Muslims

Especially important for today's Muslim world is the growth of an American Muslim community. It has origins that go back to the earliest history of Spanish exploration in the New World, but the latest chapter is written from the last half of the twentieth century. Many, many immigrants from Asia, especially South Asia, have come to the U.S. and settled in major urban areas like New York City, Chicago, and Los Angeles. Together with a large and growing African-American Muslim community, they have made Islam one of the fastest growing religions in North America.

Islam is the second or third largest religion in North America. It is certainly the second largest religion in Europe, and it dominates the African-Asian span from Dakar in Senegal to Djakarta in Indonesia. We should not be surprised then that many, many different groups call themselves Muslim. Adding to the puzzle is the absence of anyone like a Pope or a Chief Rabbi who can claim to speak for all Muslims.

Islam in America

For details on both the history and current status of American Muslims, surf over to the home page of the Muslim World, which is actually the Islamic Interlink of University of Michigan Computer Club: www.ais.org/~islam/world/americas.html. It has a stunning number of links to other Islamic sites, and also to the locations of mosques, Islamic centers, and Islamic schools throughout North America, from Canada to Mexico including all 50 states in the United States.

Some groups do have local authority figures, such as W. Deen Muhammad, the spokesperson for the Muslim American Community.

Names in the News

Do not confuse Imam W. Deen Mohammed with the other African-American Muslim leader in the headlines, Minister Louis Farrakhan. They share some history but are very different representatives of African-American spirituality today. Check out the Ministry of W. Deen Mohammed at his home page with that title: www.worldforum.com/islam.htm.

There is also the Agha Khan, the leader of the small but influential Ismaili/Shi'i Muslim community, and you can explore the Agha Khanis at www.ismaili.net.

Yet neither Imam W. Deen Mohammed nor the Agha Khan nor any one else speaks for all Muslims. The Web has become a great leveler, making it possible for even tiny groups to have their views projected as authoritatively Islamic in cyberspace. Here are some of the most prominent sites.

Independent Cultural Associations

It is not easy to thread one's way through all the groups who claim to be mega-voices speaking on behalf of all Muslims. Many are independent cultural associations or university home pages. There is a huge overlap, but the following sites seem to stand out beyond others who compete with them while also projecting a strong Muslim presence on the Web.

A FIELD Day

The site at www.ismaili.org is advertised as the First Ismaili Electronic Library Database (FIELD), and it provides insight into one of the most dynamic and socially active Islamic groups in the world.

IslamiCity in Cyberspace

www.islam.org

This one megasite provides links to other Islamic resources on the Net. It has garnered three domain names. In addition to the above address, www.islam.org, you also can find it at www.islamic.org and www.islamicity.org. What this means is that the chances are good that wherever you go in your keyword search on Islam you will come to this omnibus site. In keeping with its "city" metaphor, this site will take you to the virtual mosque on Mecca Street, where you can find links to the Qur'an, to hadith, to Islamic history, and much, much more. You also can go to the virtual market for links to Islamic commercial groups on the Web, or you can visit the CyberPort if you want to travel to other Web links. If you've got an issue on your mind, there is also a Chat platform and if you need to hear some Islamic sounds, there is Radio Al-Islam, with audio files that rank with the best on the Net. The site claims over 50 million hits in just the last year!

Al-Islam Home Page

www.al-Islam.org

Maybe you thought that all your dreams had come true on the information superhighway; no more need to surf for all sites on Islam, you could just stop at Islamicity.org. Alas, digital Islam is no more a monopoly than ground-level Muslim practices. To see how opposite a view of Islam is out there in cyberspace, go to this site, which we mentioned before because of its focus on the Imams or the Infallibles. Here is the most sophisticated Shi'i view of the world, even though it is sponsored by a group that emanates from Toronto, Canada and not, as you might expect, from the Middle East.

International Institute of Islamic Thought

www.jaring.my/IIIT

This site tries to project a multi-dimensional intellectual and cultural approach to issues underlying the plight of the contemporary Muslim world. It stresses a particular view that it labels the Islamisation of knowledge.

What Does It Mean to Islamize Knowledge?

The approach of IIIT and related Muslim intellectual foundations is to integrate all contemporary sciences, from biology to economics, within the framework of revealed knowledge, in this case, the knowledge revealed by Allah to humankind through the Prophet Muhammad in the Holy Qur'an. Not every Muslim, or non-Muslim, will agree with the soundness of this approach, but it does have substantial backers and a loyal following.

International Islamic University (Malaysia)

www.iiu.edu.my

This is the home page for the International Islamic University (IIU) Malaysia. It provides perhaps the best university site in the entire Muslim world. It includes a beautifully simple but evocative home page. It offers an array of Islamic resources as well as literature on different departments and faculty within the IIU. It tries to do what the International Institute of Islamic Thought also proposes to do: integrate revealed knowledge with the social sciences in a thoroughly modern university setting. If you clicked to its links page, you would find yourself with hyperlinks to all the major Muslim topics, including a Muslim sisters' links page.

Private Individuals

Beyond cultural associations and universities, there are multiple sites that are run by Muslim individuals for the benefit of other Muslims. They include Muslim women, Sufi groups, and minorities looking for their voice in cyberspace.

Muslim Women

There are tens of hundreds and perhaps thousands of pages by and about Muslim women in cyberspace.

We cannot begin to do justice to all of them, but we can at least mention two of the many out there.

Islam: The Eternal Path to Jannah

www.jannah.org

One of the best sites comes from a cybersavvy Muslim software engineer, Huma Ahmad. It is actually a kind of megasite or subject directory on Muslim women rather than a single-issue site. If you surf down through the nine buttons on the index of the home page for jannah.org, you will find at the top of the list a button for Sisters. If you click that button, you will find everything from general articles about Muslim women to tips on getting married to advice about dress codes, all done with a tongue in cheek sense of humor that tempers the seriousness of her enterprise. Equally extensive, and impressive, is the second button. It is labeled Mama's List, and is sometimes referred to in others sites as Huma's Mama's List.

The site is even better than the rhymes that invite you to try it. It has buttons arrayed by alphabetical title, so that you can click anywhere you want and find at your fingertips the issues for looking into resources about Muslim women on the Web. Under the letter W alone, for instance, you will find no less than 12 articles or alternative sites that have information specific to Muslim women.

Iman Al-Muminah's Home Page

http://www.geocities.com/Wellesley/3565/

Billed as an e-zine for sisters following the path of Islam, this Muslim woman's home page is attractively laid out, with a beautiful background tapestry and the color-coded topics that range from the familiar Qur'an and hadith to the less expected Adaab and Sisterhood. What is projected in both the latter two sites is a sense of Muslim women's empowerment to be who they want to be within the boundaries of acceptable but also flexible Islamic norms. It also takes on FAQs, or Frequently Asked Questions, and answers them with consistent humor as well as scriptural authority.

Sufi Surfing

Sufis are an integral part of Islamic history and contemporary practice for many devout Muslims. Their aesthetic and mystical pursuits have also attracted to their circles non-Muslims, spiritual seekers who do not otherwise identify with, or pursue, the goals of mainstream Muslims. Sufis have thus become a subject of controversy, and for that reason as well as the cyber wisdom of many practicing Sufis, they are well represented on the Web.

Who Are Sufis?

Most Sufis are Muslim mystics sincerely trying to express the deepest level of Islamic faith and practice. Yet they are little understood and too often misunderstood. Most Sufis are not spiritual loners; they belong to organized brotherhoods, also know as Sufi societies or orders.

Islamic Sufi Orders on the World Wide Web

http://homepages.haqq.com.au/salam/sufilinks/

There is no more complete index to all the Sufi orders, and their current representation in cyberspace. It is maintained by Faridudien Rice and offers a classic example of how to communicate religious views on the Web. A survey of the links here would suffice to give an introduction to both the historical background and modern day legacy of institutional Sufism.

Alan Godlas's Home Page—Sufi Links

www.arches.uga.edu/~godlas/Sufism.html

Although this is a personal home page, and subject to usual limits of permanence and constant updating, its creator is a university professor with deep commitment to Sufism and also vast experience as a Webmaster.

This site is constantly invoked as one of the best places to review the vast literature of Sufism, and also to find links to other Sufi sites in cyberspace.

Other Minority Muslim Groups on the Web

Of the many minority groups within the contemporary Muslim world two stand out for the special contempt, evoking both controversy and acrimony, linked to them. One is a would-be reformist group, the other is a gender-oriented redirection of Muslim norms and values. Both have found their space on the Web, and need to be included in any cyberprofile of present-day Muslim netizens.

Ahmadis

www.ahmadiyya.org

The scourge of Orthodox Sunni Muslims, the Ahmadis have long suffered isolation, and worse, for their views. They identify with a nineteenth century North Indian reformer. They regard him as a kind of prophet sent to modern day Muslims. Because the Prophet Muhammad is upheld as the LAST prophet, the effort to add a latter day supplement or successor to him has not been well received. This site projects the beleaguered outlook of Ahmadis, also known as Qadyanis after their place of origin in North India.

Queer Jihad

www.geocities.com/WestHollywood/Heights/8977/

This site is managed by gay and lesbian Muslims. It is a singularly bold effort to find acceptance within the Muslim fold. Some Muslims have labeled this site as insulting and misguided, yet anyone who surfs to this site has to be struck by the faith commitment of these otherwise anonymous men and women who believe in the one God, Allah, and also in his Last Messenger, the Prophet Muhammad.

Anti-Islamic Sites

One of the difficulties with cyberspace is the lack of regulation of content. Searching under the word Islam, you will encounter both screen bias and false advertising. Screen bias? Yes, the first image of Islam might not represent an actual Muslim message. False advertising? Alas, yes, because some sites try to lure you into reading them, then give you a message you did not expect, or want. Two examples represent a host of others.

Welcome to the-Good-Way.com

www.the-good-way.com

This looks like a Muslim site yet it is actually a Christian evangelical group trying to convert Muslims to Protestant Christianity.

Answering Islam

http://answering-islam.org.uk

Although based overseas in England, this site still gets a lot of global attention through the Net. It is another evangelical group attempting to show contradictions in the Muslim world view, and for what reason? To convert Muslims to Christianity, and guess what? You will find testimonials from Muslim converts to Christianity, but you will also find a debate between two converts who went opposite ways!

Muslim Resources

Whether you are trying to counter deceitful efforts at proselytization or you are look-ing for a virtual Mecca of Islamic netaphysics, you have a lot of support on the Web.

The Wisdom Fund

www.twf.org

This is a source that attempts to set the record straight about the truth of Islam, and it is probably the best counter-offensive to Biblically based efforts to refute Islam and also to convert Muslims to some form of Protestant Christianity.

Free Islamic Resources

If you haven't already discovered it, you might want to go to Free Muslim Resources. Click www.geocities.com/Athens/Agora/4229/, and you will have arrived in cyberMecca. Here is a rollerdex of all kinds of Muslim opportunities, from free copies of the Qur'an to clip art to email. You can even find scholarships to study abroad!

HIV/AIDS Treatment with Sufi Healing Method

http://www.all-natural.com/sufi.html

One would like to think that no Muslims are AIDS victims, but in fact, AIDS is a creed-blind curse that afflicts Muslims as well as non-Muslims not only in Western Europe and the Americas but also across the span of Africa and Asia. There is no Muslim Web site more extraordinary than the Barzakh Foundation as a response to AIDS. Constructed by a Sufi master from Indonesia, it issues an ecumenical invitation for AIDS-afflicted cybernauts. After you pray to God (according to your own faith out-look) and receive an air mail-sent scroll, you can connect at a globally synchronized hour to Muhammad Zuhri and hope to find a spiritual pathway (barzakh) through the horror of AIDS.

Rest and Remember

➤ Few Muslims have exhausted the resources of Islam in cyberspace, but many have helped to make Islam a cybersavvy religion as well as the second largest religion in the world.

➤ The best Web sites on Islam abound with sound information, multiple links, and also resources for non-Muslims and Muslims alike.

➤ Until cyberpolice become as frequent as highway policy, the information superhighway will have a lot of reckless drivers with license plates labeled Islam. Be wary of them, shift lanes, and get out of their way whenever you see them on the Net.

Part 5

Beyond Abraham: Cybersavvy Forms of New and Old Religious Traditions on the Net

In Part 5, you find a huge diversity of voices, all appealing to the basic human sensibility to explore, to test, and to invoke the Divine. It has no fewer than 14 chapters, each with a different voice, a different religion, a different commitment to the mysterious, the true, and the worshipful. There are Native American voices and Asian voices. There are satanic and atheist voices. There are Wiccan and Vodun voices. There are even voices from Star Wars and Scientology, both clamoring for attention as religious sites on the Web.

Chapter 23

God Is Red: Native American Spirituality

In This Chapter

➤ The oldest American spiritual tradition is starting to find an audience in cyberspace

➤ God is a constant, vital presence to Native Americans, often present as a Red Deity

➤ You can begin to explore the staggering number and varieties of Native American spirituality on the Net

---

God is red—American red, Indian red. He is your grandfather, or the stand-in for all your grandfathers dating back countless years. He dwells in your land. He is your land. He is you, and you are his.

That might be the creed for Native American spirituality. A famous student of religion once said: "When I see God I see society transfigured, I see society expressed in an abstract symbol." What he meant was that we often make our highest authority someone like ourselves. Through religion, our dead ancestors become living resources for us.

This notion is expressed in the work "The Circle of Life," by Iowa artist Frank Howell, which is shown in Figure 23.1 as it appears on the Web site at www.rt66.com/ ~bluraven/. Frank Howell was an Anglo-Iowan artist and poet who felt a special attraction to the Lakotan Sioux tribes of—where else?—Sioux City, Iowa. Though the painting is here represented in black and white, the original, which you can see by clicking the Web site, is bathed in red, from the background horse's head to the cloak worn by the wise elder who is its central subject.

Figure 23.1

Although this Web site appears black and white here, it really sports a rich array of colors that reflect Native American traditions.

What Is Ancestor Worship?

Ancestor worship characterizes about 60% of all the cultures in our world, including Native American traditions. Most of these cultures believe that the ancestors support the living, and if the living neglect their worship, the ancestors might become angry and punish their forgetful descendants.

If the God of our fathers sustains us, he sustains us not just in thought and prayer, but also in space—in the space that we call home, in our territory, our land. As the poet Robert Frost intoned at the inauguration of President John Kennedy: "The land was ours before we were the land's." But for Native Americans, the land was theirs before we (non-native Americans) claimed it as ours.

President Kennedy once said: "Our treatment of Indians…still affects the national consciousness… It seems a basic requirement to study the history of Indian people. Only through this study can we as a nation do what must be done if our treatment of the American Indian is not to be marked down for all time as a national disgrace."

In a very real sense, to begin to study the history of native Americans is to acknowledge God as red, a red ancestor who continues to live through his descendants. And he continues to live in the land, on those precious parcels of burial ground and ceremonial celebration that identify America as Native American land.

How Do I Find Native American Issues on the Web?

If you want to see a range of First Nation perspectives, you might try the American Truths page at www.americantruths.com. It sells both audio programs and book courses, and it also provides free samples. Above all, this site dramatizes new ways to understand the ongoing relationship between indigenous peoples and European Americans.

Native American Spirituality and Land

Control of Native American land has been under constant change for more than 500 years. Explorers around the time of Christopher Columbus in 1492 first occupied it. Then European settlers who arrived in Jamestown in the sixteenth century occupied it. Then soldiers from England, France, and Spain fought over it. Now it is occupied by descendants of those first European Americans, by other Americans who were first imported as slaves and then granted freedom some 140 years ago, and by the descendants of waves of European immigrants. And in addition to the European and African-Americans, are Asian and Hispanic Americans, whose numbers have increased dramatically in recent decades.

Christianity and Native Americans

Europeans missionaries knew they were competing with native spirituality, which they regarded as evil superstition inspired by Satan. Many Native Americans were forcibly converted to Christianity. Then when the United States and Canadian governments instituted policies to force natives onto reservations, they also encouraged the natives to become assimilated into the majority culture. Much ink has been spilled speculating on the high suicide rate among Native Americans, but many believe it is due to the suppression of their religion and culture by the federal governments in both Canada and the United States. Given that history, it is even more crucial to uncover the valuable historical background about the actual development of the West and the damage it caused to our country's first inhabitants.

How Many Native Americans?

Five hundred years ago, before Columbus made his discovery, Native Americans were the sole inhabitants of the modern-day areas of the United States, Canada, Mexico, and the Caribbean. They numbered several million, approximately 30, 40, or 50 million in all. The arrival of Europeans marked a major change in native society. The rigors of slavery, wars and extermination programs, and European illnesses against which Native Americans were defenseless caused the death of tens of millions. Today, the total Native American population of the United States is less than two million, and less than half a million First Nation survivors remain north of the border in Canada. There are also, of course, Indians south of the border, in Mexico as well as the Caribbean. If you are concerned about more than just the diminished number of Native Americans, you can check out their version of what has happened to some of the 240 tribes that existed until 1900. It is a monumental history project called First Nations Histories, and it is available at www.dickshovel.com/.

The best place to start may be the superb eight-part documentary series "New Perspectives on the West." Co-directed by the award-winning filmmaker Ken Burns and produced by PBS in the fall of 1996, it gives you a virtual tour of the West that includes an interactive map of the expanding American frontier from Kansas to California. You can check it out at www.pbs.org/weta/thewest/. This site does *not* focus only on Native Americans, nor does it highlight cultural practices that might fall within a broad notion of spirituality. But it does push and probe and present a non-official, largely unknown view of the American frontier where the First Nations are at center stage.

Native Americans in Cyberspace

The Native American sites in cyberspace explore all the themes of Native American spirituality, at once ancient and modern, both glorious and tragic. You will quickly discover that many of these sites resist even prevalent categories, such as religion and spirituality. Why? Because neither religion nor spirituality expresses the kind of worldview that echoes in First Nation sources. The oldest form of American spirituality (if one can call it that) is a radically different type of spirituality. It is a spirituality that is now in the process of being rediscovered at many levels, including on the World Wide Web. It does have a God. He is red and far from dead. He lives in the imagination and the lands of Native Americans. He finds his newest voice on the Net.

The Great Spirit and His Message

www.indians.org/welker/tencomm.htm

This site provides the clearest expression of the First Nations' commitment to the Great Spirit, which is embodied in the Earth. It is a creed that could be said by many ecologically minded European Americans, but for Native Americans, it resounds as a sacred mission.

Religious Tolerance Begins at Home

www.religioustolerance.org/nataspir.htm

If you are eager to find out more about the first American spiritual way without doing a lot of side surfing, you might go to Religious Tolerance, the most tested search directory I have found. Here is a much longer, more cerebral introduction to other sites, authored either by Native Americans or by Native American advocates. It also includes links in endnotes to its essay, and it explains to even the most clueless beginner why the original Americans still count as religious, even if they resist the very notion of religion as commonly understood.

Broken Threads

http://www.i-america.net/homepages/sngunn/links.html

Not everyone will welcome the use of Native American traditions, from cosmologies to genealogies, by New Age practitioners. However, check out the Broken Threads page. It provides one example of a site that has a huge amount of information about Native America resources, while at the same time allowing you to scroll down to cyberspace and cyberwitch (which is another way of talking about Goddess worshipers or Wiccans; see Chapter 26, "She Is God: Neopaganism and Wicca").

Walking Stick Foundation

www.walkingstick.org/

Similar in spirit, but with a much more practical, ecologically focused message, is the joint Web site of Jewish and Native Americans. If cyberspace can bridge communities and produce a greater whole than the disparate parts, this site might be one of its first successes. Stroll over to walkingstick.org, where you will be introduced to the Walking Stick Foundation, a nonprofit tax-exempt Jewish and Native American partnership dedicated to the recovery and preservation of indigenous spirituality.

Powwows and Festivals

http://info.pitt.edu/~lmitten/indians.html

If there is one part of Native American culture that has made it into mainstream European American consciousness, it is the powwow—the coming together of Native

Americans to share stories, dreams, concerns, and challenges. It is now possible to track powwows, thanks to Lisa Mitten, a Social Sciences librarian at the University of Pittsburgh. Her site, which is regularly updated, not only provides local information about powwows and festivals, but also covers First Nation art, music, and cultural activities on a broad scale.

Native American Tribes: Information Virtually Everywhere

www.afn.org/~native/

No joke, this is really the name of a useful, if very spartan Web page that provides topical links to most of the other facets of First Nation culture that you may not have found elsewhere. It is maintained by another librarian, this time at the University of Florida. Having had a Native American co-worker, she became intrigued by all the available information about the original Americans, so she put together this site. It even gives a list of all the radio stations that broadcast Native American programs. Not surprisingly, most are out in the Far West or the Southwest, but stations do exist in Alaska and, of course, Canada.

Native American History Archive

www.ilt.columbia.edu/k12/naha/

If your interest is strictly in history, you might want to visit the Institute for Learning Technologies of Teachers College, Columbia University. Its Native American History Archive is bursting with information about interactive learning on the Net and other material about Native American organizations.

Native Americans—Internet Resources

http://falcon.jmu.edu/~ramseyil/native.htm

Maybe you're short on time, and you just want to get the quick ABC's for a class project. Then you might try an alternative site that is maintained by Inez Ramsey, an Emeritus Professor of Library Sciences at James Madison University. The site is called Native Americans—Internet Resources. Its creator intended this site for young adults, but this site provides basic electronic resources for classroom instruction on the First Nations. It also includes their religious rituals and spiritual pursuits, although they are often folded into history or culture or society instead of being listed separately.

Native American Art

www.hanksville.org/NAresources/

If religion is as close to art as it is to literature, Native American spirituality has a claim to being among the most aesthetically developed traditions of humankind. It encompasses all kinds of art, from pottery and baskets to textiles and prints, with countless local expressions that defy easy generalization.

Fortunately, one of the oldest sites on Native American resources, appropriately titled the Index of Native American Resources on the Internet, provides not only a cornucopia of links to other sites but also an entire section on Native American art. Maintained by Karen M. Strom, from Hanksville, Utah, this site gives you almost more than you can absorb. Whether you're looking for individual artists, galleries, museums, or home pages, you'll find them all here, including World Wide Web Virtual Library resources. Be prepared to go slow, however; this site is so loaded that it takes a while to scroll through its buttons. But if you had to linger on just one figure, it might be the one shown in Figure 23.2.

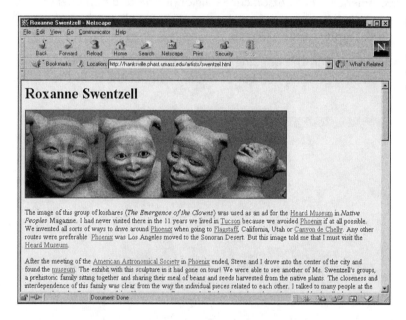

Figure 23.2

"The Emergence of the Clowns" is an example of the art you might find at this site.

This stunning evocation of four clowns in related but puzzling postures is the work of Pueblo artist Roxanne Swentzell. Raised at Santa Clara Pueblo in New Mexico, Swentzell observed the emergence of black-and-white striped clowns from the community's underground ceremonial houses during ritual celebrations. Why clowns? Because according to one Pueblo tradition, clowns led the people from the underworld through the earth navel into the middle world where they still live. The clowns symbolize the four directions, and they still look dazed—even amused—at what they see around them!

Native Americans and Others

Maybe you're not of Native American descent, and maybe you still think of Native Americans as Indians from the Wild West, always being chased by cowboys or killing innocent settlers. Yet there is a new, growing interest in the perspective of Native Americans as the First Nation of this vast continent. Because there were many Native American tribes, there were really several *first* nations. However, they had much in common, including practices that can be, with care and caution, labeled religious or spiritual. You have come to the right place to begin to discover them on the Net.

Rest and Remember

➤ You cannot fully understand American history without knowing of the 240 or more tribal groups who were here before Columbus arrived.

➤ Although Native Americans did not practice religion in the traditional sense, they had a worldview and a set of expectations and rituals, all of which sustained them as tribal groups, both large and small.

➤ You can begin to understand the ongoing legacy of the First Nation by exploring the ample and growing number of resources about them on the Net.

NO THANK YOU.

Chapter 24

There Is No God: Atheists and Agnostics, Freethinkers and Humanists

In This Chapter

➤ Atheists and agnostics are not identical, but they share many common sites in cyberspace, along with freethinkers and humanists

➤ The most celebrated atheists have contributed much to history, and also have their supporters on the Net

➤ Most people who want to find out more about atheists, agnostics, freethinkers, or humanists are going to be surprised at how much there is to learn from them, even if you do not share their viewpoint. You can learn a bunch about them on the Web

Very few people at the end of the last century thought that atheism had a significant following, despite the excitement generated by Mr. Darwin and his evolutionary theories. Now, a century later, in the aftermath of a major explosion of scientific knowledge and also a major experiment with government-sponsored atheism (in the former Soviet Union and also the People's Republic of China), more people have had to consider the argument made by and for atheists. I'll begin by discussing a worldview that has much in common with atheism. It is known as objectivism.

The Objectivist Approach to Life

Have you ever thought about what Ayn Rand and Alan Greenspan have in common? Both subscribe to a worldview known as *objectivism*. Is it really atheistic? Some folk would just label objectivism and objectivists as a new philosophical movement. It is, to be sure, but it is also part of an old philosophical tradition that was identified from the time of the Greeks as atheism. Atheists have no need for gods, and most of them reject anything to do with the supernatural.

What do atheists believe in? Well, if you follow the line of thinking of Ayn Rand, then it is stark reason and unbridled egoism. Whether you go to her best selling novel *Atlas Shrugged,* or you explore one of her other books such as *Introduction to Objectivist Epistemology* or *The Virtue of Selfishness*, you will find the same message: There is no reality beyond this world, there is no force greater than the human ego.

Ayn Rand does have a philosophical hero. It is Aristotle. Ayn Rand believes that Aristotle had proved both that the universe or material world exists independent of human consciousness and also that there is no consciousness apart from the material world.

What's the Big Deal with Ayn Rand?

If you've not heard of Ayn Rand before, and you associate atheism with some other major figure of European or American history, then you might want to go and check out one of the several Web sites dedicated to her. The Ayn Rand Institute, also known as the Center for the Advancement of Objectivism, has its own Web site: www.aynrand.org/. Its appeal is especially directed to college students.

Most organized religions, and also some other schools of thought, such as Platonism and German idealism, come to a different conclusion. They argue that consciousness can create its own reality. In a God-centered world, there is the further notion that above nature there exists a consciousness superior to the material world and also beyond the reach of the human intellect. It is the God principle, and that is the principle that all atheists, including Ayn Rand and her followers, reject.

Atheism Light

One of the great things about About.com is its guide system, and there is also a guide for atheism/agnosticism at http://atheism.miningco.com/. You will find many sites to explore, and they will give you an alternate reading of religious history, mostly from within Christian circles. The most intriguing of these links are those that follow.

The Benefits and Hazards of the Philosophy of Ayn Rand

That's right, Ayn Rand has her detractors as well as her admirers. The essay found at http://216.98.133.68/fs/ayn.shtml is written by a man who had worked closely with Ayn Rand, but then broke off from her in 1968, Dr. Nathaniel Branden. So this is not a flimsy off-the-cuff response to her thought, and it does put objectivism into a broader light than you'd get from within the Ayn Rand Institute.

The Atheist Celebrity List

So are you really tired of Ayn Rand but you still want to know who are the other high-flying atheists past and present? Well, then you might want to surf through About.com till you come to the Celebrity Atheist List at www.primenet.com/ ~lippard/atheistcelebs/. You might be surprised at the names you find there.

This site gives two lists. The first is huge, and it is labeled *The Atheist And The Materialist*, that is, those who have no need for gods and some who have no need for the supernatural. It includes such screen stars as Ingemar Bergman, Marlon Brando, and Jack Nicholson. It includes big-time investors, such as Warren Buffett and Bill Gates. It even includes a politician, Fidel Castro.

The other list is smaller, and it is labeled *The Agnostic And The Ambiguous*, that is, those who call themselves agnostic and those from whom we don't have enough information. Among their number are the Harvard Professors E.O. Wilson, Stephen Jay Gould, and Alan Dershowitz, along with their MIT neighbor, Noam Chomsky. There is also a politician, Mikhail Gorbachev, and two religious leaders, the Dalai Lama and Rabbi Sherwin T. Wine, founder of the Society for Humanistic Judaism (see later in this chapter).

Home Page for the North Texas Church of Free Thought

If you aren't laughing yet over the variety of candidates for the atheist and agnostic rolls, then you might have to read a bit of the Revised Book of Genesis from the North Texas Church of Free Thought at http://church.freethought.org/ 9701.creation.html, shown in Figure 24.1. It has taken upon itself the delicate job of tasteful satire. Some anti-religious humor just goes way over the top, and you will have to be careful to avoid such sites on the Net if you are offended by some over-done barbs. But this one comes within the bounds of decency, at least for most folk.

Gay and Lesbian Atheists and Humanists (GALAH)

If you want to find something akin to an activist agenda for crusading atheists, along with humanists and agnostics, you might look at the 11 Things You Can Do to Fight the Religious Right at www.serve.com/tgkindc/11things.html. In addition to targeting groups that support the Religious Right, it also has a newsletter that updates current issues or events where the voice of Gay and Lesbian advocates can be heard and can possibly make a difference.

Figure 24.1

The Book of Genesis—Revised, Chapters 1 & 2. To update the Book of Genesis, this society of professed unbelievers tries to do a version of the first two books of the Hebrew Bible that includes the discoveries of modern science, although always with more than a bit of tongue-in-cheek flavor to their revised scripture!

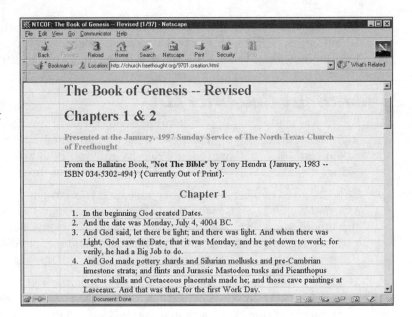

What's the Difference Between Agnostics, Atheists, and Humanists?

Until the nineteenth century, any one who was an agnostic also was considered to be an atheist (one who believes in no god). It was then that a British freethinker named Thomas Huxley coined the term agnostic. And much has been debated since then about what an agnostic is exactly. An agnostic can just be someone who says, "I don't know if there is a god," and tries to find out by using logical thinking and scientific fact gathering. But an agnostic also can be someone who says, "I can't know," and argues that no matter how good your method or how many facts you produce, you can't know some things, like the nature of God.

Humanists, on the other hand, can be either religious or secular. Even when they are religious, though, they assert that what is crucial about religion is its function. We cannot have a moral society without religious foundations, they claim, but then they quickly add: "There is more to religion than God talk; it is the function not the content of religion, ethics not metaphysics, that counts as *true* religion." Hence most Unitarian Universalists (see Chapter 18, "Beyond Protestantism") could be called humanists rather than agnostics or atheists.

Atheism Heavy

After considering all these avenues to the profile and practice of atheism, you might be ready for some heavy lifting. You might want to enter into some of the debates in which atheists themselves engage about the meaning of life, the respective roles of science and religion, and the separation of church and state. If so, you might be ready for a site that declares itself to be the most heavily trafficked non-theistic site on the Web. You might be ready for the Secular Web.

The Secular Web

www.infidels.org/

It is hard to top Infidels.org for good graphics, thoughtful material, extensive networking, and interdisciplinary flair.

The Secular Web: www.infidels.org/

You will find other sites that carry the banner for modern day infidels, but none that has so many links to other sites, plus a monthly newsletter and a Web ring.

Especially useful is Infidels.org's list of FAQs (that is, Frequently Asked Questions), shown in Figure 24.2. Can you imagine any group that would be self-critical enough to field a question about its limits, such as Why do Internet Infidels focus so much on Christianity?

The answer is a blunt admission that most of the pro-God, pro-religion sources on the Net, as in society at large, are Christian, and so the response of Infidels, including Internet Infidels, has been to Christian opponents. But then the Infidel spokesperson quickly adds, "We've been thinking of Islam, Judaism, and Mormonism, too, so let's move on against them as well!"

Figure 24.2

*When you go to the Infidels.org main page, click the **About** link to access this FAQ at the bottom of the page.*

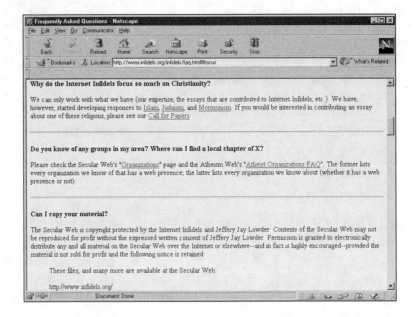

Why do the Internet Infidels focus so much on Christianity?

We can only work with what we have (our expertise, the essays that are contributed to Internet Infidels, etc.). We have, however, started developing responses to Islam, Judaism, and Mormonism. If you would be interested in contributing an essay about one of these religions, please see our Call for Papers.

Do you know of any groups in my area? Where can I find a local chapter of X?

Please check the Secular Web's "Organizations" page and the Atheism Web's "Atheist Organizations FAQ". The former lists every organization we know of that has a web presence; the latter lists every organization we know about (whether it has a web presence or not).

Can I copy your material?

The Secular Web is copyright protected by the Internet Infidels and Jeffery Jay Lowder. Contents of the Secular Web may not be reproduced for profit without the expressed written consent of Jeffery Jay Lowder. Permission is granted to electronically distribute any and all material on the Secular Web over the Internet or elsewhere--and in fact is highly encouraged--provided the material is not sold for profit and the following notice is retained:

These files, and many more are available at the Secular Web:

http://www.infidels.org/

Humanistic Judaism

The humanistic alternative in Judaism has already arrived in the person of Rabbi Sherwin T. Wine. In 1969 he helped form the Society for Humanistic Judaism, found on the Web at www.shj.org/. He is now Dean of the International Institute for Secular Humanistic Judaism in North America, as well as the author of several books, including *Judaism Beyond God*.

Alternative Islam

We've already clued you in about About.com: It has a human guide, and he directs you to all kinds of sites that involve atheists and agnostics, humanists and free-thinkers. But even after you have surfed through site after site, you will not find material on Islam unless you go to the button marked "Islam" in the left column of the box on his home page. After you do, you are in for another set of visits that will leave your head spinning about the world's second largest religious community after Christianity (see Chapter 22, "There Is No god but God: Islam"). I cannot list all these sites, but one or two cry out for special mention.

The International Society for Islamic Secularization

This Society has a Web page at www.secularislam.org/. Its site gives no background information about its place and date of origin, nor its founding members. Yet it has a very broad agenda, from separation of mosque and state to protection of minorities to advocacy of women's rights. In fact, many of the other sites that you will find in About.com are actually links contained within this megasite. Its influence is impossible to gauge, but its very existence on the Net proves the availability of diverse views on even the most delicate subjects.

SuralikeitAffair

Unlike the preceding site, the Web page at byrden.com/suralikeit/Sura.shtml has its author's fingerprints all over it. He is David Byrden, an electronic engineer, a professor, and a certified Java programmer. He has apparently decided that the crisis of freedom of speech is his own war to wage as a freethinker in a democratic, liberal society. He has made it his mission to publicize the AOL action to close down a site that was trying to elicit from viewers Qur'an-like verses. That is, the site sought modern day compositions that looked like those Arabic verses revealed to the Prophet Muhammad back in the seventh century CE (see Chapter 22).

There might be more delicate issues involving blasphemy and human rights, but this ranks up there with Piss Christ (the painting that showed just that!), and it far exceeds the offense felt by some Christians with the movie "Last Temptation of Christ." But again, in the name of both atheism and the Internet, we now have a site dedicated to showing the limits of freedom within orthodox Islamic notions of scripture. Do you remember Salman Rushdie and *The Satanic Verses* controversy back in the late 80s and early 90s? Were Suralikeit to become a major public issue, David Bryden would be as much in risk in public as Salman Rushdie, yet Professor Bryden closes this Web site by asking Egyptian respondents for good places to visit while on a trip to Egypt!

Why Atheism?

Whether you prefer Atheism Light or Atheism Heavy, you might consider this: the debunkers, the scoffers, the unbelievers—all are struggling with the same life-and-death issues as other folk. They just don't find any satisfaction or solace in the avenues that we call religion, most of which involve belief in some consciousness beyond the here-and-now, whether you call it God, Being, Spirit, Self, Other, Unknown, Unknowable.

Some like it hot, some like it cold, some say yes, some say no, but even the naysayers have found a space on the Net, and we would all be the poorer for not noting their contribution to cybersavvy spirituality.

Rest and Remember

➤ Atheism is not alone in opposing organized religion or God talk. Agnostics, humanists, and freethinkers, as well as atheists, share sites on the World Wide Web.

➤ The best sites on atheism combine serious analysis of issues with an attempt at light-hearted banter, including self-mockery; laugh at yourself and the world will laugh with you—this phrase could be a cybersignature for some atheist Web pages.

➤ While Christianity remains the favorite target for unbelievers, there is also an effort to look beyond God in Judaism, and also an effort to look behind the Qur'an in Islam. Neither effort is mainline, but both are represented on the Web.

Chapter 25

God Is Black: Farrakhan and Rastafarians

In This Chapter

➤ The Nation of Islam preaches that God is black; so do the Rastafarians

➤ Both the Nation of Islam and Rastafarians are influenced by powerful black leaders, and also by links to Africa as a homeland

➤ Don't overlook the impact of media, including the Net, in getting out the message for both followers of Louis Farrakhan and the Rastafarians

---

Although it may seem strange at first to place any other religious community in the same chapter with the outspoken Minister Louis Farrakhan, I have tried to make sense of his views of God by looking at their racial accent. I have found that the God of Minister Farrakhan resembles the Lion of Judah worshipped by Rastafarians. Both are African, both are black, and so together they help us understand a powerful construction of the Almighty as Black.

Nation of Islam or Farrakhanism?

Is the Nation of Islam a part of the large global religious tradition known as Islam? Perhaps. Could it also be part of a racial protest movement within the United States that invokes the name Islam but is not Muslim? Perhaps.

Perhaps.... Perhaps.... You want a definite answer: *yes* or *no*, but we are trafficking here in a gray area. There is no simple way to define the Nation of Islam. You must ask yourself, and you must answer for yourself: Who is Louis Farrakhan? What does his group stand for? Are they really Muslim?

If you decide to surf the Web to find the answer, you might go where you've already been. You might go to the Ontario Consultants on Religious Tolerance (OCRT: www.religioustolerance.org). There you find reference to the Black Muslim Movement (BMM), but not to Louis Farrakhan or the Nation of Islam. And even there, the information is somewhat obscure. To find the information on the BMM, click **Other Religions** on the main page, click **Islam** on the next page, and then page down to the correct section of "Schools within Islam."

And what is the Black Muslim Movement? It is the antecedent to the Nation of Islam. OCRT tells us that it is largely a black urban movement in the U.S. One driving force was a rejection of Christianity. Why? Because Christianity was the religion of the historically oppressing white race.

Wallace Fard started the BMM. Fard built the first BMM temple in Detroit back in the 1930s. Elijah Muhammad (born Elijah Poole) established a second temple in Chicago and later supervised the creation of temples in most large cities with significant black populations. All the BMM temples taught that blacks were racially superior to whites. They also believed that a racial war was inevitable. The charismatic Malcolm X became their most famous spokesperson. Long before Spike Lee made a movie of his life, Malcolm X had become a hero to many African Americans, and after a pilgrimage to Mecca, the central city of Muslim devotion, in 1964, he tried to reverse the BMM's anti-white beliefs.

Wired Monk

Who Was Malcolm X?

Malcolm X was part of a Black Liberation Movement that was larger than the Black Muslim Movement. It is sometimes better to approach a legendary hero by looking at his link with another legendary hero. This is the approach taken by Alton Pollard, a Religious Studies Professor at Wake Forest University. Pollard wrote an article titled "Martin and Malcolm and the African–American Struggle." It was published by the Union Seminary Quarterly Review (USQR), and you can read it at www.uts.columbia.edu/~usqr/pllrd.htm.

But did Malcolm X succeed? The BMM in its earlier years had deviated significantly from traditional Islamic beliefs. Unlike traditional Islam, the BMM was not racially tolerant; it was for blacks only. The BMM leaders, from Elijah Mohamed to Louis Farrakhan, were regarded as something akin to prophets, while in Islam the last prophet was the Prophet Muhammad.

Still, if you follow another tradition from Malcolm X, you will be led not to Louis Farrakhan but to Imam Warith Deen Muhammad. The Son of Elijah Muhammad, he also claims Malcolm X as his role model. He is a broad-minded African American Muslim leader, who is striving to bring African American Islam into both the mainstream of American society and into the center space of Islamic faith. For more on his role as a Muslim spokesperson, see Chapter 22, "There Is No god but God: Islam."

Louis Farrakhan As a Black Nationalist

Louis Farrakhan also claims the legacy of Malcolm X, even though Farrakhan has not reversed BMM's anti-white beliefs. His is a racialized view of Islam, so much so that many who attack him do not even refer to his following, and the organization he has built up, as the Nation of Islam. Instead, they call the movement that Farrakhan spearheads Farrakhanism.

Throughout the United States Louis Farrakhan is a very public figure. In Fall 1995 he attracted hundreds of thousands of men to his Million Man March in Washington, D.C. He received national and international publicity for weeks, yet the total membership of the Nation of Islam might be as low as 10,000, while the total African American Muslim population is above two million!

Figure 25.1 shows how the Institute of Islamic Information and Education, which is a mainstream Muslim group based in Chicago, reviles Farrakhanism in one of its publications.

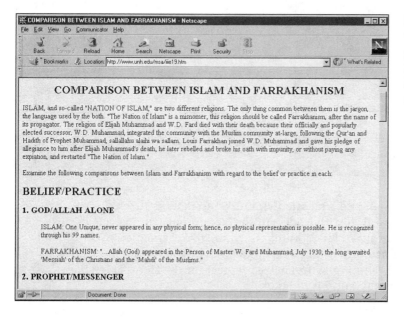

Figure 25.1

This Web site gives the mainstream Institute of Islamic Information and Education's take on Islam and Farrakhanism.

Islam is not Farrakhan(ism). For many American Muslims, the constant need is to maintain the distance between Farrakhan—his beliefs, his practices, and his organization—and mainstream Islam. While the site pictured previously, www.unh.edu/msa/iiie19.htm, gives you a head-to-head comparison, if you type in Farrakhanism under any search engine or subject directory you will find similar contrasts being made. The gap would seem to be unbridgeable, as long as Farrakhan continues to embrace W. D. Fard as God and Elijah Mohamed as his Prophet.

Farrakhan As the True Successor to Elijah Muhammad

Could Farrakhan be who he says he is? Could he be both a Black Nationalist with a black God and a black Prophet, and also a genuine Muslim? That is the story we find when we go to the site maintained by the Nation of Islam, www.noi.org. If you click **General Information** and then **Louis Farrakhan**, the page opens with an attractive photograph of Louis Farrakhan, accompanied by a story that is even more attractive, as shown in Figure 25.2.

Figure 25.2

Louis Farrakhan is praised on the Web site of the Nation of Islam.

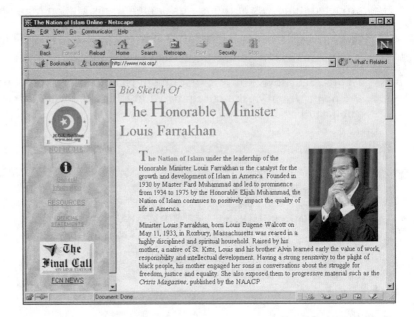

As a Caribbean immigrant and a talented violinist, Farrakhan struggled all his life to combat racism. He worked with leaders of the Nation of Islam, especially with Malcolm X. After the death of Elijah Muhammad in 1975, Farrakhan tried to follow Warith Deen Muhammad. After three years, however, he found that he had to chart his own path, a path beginning with renewed respect for the Honorable Elijah Muhammad, his teachings, and his program.

What this has meant is restating a belief system that sees the first humans as a race of black people. It is from this group, also known as the Original Man, that white people were created through a genetic experiment that took place 6,000 years ago. Elijah Muhammad claimed that whites would rule the world for 6,000 years and then be destroyed at the end of their time by blacks. He said that 'Judgement Day' means that at the end of time, the Gods, all of whom are black, would destroy the entire white race, also known as the devils, and then the black Gods would establish a permanent Paradise on this earth. It would be known as the Nation of Islam.

While this is far from the world view and belief system of mainstream Muslims, Louis Farrakhan continues to identify himself and his followers as Muslims, and the places they worship are labeled mosques. Farrakhan also includes among the world leaders with whom he visits a few Muslim heads of state, the most notorious being Muammar Qaddafi of Libya.

The Nation of Islam Beyond America?

If you have still not made up your mind on the status of the Nation of Islam as a Muslim organization, you might visit the official Web site at www.noi.org. It does include the traditional Muslim invocation of God's name, and it refers to Louis Farrakhan throughout as a distinguished Muslim minister. But when you look at the resources bar on left side of the home page, you find that overseas there are only two sites: London, England and Accra, Ghana. Ghana? Does the Nation of Islam have a mission there? Well it's not clear, because the site mostly promotes tourism in Ghana, an ideal vacationland that is said to be beautiful, ancient, and timeless. Discover Ghana, discover yourself. Okay, but what of Islam? It's not there.

So is there any last clue on Minister Farrakhan and the Nation of Islam? It is perhaps to keep uppermost in your mind the power of the press, the media, and, yes, cyber-space to shape views. It is not rare to go surfing under the word Islam and to find the Nation of Islam as one of the first sites that you discover. This is an example of what we call screen bias. Try making such a search on Infoseek (www.infoseek.com) and find out for yourself.

Even in a streamlined portal such as About.com you will not easily find the name Warith Deen Muhammad, while Louis Farrakhan's name is there click after click. But keep in mind that such a screen bias does not automatically mean that Farrakhan is a more important African-American leader, or that he is more representative of Muslim teaching than his neighbor and rival Warith Deen Muhammad.

Rastafarians

Like the Nation of Islam, or Farrakhanism, Rastafarians are tied to Africa. Their most important belief is that the emperor Haile Selassie, who ruled Ethiopia till 1974 and then died mysteriously the next year, was no mere emperor: He was God. The name Ras is Ethiopian for Prince, while Tafari is the formal name by which Haile Selassie ruled. When he was enthroned in November of 1930, the event was seen as culminating a centuries old dream. It was seen to be a biblical enthronement of Ras Tafari as His Imperial Majesty. The Emperor Haile Selassie I became King of Kings, Lord of Lords, and Conquering Lion of the Tribe of Judah.

Rastafarians (or Rastas, as they often call themselves) see Ethiopia itself as having divine significance. It is the promised land. It is the place in Africa to which all blacks should be repatriated when the biblical story unfolds into its final chapter. Just as the children of Israel were rescued from captivity and led into Egypt, so black people around the world will be freed from the slavery and oppression they now experience and returned to Ethiopia.

Sound strange? Not if you are from Jamaica, for during his long reign, Haile Selassie set aside several hundreds of acres in Ethiopia. He reserved this huge chunk of real estate for the people of Jamaica to inhabit when they returned to Africa.

Food for Thought

Haile Selassie—Man or God?

For a brief history into the connection of Garvey to Jamaica to Rastafar, or Haile Selassie, you can find few thumbnail portraits better than the Rastafarianism page at http://psychicinvestigator.com/Relig/Christ2.htm. But what this site omits is the continuous investment of Haile Selassie with divine powers through the verses of the great song master Bob Marley. To find out about the real Haile Selassie you have to go from conventional history to popular culture, where a song of Bob Marley will introduce a speech by Haile Selassie, and lend it an air of plausibility that is mind tingling. Check it out at www.in.tu-clausthal.de/~wallner/marley/him.html.

Marcus Garvey

The idea of the black race returning to Africa is often identified with Marcus Garvey. He was a magnificent orator and visionary whose views gained popularity in Jamaica in the early 1920s. He preached not only a return but a coming together of all Africans. So popular was Garvey that early Rastafarians called themselves Garveyites. Garvey is sometimes referred to as a John the Baptist, leading blacks to someone greater than himself, namely, Haile Selassie. Garvey also was seen as a Moses-like figure, leading blacks from Diaspora to the new Zion, a Zion in Africa that would be restored to them after centuries of dispersal, slavery, and oppression.

Garvey himself enjoys considerable fame on the Net, but to explore his full significance for the Rastafarian movement, you might have to break down and go back to print sources. Many such sources are available at www.onedropbooks.com. It is a site totally dedicated to the message and spiritual lives of Rastafari heroes/prophets.

Garvey, who is also known as Marcus Mosiah Garvey, is featured there, along with the Lion of Judah, Haile Selassie.

Rastafarians and Christianity

As can be seen, there is a close tie to Christian themes of redemption and deliverance or salvation in the thought world of Rastafarians. God revealed himself to humankind through prophets, Moses, Elijah, and then Jesus. The climax of his prophetic revelation was Ras Tafari (Haile Selassie), and it is thought that Jesus himself predicted the coming of Haile Selassie.

Yet Rastafari is an independent religious movement, with no ties to mainstream Christian denominations. Its numbers are calculated with wild abandon, but they probably number about 70,000 in Jamaica and another 180,000 scattered to various parts of Europe, Africa, and North America. For all the various guestimates, check out www.adherents.com/Na_349.html#2420, but be prepared to scroll down until you come to the actual Rasta counts.

Why Those Dreadlocks?

If there are two things that characterize all Rastafarians, it is smoking marijuana as a sacrament and wearing dreadlocks. Rastas often speak of marijuana as a holy sacrament, and it's central to their religious ceremonies. They claim that its use can be confirmed from the Bible. There are, after all, many verses in the Bible that refer to herbs or cane, and what is meant, according to Rastas, is marijuana.

Similarly, there is a Biblical justification for dreadlocks. It comes form the Book of Numbers, Chapter 6, verse 5. Referring to Samson, it says, "All the days of his vow of separation no razor shall come upon his head; until the time is completed for which he separates himself to the Lord, he shall be holy; he shall let the locks of hair of his head grow long." Dreadlocks then become a biblically justified way of separating oneself from normal society. They are also symbolic of strength, identifying Rastas with the hairstyle of the Mau-Mau warriors of Kenya.

The picture of the dreadlocked man shown in Figure 25.3 is part of the permanent teaching resources on Africa to be found at the Smithsonian Institution in Washington, D.C. Here you will find a magnificent Smithsonian Exhibit on Dread History: the African Diaspora, Ethiopianism, and Rastafari, which you ought to check out in full.

Figure 25.3

The Dreadlocks look is captured here.

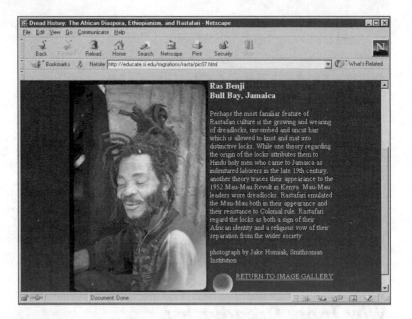

Bob Marley and Reggae

Part of the popularity of Rastafarians in the United States is linked less to their religious beliefs than to their musical style. Reggae comes out of the Rastafarian worldview, and it has found its own prophet in Bob Marley, even though Marley did not introduce Rastafarianism to the United States through his inspirational music until the late 1970s. Some Rastas are quick to point out that while Marley did more to popularize and spread the Rasta message world wide than any other single individual, neither Marley nor reggae music represents the roots of the Rastafari experience. Reggae, as a music of populist black protest, emerged in Jamaica only during the early 1970s. Rastafari in Jamaica had been evolving an African-oriented culture based on their spiritual vision of repatriation to the African homeland since Haile Selassie's coronation in Ethiopia during the 1930s.

Still, Marley's significance would be hard to underestimate. Why bother to explain it in black-and-white prose when you can discover it for yourself by checking out Ras John's Robert (Bob) Nesta Marley's Livification Page at `http://Page@reggae.com/`? No, that is not a misprint or misspelling. When you click the Reggae Music page at `http://reggae.com/regtour/marltour.htm` you will find the most extensive map to the life and work of Bob Marley, and it is a site livicated to the leading prophet of Reggae. Livicated means dedicated to the living, to the making alive, of someone, in this case, Bob Marley.

More on the Spirituality of Reggae

You might want to know more about Babylon, Zion, or Jah. You might want to learn why Rastas livify their heroes. If so, check out http://debate.uvm.edu/ RhetReggae.html, which provides information about a full course on Reggae Rhetoric offered by Professor Alfred C. "Tuna" Snider, an expert on Reggae who teaches at the University of Vermont. If you can't make it to school bring the school to you, and get with the beats of this amazing musical style and the religious tradition that it fosters.

Resources

There are countless sites on Reggae and on Rastafarianism if you are willing to spend some time surfing the Net. We have highlighted the best that we have found, but if you explore the Yahoo! listings at http://dir.yahoo.com/Entertainment/Music/ Genres/Reggae/ you will find out that the legacy of Bob Marley lives on the Net as well as in many circles of Rasta and Reggae devotees. You also might explore the Rastafarian sites listed by Yahoo.com under the following subdirectories: Society_and_Culture, Religion_and_Spirituality, Faiths_and_Practices, Christianity, Denominations_and_Sects, and then Rastafarian. It takes a bit of patience, but there is a lot to be found at the click of a button (or rather several clicks).

Another resource that you might find especially useful in tracking Rastafarianism on the Web is the search engine at www.c4.com (formerly Cyber411). Try searching under Rastafarianism. It checks a number of other search engines to give you a vast sampling of what is out there on the ground to be shared with the legatees of the Lion of Judah, and Bob Marley.

There is no direct link between Rastas and followers of Louis Farrakhan. However, powerful black leaders from the 1930s shaped both of the movements discussed in this chapter, and both movements honor a deity whose racial definition empowers his followers. You do not have to be part of either movement to visit their Web sites, and you don't even have to be a music lover. But if you do visit some of these sites, you will discover a vast world of alternative thinking about present day society, and also about the world to come.

Rest and Remember

➤ There is no Black Nationalism that does not have a religious counterpart, and it often includes devotion to a black deity or deities.

➤ Two of the major sites for worship of the Black God of Biblical and post-Biblical history are the Nation of Islam and Rastafarianism, and each of these sites can be explored on the World Wide Web.

➤ The musical tradition that informed Louis Farrakhan is not the same as the Reggae of Bob Marley, but both influenced their religious outlooks, and both are available through the Net.

Chapter 26

She Is God: Neopaganism and Wicca

> **In This Chapter**
>
> ➤ Neopagans are a part of the contemporary religious scene
>
> ➤ The Wiccan group is so large that they might soon be considered a separate group
>
> ➤ Asatru and Druids are upcoming Neopagan communities

It's hard to imagine a group that has become more familiar with cyberspace, and projected a more vivid image of itself on the Web, than those known as Neopagans or Wiccans. Their strong accent on feminine resources, both divine and human, is matched by a zest for artwork and ritual creativity. The Web sites that follow provide the outline of Neopagan "netaphysics," but they do not exhaust its potential.

Neopaganism

She is God, the goddess and the creator. She is a mother, a maiden, a crone. She is a warrior, a protectress, a peacemaker, a spirit, the earth. She is the world. She is God.

Before Judaism, before Christianity, and before Islam, there was paganism. Various pantheons of deities were celebrated and feared. Magic and ritual were part of life. The earth was revered and the goddess ruled. Now she has returned in the form of Neopaganism. Her many forms are once again evident, and ancient rituals acknowledging her power touch the hearts of thousands of believers, while also shaking up traditional believers. Nowhere is this more evident than on the Internet. And while the modern pagan voice might be small—at least compared to traditional religions—its echo is reverberating throughout the world. It draws believers from every race, culture, and walk of life.

So what is Neopaganism? For starters, it's paradoxical. Labeled a new age religion, its roots are deeper than those of our most established religions. Countercultural?! Some say so, but paganism inspires mainstream culture with major moments and monuments: Christmas and the Christmas Tree, Spring and the May Pole, Winter Solstice and the Yule Log. The Pagan Wheel of the Year is a calendar of eight holidays, some with more familiar names than others. From Yule to Samhain, Figure 26.1 shows the pagan calendar, as seen at the Witch's Voice (www.witchvox.com), in all its splendor.

Figure 26.1

The eight seasons frame the holy year for Neopagans but also for others who observe life's seasonal rhythms.

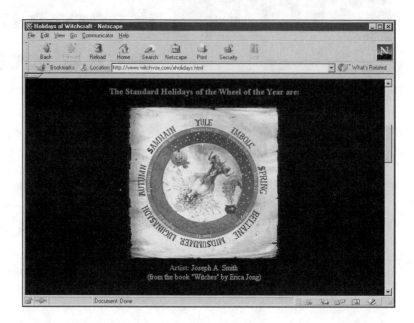

With all of the negative connotations of anything labeled pagan, you might ask yourself: how did this resurgence come to be? Why would anybody in the modern world be drawn to paganism? What is it that's unique enough to inspire the passionate belief of some while firing up the passionate resistance of others? For one thing, there's the focus on the feminine energy and feminine incarnations of the divine. Pagans also respect the power of the earth and see the whole universe as sacred.

Doesn't sound traditional? You're right: Neopaganism is not traditional and many of its tenets fly in the face of conventional thought and religion. Yet, at the same time, these novel focuses complement the increasing awareness of feminist and ecological issues. In this way, paganism can provide healing, support, fulfillment, and affirmation.

So what kinds of people are involved in Neopaganism? The answer is all kinds. Some were born pagan and have been raised in the practice. Others have come on their own, seeking affirmation, religious experience, and personal spirituality that they could not find elsewhere. Not all structure their lives around pagan practice. Some are casual practitioners or passive sympathizers.

But, above all, most pagans are good people. Too many non-pagans still believe that visions of Satanism, crusades, animal sacrifice, idolizing, bad magic, and witches define paganism. They don't. Take note: mainstream pagans—and most pagans ARE mainstream—are no more Satanists than mainline Protestants are followers of David Koresh!

If paganism has made a resurgence, it is partly through books. Just walk into your local bookstore and you'll see tons of books on topics closely related to Neopaganism. But it is the Net that has brought Neopaganism way up in the popularity charts. Look at the site Witch's Voice. According to `www.hitbox.com`, it is the most popular religious Web site.

For the person encountering paganism for the first time, some of the more general religion sites provide good objective information and some great links. For general information on the history of paganism and society's perception of it as well as the characteristics of its different subsets

Wired Monk

The Witch's Voice

There is no better way to explore the many positive facets of Neopaganism than through `www.witchvox.com`. Explore this site and find the wonders of a new world, if you're not a Neopagan, or else, if you are already, check out this version of a familiar world teeming with new and hopeful opportunities.

such as Wicca, Asatru, and Druidism, turn to Religious Tolerance. For Neopaganism, you can do no better than `www.religioustolerance.org/neo_paga.htm`. But if you want to find out about Wicca, see `www.religioustolerance.org/witchcra.htm`. Another good site for Wicca is `www.about.com` (after you are at the home page, select **society/culture**, **religion/spirituality**, and, finally, **paganism/witchcraft**). Although the site itself does not offer a lot of textual information, there are well-organized links to just about every topic you could want to know about these subjects. The same could be said of Yahoo!'s section at `dir.yahoo.com/Society_and_Culture/Religion_and_Spirituality/Faiths_and_Practices/Paganism`.

Neopagan Traditions

Neopaganism itself is made up of innumerable different traditions, most of which have strong presences on the Internet. Truly, not all pagans are the same. Neopaganism is Asatru, or Norse Paganism, Celtic Druidism, Goddess worship, and Wicca. All are revivals of ancient traditions of polytheism or duotheism. They focus on worship in nature and the personal experiences of the worshipper. They seek not to dominate the earth but to honor it and to celebrate the seasons as one celebrates holidays. They seek to open the door to multiple deities, multiple spiritual powers, and multiple ways of worship. The specific traditions vary in the specific rituals and deities they use and the cultures from which their traditions originate, yet they all share a common understanding.

Asatru

Drawing on the heritage and religion of ancient Viking and Germanic tribes and their extensive pantheon of gods and goddesses, Asatru, or Norse Paganism, is a thriving religious community today. You can find some of their largest organizations on the Internet. These sites also contain information on the beliefs and history of the tradition as well as its practice today.

The Ring of Troth

asatru.knotwork.com/troth/

The Ring of Troth is one of the largest North American Asatru organizations. It is also the official site for this group. Everything you need to know or might find of interest about Asatru is likely to be here.

Asatru Folk Assembly

www.runestone.org

You also might want to consult the Asatru Folk Assembly. At this site you'll find out about meeting times, you'll be able to download essays from the Runestone Magazine, and you'll have immediate access to a catalog on other pagan publications. Who started this group? A guy named Steve McNallen and his home page also is available at this site.

Irminsul Aettir Asatru

www.irminsul.org

If you still want to know more about Asatru, especially if you're from the Northwest, then you might want to consult this dark-toned but beautifully constructed site. It has a contact map, library, and scads of information about Neopagan activities in Seattle and neighboring areas.

Celtic Druidism

Celtic Druidism is another tradition hailing from Europe. It also is marked by some of the highest quality, most colorful sites on the Internet. Only a few can be mentioned here.

Ár nDráiocht Féin Fellowship

http://www.adf.org/homepage.shtml

Here you can find rituals and chants for your own practice, as well as membership information. With pictures from past gatherings and study programs, this site is full of resources, not to mention beautiful graphics.

Druidism Guide

www.uoguelph.ca/~bmyers/druid.html

This site is geared toward the solitary practitioner or anyone interested in the practice of Celtic Druidism. With a rich and well-organized overview of the history of this tradition as well as its lore, practices, and customs, the site is very educational.

Aisling Association of Celtic Tribes

members.aol.com/AislingACT/index.html

A group of Celtic Reconstructionist Pagans, the ACT's Web site offers membership as well as educational material. Visit their site and read about their tradition and their activities. Also of interest is a write-up of their liturgy and rituals.

Other Traditions

Just when you thought you'd heard more about pagans than you ever imagined, or wanted to know, here are a couple more.

Church of All Worlds

www.caw.org

The site features an online bookstore, branch directories, and a suggested reading list. It also boasts two online magazines, including one geared toward pagan children.

Covenant of the Unitarian Universalist Pagans

www.cuups.org

This site looks surprisingly like any Protestant organization's site! With its lighter colors and conventional organization, this site is an enigma for pagan sites but a good one nonetheless. This site features extensive explanations of the beliefs of this group as well as event listings, directories, and a Webring. For more information about Unitarian Universalists see Chapter 17, "Mainstream Protestants: Pentecostals."

Wicca

Deserving its own section due both to its size and to its incredible presence on the Internet is Wicca or Witchcraft. While it can be labeled as Neopagan, Wicca is large enough to be a tradition of its own.

Wicca, or witchcraft, involves the practice of *the craft*, magick and spells. Focused around the eight Sabbatts or days of celebration, Wiccans practice in solitude or in covens. The Wicca Rede is simple: "If it harm none, do what thou wilt." This principle reflects the positive and healing nature of the witchcraft. It is good magick, not harmful spells and tricks as it has been so often portrayed.

The Wiccan sites on the Internet are as remarkable as they are plentiful. As mentioned previously, the Witch's Voice at www.witchvox.com is my top pick in this category. Visit this incredible site for everything from spells and rituals to current events. It is extremely large but pretty easy to navigate. It also contains links to hundreds of other Wiccan and pagan sites where you can find everything from how to be a pagan parent to where to buy your necessary tools. Three other sites that are similar in magnitude and valuable resources in their own right are listed next.

The Witch's Brew

www.witchs-brew.com

This site offers an online community for Wiccans with a contact page, a birthday club, and an online store. One of the biggest features on this page is the Book of Shadows with everything from laws and rules of witchcraft to actual spells and rituals.

The Witch's Web

www.witchesweb.com

Focusing on news, education, and networking, the Witch's Web is another online community for Wiccans. Though this site is currently under construction, if you make it to the site map, you can find all you need. The Witch's Web's Online Shop offers supplies and books and the Book of Days, which is a 365-day calendar with holidays, events, and even birthdays for the Wiccan community.

Circle Sanctuary

www.circlesanctuary.org

Strong on graphics but weak on organization, the Circle Sanctuary, shown in Figure 26.2, nonetheless provides valuable resources for its visitors. The site offers several online magazines, a national directory of pagan organizations, and even information about the Sanctuary's Nature Preserve in Wisconsin! As captured in this image from www.circlesanctuary.org, the central focus is the circle. The circle on the ground that attracts the circle from the sky. The glowing circle. The moon.

Covenant of the Goddess

www.cog.org

This neatly organized and clear site provides yet another set of resources for Wiccans and pagans from all walks of life. The COG recently added a new feature to their site for the New Generation of Witches—Wiccan teens. This is a fantastic resource for those younger people recently drawn to the craft and looking for more information. For older or more general audiences, the COG main page provides similar resources.

Figure 26.2

The moon as filtered through Stonehenge is a magnet not only for Circle Sanctuary but also for all Neopagans.

Neopagan Resources at Your Fingertips

The Internet is invaluable for the Neopagan. It is private and it is global. Through the Internet, a lone practitioner, who would otherwise have lacked a community, could find one online. Here Neopagan believers and those who are interested can learn about the craft, the rituals, the history, and the beliefs without leaving their home.

There is no better way to explore what Neopaganism is, or can be, than to look at its Net resources. They are plentiful, whether you are shopping for ways to make your own magic, or just want to surf some more in technopagan turf. You might have a special interest in connecting to groups or networking, and you might also want to know how to counter all the nasty things said about pagans in some sectors of modern day America. Resources on all these topics lie just ahead.

Buying Tools and Other Products

The practice of paganism is nothing if not hands-on. If you are serious about learning rituals and practicing spells and charms, you'll need the proper tools. Here are two sites to help you along.

New Moon Occult Shop

www.newmoon.uk.com/newmoon.htm

These tools aren't for everybody, but if you're eager to check out the ways that Wiccans or other Neopagans actually perform rituals and cast spells, you might want to check out The New Moon Occult Shop. After you log on you will find loads of supplies you can buy over the Internet, in complete privacy.

Witch's Voice

www.witchvox.com/links/webshops.html

But you want to find out still more about the kind of Web resources that range beyond the usual occult fare. As with almost every topic that concerns Wiccans or other Neopagans, you can do no better than go to the Witch's Voice once again. Among its other valuable qualities, the site Witch's Voice has links to many other commercial sites; it also gives brief descriptions of their specialties and contents.

Connecting to Groups and Needs

You might belong to a particular group or have specific Neopagan needs. Here are three rather specific and very interesting sites you might try.

Pagan Parenting Page

www.jazgordon.com/pparent/

Are you a parent, or about to become a parent? This site is chock full of resources for pagan parents and kids—advice, activities, and support.

Military Pagan Network

www.milpagan.org

Are you a pagan in the military? At this site you will find an organization devoted to serving the needs of the pagan military community. It is a political action group, but it is also a support system for those in this position.

Pagan Rock Bands on the Web

www.geocities.com/SunsetStrip/Balcony/2570/pagrock.htm

Maybe you just want to rock to shamanic tunes? If you're looking for a truly fun site, this one's for you. It provides all the links you need to locate and even listen to rock bands across the World Wide Web.

Search Engines, General Sites, and Links

So, you are still looking for a community. Perhaps you can't find that support that you sense MUST be out there. Above all, you want to avoid persecution, and regain a sense of wholeness. Then you might be looking for the kind of megasites that connect you to just about everyone and everything pagan. Here are a few of the best.

Pagan Top 100

www.pagansunite.com/pt100/list.html

No one can match the Witch/Pagan Resources Pagan Top 100. It does just what its name promises: ranks pagan sites and gives great descriptions of what can be found there. The format is clear and helpful, as you can see in Figure 26.3.

Figure 26.3

The Pagan Top 100 pro-vides not only great links, but also helpful descrip-tions and frequently updated ratings.

WiccaNet

www.wiccanet.com

Similar to a larger search engine like Yahoo!, WiccaNet is a simple but useful site for general searches and basic resources. You can find your information by either doing a search or by clicking one of the subheadings that range from Books to Graphics to Herbs.

Don't Overcharge Your Magick Wand!

Sometimes there is too much for a person to absorb easily or quickly, but for the patient seeker, it will be worth the effort. See the Avatar Search engine for the Occult Internet at www.AvatarSearch.com. Remember, though: it is most useful as a ready resource if you know specifically what you're looking for.

Networking and Webrings

Did you recently move into the neighborhood and you want to find out who your Neopagan neighbors are? Or, are you a new pagan who is looking for a kindred spirit? Here are a few pages that'll help you network and connect with others.

Green Pages

www.oakgrove.org/GreenPages

Search the Green Pages for a group in your area, an online store, or upcoming events. This is a general site featuring all sorts of useful pagan information and ways to network with other pagans.

Pagans Online

www.pagansonline.com

Beyond all the myriad ways to network and interact with other pagans, if you want to find just one site that might do it quick, then try Pagans Online. This site features chat rooms, mailing lists, and information on pagan events.

Pagan Webweaving

www.hue.org/paganww

At this site, you can find the ultimate networking possibilities. Post a message or respond to another's via email with the click of a button.

News Stories and Rejoinders to Anti-Pagan Press and Discrimination

There is always the possibility that you have to contend with all those bad vibes that other folk are projecting towards pagans. Check out these sites for pagan responses to anti-pagan press.

Beware of Pagan Bashers!

Sound Doctrine? There are still those who think pagan equals heretic or worse; for these views, often voiced by advocates of a zealous Christian outlook, see www.sounddoctrine.com/ptimes/, an anti-pagan Christian site.

Wren's Nest

www.witchvox.com/xwrensnest.html

Check out this site for current issues facing pagans. Here you'll find essays from the pagan perspective responding to recent news stories relating to discrimination against pagans.

Witch's Voice

www.witchvox.com

If you have a more relaxed view of what you want to do, but you are still a news junkie, you might look for weekly updates on pagan-related news items at the Witch's Voice home page.

Pagan Educational Network

www.bloomington.in.us/~pen

If you want to get involved in fighting discrimination against pagans, this is the site for you. PEN is an activist organization devoted to educating the public about paganism and ending the myths about this religion. This attractive site offers ways to get involved and a vast array of resources at your fingertips.

A Last Look at Neopagans

Whether you're a Christian wanting to finally find out what all the fuss is about or a new pagan looking for some like-minded people in your area, the Internet is an invaluable resource. While pagans continue to face discrimination and persecution throughout the world, their modern resurgence has been remarkable. The Internet provides a forum for information, community, and understanding that Neopagans might otherwise not have found. You could say that the most recent incarnation of the Goddess has come through the World Wide Web!

Rest and Remember

➤ Neopagans are part of the contemporary religious scene, and most of them are cool folk.

➤ Neopagans are as diverse as almost any other religious group, and Wiccans are so big that they could—and maybe should—be considered a separate group. Asatru and Druids are two other major Neopagan communities.

➤ You can find more Neopagan resources on the Net than at your local bookstore, and a good place to begin is with the highlighted sites in this essay.

Chapter 27

God's Many Prophets: Bahais

In This Chapter

➤ Bahais trace their roots to nineteenth century Persia, but today the religion has a global following

➤ Bahais believe that there is in essence only one true religion. As the latest in a long line of messengers, Bahaullah is the culmination of divine prophecy

➤ Bahai faith is centered in the Holy Land, but their sense of community is cemented in cyberspace

---

There are many religious traditions linked to Iran: Muslims, Zoroastrians, and Bahais. Bahais are the most recent, but they have a very broad reach, and many Bahais have now joined the ranks of cybernauts, making their presence felt on the Web as well as in diverse parts of the globe.

Historical Development

Bahai is a colorful and dynamic religion with approximately six million members worldwide. Bahais are found in more countries and territories than any other religion except for Christianity. There are about 2.5 million adherents in India, 130,000 in the United States, and 15,000 in Canada.

Today Bahai is a truly global religion, but its historical roots are found in nineteenth century Persia. The religion draws its name from its founder. His name was Mirza Husayn Ali-i-Nuri, but he is better known by the honorific title Bahaullah, or "Glory of God." For more information on the "Greatest Name," stop by The Greatest Name at http://bci.org/prophecy-fulfilled/grstname.htm.

Bahaullah was himself a follower of the charismatic and controversial Shi'i Muslim leader known as the Bab.

Who Was the Bab?

Bahai traces its roots to Islam. Shiite Muslims believe that there were 12 legitimate descendants of the Prophet Muhammad know as *imams*. The twelfth *imam*, known as the Bab (meaning Gate), disappeared in the ninth century. Shiites around the world await the triumphant return of their lost leader as the Messiah. In 1844, a young Persian man named Ali Muhammad declared himself to be the Bab. He quickly gained a large following. Predictably, the clergy and government resisted his claims. They saw the Babis as a serious threat to orthodox Islam and their own authority. As a result, the Bab was arrested and executed by a firing squad in 1850. His disciples also were persecuted, and an estimated 20,000 of them were killed. The Bahai movement arose amidst this persecution. Sadly, in Iran the persecution of Bahais continues to this day. For more information on the Bab and Bahai's relationship to Islam, see Islam and the Bahai Faith at `http://bci.org/islam-bahai`.

Before his death, the Bab announced that there would be a new leader greater than himself to carry on the work of establishing a universal religion. Shortly after the Bab's execution, Mizra Hussain Ali publicly declared himself to be the awaited Prophet, Bahaullah.

Like his predecessor, Bahaullah faced stiff resistance from the political and religious establishment. In fact, the last 40 years of his life were spent in prison or exile. His final 22 years were behind bars in the prison city of Acre. Today his tomb complex in the Holy Land forms the center of the world headquarters of the Bahai faith. Want to learn more about Bahaullah? For a cyberspace biography of his life, visit a site called Bahaullah—A Statement by the Bahai International Community found at `www.bahai.com/Bahaullah/glory1.htm`.

The story of Bahai does not end with Bahaullah. After Bahaullah, his own son, Abdul Baha (Servant of the Glory), assumed the mantle of leadership. Abdul Baha expanded his father's teachings and actively spread the Bahai message throughout the world. He, in turn, was succeeded by his grandson Shoghi Effendi (The Guardian), pictured in the Web site shown in Figure 27.1.

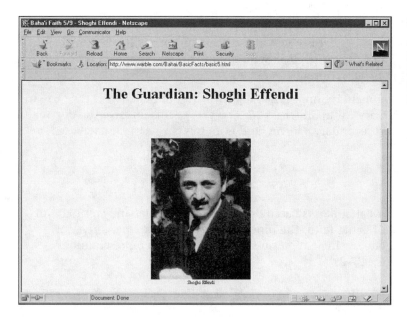

Figure 27.1

A picture of Shoghi Effendi from the Bahai Faith Basic Facts pages at `www.warble.com/Bahai/ BasicFacts/basic5.html`.

It was Shoghi Efendi who firmly established an administrative system to oversee the religion. He died in 1957 without naming a successor. Since that time, the Bahai religion has continued to thrive and expand under the guidance of an elected legislative body based in Haifa, Israel.

Is your brain bursting at the seams? Bahai history is certainly complex. But it's fascinating too. If you want to find out more, surf over to the following informative Web sites.

The Bahai Faith

`http://religioustolerance.org/bahai.htm`

This site offers a broad but informative introduction to Bahai history, beliefs, and practices. It also includes numerous links to other interesting pages.

The Central Figures of the Bahai Faith

`http://bounty.bcca.org/~cvoogt/central_f.html`

Fascinated by the stories of the early leaders of the Bahai community? This Web page provides access to a mass of information about the life and times of Bahaullah, Abdul Baha, and Shoghi Effendi.

The sacred literature of Bahai consists of the writings of its founding fathers. All together, this corpus comprises hundreds of texts. The most important of the Bahai scriptures, however, were written by Bahaullah himself. These include the *Kitab-i-Aqdas* (Most Holy Book), which describes Bahai laws and institutions, the *Kitab-i-Iqan*

(Book of Certitude), a collection of his revelations, and the *Book of Covenant*, in which he offers a clear interpretation of his own writings and authorizes the legitimacy of his son, Abdul Baha. Since the death of Shoghi Effendi, no one has been officially authorized to interpret Bahai scripture.

For translations and commentary on all the major writings of Bahai, visit the "Bahai Academics Resource Library" at `http://bahai-library.org`. This massive site documents both primary and secondary sources, and even offers a research database for scholars.

Doctrine

The religion founded by Bahaullah is based on the tenets of social and spiritual universalism. The symbol of Bahai faith, the nine-pointed star, represents universal unity—nine being the largest single-digit number. You can see a representation of the Bahai star in Figure 27.2.

Figure 27.2

The Bahai star, with the Greatest Name at its center. For more beautiful images, visit the Bahai Graphics Gems Web page at www.arkapple.com/gems.

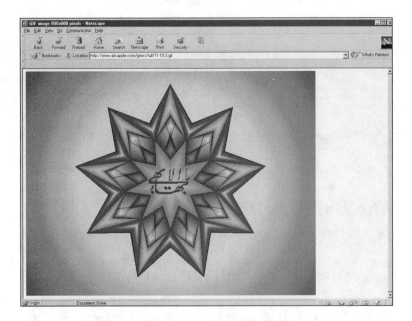

Bahais view God as transcendent and unknowable. Yet, Bahais assert that God remains active in human history. He has sent—and will continue to send—prophets to teach and guide humanity. The Great Manifestations of God in history up to this time are nine in number: Abraham, Moses, Krishna, Zoroaster, Buddha, Jesus, Muhammad, the Bab, and Bahaullah.

As this list suggests, Bahais believe in an essential unity to the world's religious traditions. This is not to suggest that Bahais ignore spiritual boundaries and differences between religious traditions. So how is this paradox resolved? Bahais hold that divine prophecy is tailored to fit the circumstances that each successive Messenger encounters. When the times change, so do the teachings. But although religions differ in the details, the essential message remains the same.

As the latest in this line of Divine messengers, Bahaullah represents the culmination of prophecy. Bahais view his teachings as the most up to date and enlightened guide to social and spiritual life. In Bahai belief, prophecy is a continuous, evolving process. There can be no final revelation and no final prophet. But devotion to the person of Bahaullah as the most recent manifestation of Divine will is the focus of Bahai piety. For this reason, his name—written in Arabic script—is at the center of the nine-pointed Bahai star.

Baffled by All This Prophet Talk?

Not to worry. Just ride the hyperspace wave over to http://bci.org/prophecy-fulfilled. The Bahai Prophecy Fulfilled Web page offers articles and essays detailing the Bahai perspective on all the world's great religions.

The Bahai faith is largely practical in orientation. Instead of complex theology, it stresses ethical and social teachings. All Bahais are called upon to put their faith into action in their daily lives. Every day is viewed as a Judgement Day of their conduct. Bahais believe that the final trial comes at death when each immortal human soul is called to account for its worldly deeds. The more pure the soul was during life, the closer its proximity to God. Hell is defined as the absence of the Divine presence. In short, Bahais view the world as a testing ground. Doing good here and now is the key to eternal paradise.

Since its inception, Bahai has promoted gender and racial equality, freedom of expression and assembly, and scientific exploration. Bahais are urged to pursue education, live a monogamous lifestyle, and avoid the use of alcohol and narcotics. More broadly, Bahais are called to actively promote world peace and international understanding. They believe that there will eventually be a single world government, led by Bahais and grounded on the faith's doctrines and administrative framework. Social, political, and spiritual universalism is the ultimate goal.

Ritual Life

Membership to the Bahai community is open to any person who accepts the teachings of Bahaullah and professes faith in him. Bahai does not have professional priests, monastic orders, or official sacraments. While the faith avoids complex rites of passage and religious rituals, followers do observe certain basic practices. At the center of Bahai faith is daily prayer.

Where Do I Find the Calendar of Bahai Prayer?

For insights into the form and function of Bahai prayer, stop by the Bahai Prayers Web page at `http://bounty.bcca.org/~glittle/prayers/index.html`. This site documents a host of general, occasional, and obligatory Bahai prayers. It also provides HTML formatted prayers that can be downloaded as a ZIP file.

The Bahai ritual calendar is highlighted by certain ritual events that all strengthen individual piety and cement communal solidarity. For example, Bahais observe nine holy days during the course of the year that commemorate key dates in their history. These include the birthdays and death anniversaries of the Bab and Bahaullah, as well as the dates on which they both publicly declared their spiritual missions. An additional 19 days each year are marked for fasting. On these days, from sunrise to sunset, Bahais abstain from all food and drink.

At least once in a lifetime, Bahais also are expected to make a pilgrimage to the Holy Land. There they visit the shrine of the Bab in Haifa as well as the houses in which Bahaullah lived.

Want to learn more about Bahai pilgrimage? Visit the informative site Bahai Pilgrimage to Israel found at `http://metalab.unc.edu/Bahai/Pilgrimage/pilgrimage.html`.

Local Bahai communities hold regular meetings for worship and social interaction. These meetings are led by a respected, unpaid person from the group. They typically include readings from Bahai scriptures, prayers, and discussions of religious topics. Most individual and communal Bahai worship is centered on the home. Even so, spectacular examples of public houses of worship can be found throughout the world, such as the one pictured in the Bahai Computer & Communication Association Web site (`www.bcca.org`), shown in Figure 27.3.

Bahai temples are all constructed according to designs created by Bahaullah himself. They have nine sides and are surrounded by beautiful gardens, complete with trees, flowers, and fountains. Bahai temples serve as centers of worship, but they also are used for educational, charity, and social gatherings. Contributions for their construction and upkeep come exclusively from within the Bahai community, and must be given voluntarily.

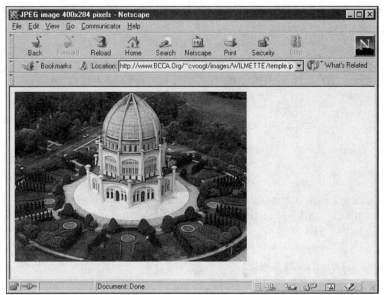

JPEG image 400x284 pixels - Netscape

Figure 27.3

This image on the Bahai Computer & Communication Association Web page shows a nine-sided Bahai temple.

Community

The Bahai faith maintains an elaborate network of official administrative institutions. Bahaullah himself established their forms and functions. At the local level, every Bahai community with more than nine adult members elects a Local Spiritual Assembly to oversee its affairs. The next level of administration is the National Spiritual Assembly, which also is elected annually. The global governing body of Bahai is the Universal House of Justice, housed in Haifa, Israel. Election to this ultimate administrative body occurs every five years and is restricted to male members.

Beyond these official institutions, Bahais cement a sense of collective identity through personal and professional networks. For examples of how Bahais around the world are building virtual communities on the Web, surf by the following sites:

Bahai Organizations

A Bahai Faith Page

http://bounty.bcca.org/~glittle

This massive site offers meta-indexes with links to all types of Bahai organizations. From college and youth clubs to professional associations, from bookstores and businesses to history and cultural activities—you can find everything here.

The Bahai Faith Index

http://bounty.bcca.org/~cvoogt

This site offers an equally appetizing menu. It is run by Casper Voogt, a young Dutch architectural student at Georgia Tech University. Like the Bahai Faith Page, this site is housed at the Web page of the Bahai Computer and Communication Association (BCCA).

"The Bahais" Magazine

http://bahai.com/thebahais

This is the official magazine of the Bahai World Faith, sanctioned by the Universal House of Justice. It is available online in numerous languages and contains a wealth of interesting and informative articles.

Spirituality-Bahai Faith's Home Page

http://home.talkcity.com/ParadiseDr/spirituality-bahaifaith/

Want to meet Bahais from around the globe? At this colorful site, shown in Figure 27.4, you can build cyberspace friendships and discuss Bahai faith in the chat room. People of all religious faiths are welcomed.

Figure 27.4

This colorful site welcomes people of all religious faiths, inviting them to learn about and discuss Bahai beliefs.

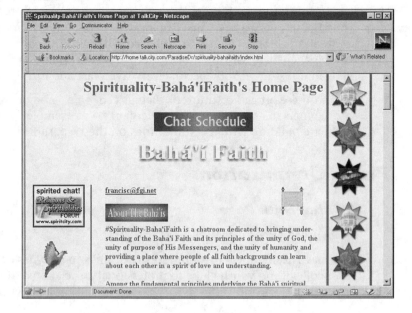

Bahais in India

www.bahaindia.org

One of the world's largest and most dynamic Bahai communities is found in the Indian subcontinent. This site is the official Web page of the National Spiritual Assembly of the Bahais of India. It offers informative articles and numerous links.

Bahais in the United States

www.us.bahai.org

Bahai's have a growing presence here in America as well. Drop by the Bahai Faith page to learn about the religion, American style. In the United States, the National Spiritual Assembly is located at the site of a Bahai House of Worship in Wilmette, Illinois.

Conflict and Dissent

Bahai, like all religious traditions, has experienced moments of internal conflict and dissent. Schisms developed within the community from the beginning. Some Bahais refused to accept the legitimacy of Abdul Baha and Shoghi Effendi as the rightful heirs to Bahaullah's authority. Today, as we have seen, the vast majority of Bahais follow the Bahai World Faith administered by the International House of Justice in Haifa. Numerous splinter groups also exist, however, each claiming to represent the true Bahai faith. For a discussion of these fringe groups, and links to their Web pages, see the Bahai Faith Web page at http://religioustolerance.org/bahai.htm.

Several critics, some of them ex-Bahais, also have attacked Bahai authorities for failing to practice what they preach. The excommunication of certain gay and lesbian members, the exclusion of women from serving on the highest religious court, and the censorship of Bahai publications—all have been frequent targets of criticism.

Not Everyone's Talisman

Recently, a clash between a group of scholars and the Bahai World Center resulted in the closing down of an online mailing list known as the "Talisman." For a summary of this highly publicized controversy, see Articles on *Talisman* History at http://bahai-library.org/newspapers/gnosis.talisman.html.

It would be a mistake, however, to see this criticism as evidence that the Bahai tradition has been undermined. Despite dissenting voices, Bahai remains a dynamic and growing religious community on the global stage.

Rest and Remember

➤ Bahais are followers of a relatively new Persian religion that spans from East to West in its membership and outlook.

➤ Bahais believe in a prophetic cycle, which links them to many of the world's great spiritual traditions.

➤ Cyberspace connections on the Net bring Bahais closer together—personally, professionally, and spiritually.

Chapter 28

No Self, No God: Buddhists

In This Chapter

➤ Buddhism is one of the major Asian religions, with more than 300 million fol-lowers worldwide and a very active presence on the Web—It is also one of the fastest growing religions in the United States

➤ Of the major groups within Buddhism, not all accept the same scripture, fol-low the same teaching, or link themselves to one another, in real space or cyberspace

➤ Among the most prominent features of Buddhism on the Web are two activist, missionary groups with almost opposite aims: Engaged Buddhism and Soka Gakkai

It's impossible to imagine the variety of spiritual practices that are conveniently labeled 'Buddhist'. In this chapter I will try to introduce you to the major strands, but I will not, nor could I, exhaust the possibilities that you will uncover for yourself as you enter more fully into this ancient religious worldview.

Buddhism 101

Okay, so life is a big circus: But no joy ride ever lasts. What is good and fun comes to an end. And most spook houses, however scary, also have an exit that you come to sooner or later. Even horror doesn't last.

And that's what Buddha, who was also known as Siddhartha or Gautama, said 2,500 or so years ago. He said it in India, and his teachings spread across Asia, profoundly affecting the cultures shared by millions of people. This cultural influence is proven by the number of statues of Buddha scattered across Asia. You can see images of two of these in Figure 28.1.

Figure 28.1

Here we see two images of Gautama the Buddha. The central experience of Buddhism is Enlightenment. The first Enlightened being in this cycle was Gautama Buddha. In the lower stone image, note especially the eyes and forehead.

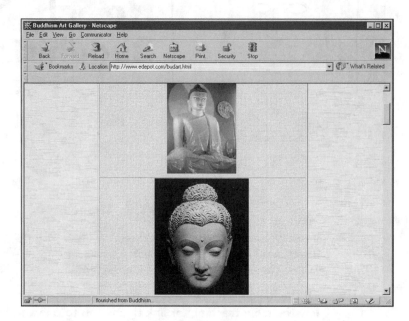

Centuries after Buddha preached his philosophy, a German novelist named Herman Hesse put together the same message in a compelling novel titled—what else?—*Siddhartha*. Many folk still read *Siddhartha* as the best explanation of why life is a big circus with rollercoasters and funny houses. Figure 28.2 shows a Web site devoted to the Hesse play.

Because we live our lives with a mind and a vision, we do not always see the fleetingness of all around us and all within us. We think that we are real. We see that we have time—opportunity, fame, wealth, power—ahead of us. We kid ourselves, and so we suffer.

Yet life, like the circus, closes down or comes to an end. We die. No matter who we are, where we go, or what we do, we die and the body goes. Either it goes under the ground and is recycled with other life, or it goes up in flames and becomes some little pot to be buried or kept around—even as other living creatures ignore that their fate is the same: under the ground or up in smoke. (Of course, some will drown at sea or believe they go off into outerspace, like the members of Heaven's Gate (see Chapter 36, "New Religious Movements"). No one really knows what happens after death, but the very mystery of life beyond death stands at the core of Buddhism, as it does in all major religions.

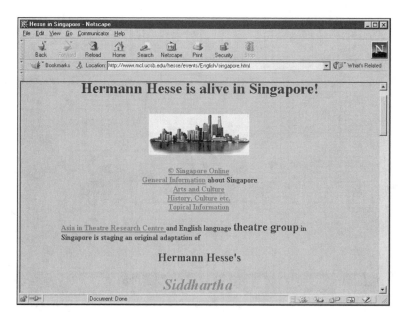

Figure 28.2
Siddhartha *was recently staged as a play in Singapore.*

The Four Noble Truths, the Eight-Fold Path

The Buddha saw four truths, but he did not quite see them as the basis of a religion. In fact, the Buddha rejected the religion into which he was born, Hinduism, in order to get *beyond* religion.

In ways more like a doctor than a preacher, he outlined what came to be known as the Four Noble Truths. He observed: Life sucks and people suffer. He diagnosed: To get beyond the bad vibes and suffering, you have to give up wanting—wanting people, wanting things, wanting to live forever. He prescribed: The way to give up desire and go beyond suffering is to find the center, the point in between despair and greed. He clarified: At the center is the eight-fold path. You don't go around being a monk all your life, but you don't follow Mr. Rockefeller, Mr. Gates, or Mr. Gekko as your model folk either. What you do when you've found the four truths is to recognize that they are all noble and all connected to the eight-fold path. So you follow the path.

The path has eight stages, which hive off neatly into three medical-like phases. The first two are internal: Think right, and feel right. The next three are external: Talk right, act right, and hold down the right job. Then the last three are *really* internal. They are internal, like the first two, except they include all of who we are and not just what we imagine. So the last three stages are integral as well as internal. They require us to do good, to focus on the good, and to aim high, higher, and higher still.

There are a lot of ways of translating the four noble truths of Buddhism. One is to make fun of the seriousness of all endeavors to find truth and peace of mind. The Web site Dharma the Cat, `www.dharmathecat.com`, shown in Figure 28.3, demonstrates a good way beyond the usual approach to life or Buddhism.

Figure 28.3

Dharma the Cat: the Dharma Doctor for the cyberage.

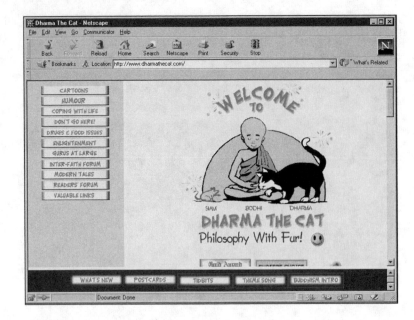

Dharma the Cat begins with the four noble truths and ends with the eight-fold path.

Wired Monk

What Is the Eight-Fold Path Again?

Go to the cat, the Dharmacat, to see how it describes the eight-fold path. Check out www.dharmathecat.com and you will find that the path comprises the following:

➤ The first two stages: right view and right purpose.

➤ The next three stages: right speech, right conduct, and right livelihood.

➤ The crucial final three stages: right effort, right mindfulness, and right concentration.

None of this has to do with the soul, and Gautama even seemed to say that soul talk, like God talk, was a hindrance more than a help when it came to finding life's deeper meaning. The higher you aim, the less you need intermediate concepts or old-speak, like soul, God, and religion. What you find instead is the space (sunyata) that is both empty and full. What you find is enlightenment (nirvana).

Who Are the Buddhists?

A lot of folks have taken this message to heart. Many, of course, are Asian. They live in South, Southeast, and East Asia. They come from countries like Tibet or India, Vietnam or Thailand, China or Japan, and even Russia. They number maybe 300 million. But there is also a growing number of Buddhists in Russia and also in America. Thirty-five years ago you had to look far and wide to find a Buddhist center; there were maybe 20 or 25 in all North America. Now, on the cusp of the next millennium, there are more than 650 known Buddhist centers, and probably many more too small to count or be registered. How many Buddhists are in America? Maybe 600 to 700 thousand, many of them Asian immigrants, but others are Americans from other ethnic groups and religious traditions.

Getting Introduced

The Buddhists were among the first people to bring their wisdom to the Web. Therefore, it is no surprise that the introductory Web sites on Buddhism are many and splendid. For the first-time visitor to CyberBuddhism, in addition to the Buddhism Intro section of the Dharma the Cat site mentioned earlier (www.dharmathecat.com), your best bets might be the following sites.

Tricycle.com

www.tricycle.com

Tricycle.com is an electronic, interactive version of a popular magazine by the same name. If you want to explore the options for understanding Buddhism as a historical experience, worldview, and living practice, you'll find what you need here. Especially notable are all the references and links to Zen Buddhist Centers, but you can also find info about other Buddhist groups at this e-zine stop. Just click the Tricycle.com home page and go to Buddhism 101!

Buddhanet.net

www.buddhanet.net

If you want an online Cybersangha (Buddhist community), you have to either go to Australia or get Australia to come to you. And it does when you check out this site.

Buddhanet.net

There's nothing more like nirvana than this site. It gives you a quick, fun, and rewarding way to get into a Buddhist mindset. You'll also find Buddhist computer art, a Buddhanet kids magazine, and *Buddhazine* (mostly for adults). Although its content is pitched to Australia and Southeast Asia, it also has many sites that link to Western Europe and North America, illustrating just how cybersavvy many of the current exponents and practitioners of the Buddha's teaching are.

Tibetan Buddhism (Vajrayana)

The Web contains so much to see about the Tibetan Buddhist or Vajrayana tradition that you could spend most of an afternoon and get through only a fraction of the *good* sites. For example, the site About.com, which has its own Buddhist guide, provides more than 60 sites on the Dalai Lama alone!

Check out `buddhism.about.com`. While you are surfing, take note that on the topic bar to the left of the page you'll find another set of sites for Tibetan schools. But surprise, surprise: The Dalai Lama is not explicitly covered in any of them. So where do you go for help?

Our suggestion is to start once again with OCRT at `www.religioustolerance.org`. Why? Because not only will you get an overview of the geographical spread and population of Buddhism from the Southern, Eastern, and Northern parts of Asia, but you will also discover that the Dalai Lama relates to the Gelug or Gelugpa school of Tibetan Buddhism. This school is but one of five schools of Buddhism in the region just north of India now occupied by China.

Armed with this information, you can and should now go to the site maintained by the Tibetan government in exile. Remember that the Dalai Lama is a political as well as a religious figure, so he is noted here under a site that is labeled Tibetan *government* in exile. Graphically this site is not much, but it does have good links, and it is packed with information if you know where and how to find it. So click `http://tibet.com`, and then scroll down further and click `http://www.tibet.com/Buddhism/gelug.html`.

When you've absorbed all that info, you can go back to `www.buddhism.about.com` and click its topic bar for Tibetan schools. There you'll find four schools of Tibetan Buddhism: Not only Gelugpa, but also Nyingma (the oldest), Sakya, and Kagyu or Black Hat Tantric.

And when you're all done, you may want to settle for just a picture of the Dalai Lama so you can see what he looks like in his current physical incarnation. Even here you have a wealth to pick from. The following figure, projected at www.tibetimages.co.uk/ dalailama.html, shows you a British site dedicated to providing images of His Holiness in Figure 28.4.

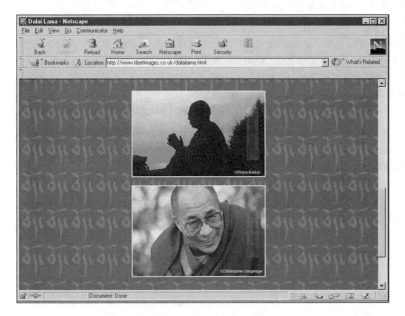

Figure 28.4

There is simply no way to reduce the best-known figure in Buddhism among Westerners to one picture.

American Faces of Buddhism

Like most things in contemporary America, Buddhism offers you different flavors. You want insight? Try Theravada. After all, it bills itself as the original form of Buddhist teaching. You want to take the path of compassion? Try Mahayana, which includes Zen. Maybe you're interested in the Dalai Lama or tantric practices? Then you'll want to explore Tibetan Buddhism (Vajrayana). Chances are that if you are *really* American, you may want your own personal flavor. You can find that, too, on the Net: It's the American twist on Buddhism, and it goes by the name of Buddhayana.

Buddhayana

The term sounds like vintage New Age religion. Take a word with one clear meaning: Buddha, enlightened one. Add to it a suffix with another clear meaning: -yana, vehicle or mode of transmission. What do you get? A new mixed word, Buddhayana, the vehicle for conveying the teachings of the enlightened one or Buddhism.

At the Buddhist Information Services of New York, www.bodhiline.org/Directory/, you can see how Buddhist teachings and practices are carried out at one center in North America. Yet there isn't a specific U.S. site on the Web for Buddhayana, this new projection of Buddhist teaching and practice. It is often defined as nonsectarian Buddhism, or mixed traditions from other groups, such as Theravada, Zen, and

Tibetan Buddhism. The Web site Bodhiline.org is, in fact, closely linked to Tibetan Buddhism and the Dalai Lama. However, it offers links to other sites, among them Maitri Dorje Gay and Lesbian Buddhist Society (http://www.geocities.com/WestHollywood/9033/). The latter site offers Buddhist meditation as a resource for gays and lesbians.

If you do want to find a full-blown Buddhayana Web page, a fine example comes from Holland. The site is run by a group of Dutch Buddhist monks and nuns that established a school, meditation center, and publishing house back in the late 1970s following the Theravada tradition. Appealing to all sectors of Dutch society, they called it the Buddhayana Centre Netherlands. You can check out its home page at http://apollo.virtual-pc.com/buddha/buddhayana.html.

Engaged Buddhism

http://www.igc.org/bpf/ineb.html

The International Network of Engaged Buddhists locates itself at the intersection of world activists. Its Net site is actually a subset of the Institute for Global Change (IGC). It, in turn, has a downstream Web page that lists all the other Buddhist-related activist sites.

Wired Monk

Interested in Buddhist Causes?

You'll find a wealth of activist possibilities on the Web. We recommend that you begin with The Buddhist Peace Fellowship at www.igc.org/bpf/activist.html. It highlights human rights, women's rights, and nuclear weapons freeze campaigns.

The International Network of Engaged Buddhists was founded in 1989 to promote inter-Buddhist and inter-religious understanding and cooperation, to provide information on Buddhist and other socially active groups, and to develop workshops. It includes not only photos and membership information, but a wide engagement with the resources for broad-scale activism. One of its most notable exponents is the Vietnamese Zen monk, Thich Nhat Hanh. He is a prolific author with his own sangha (monastery) in France. His school also has a branch in Vermont (Green Mountain Dharma Center). Both the French and American retreats can be explored at Thich Nhat Hanh's Web site, the Plum Village home page: www.plumvillage.org.

Soka Gakkai

www.sgi.org/home.html

An offshoot of Buddhism related to the Japanese monk Nichiren, the Soka Gakkai has had a long and bumpy history in the twentieth century. It was linked to Japanese nationalism during World War II, and it still has a reputation of aggressive opposition to all outsiders. At the same time, however, it has become one of the most zealously proselytizing forms of Mahayana Buddhism.

You can explore the public profile of Soka Gakkai by examining the site at www.sgi.org/home.html. As its name suggests, Soka Gakkai International Public Information Site projects its image of both the Buddha and world affairs through this user-friendly cyberpath. After all, it is Buddhist, and it favors peace, education, and human rights.

What Could Be Wrong with Soka Gakkai?

What could be wrong with Soka Gakkai? Seemingly nothing. And yet there are so many allegations of excessive force, and perhaps criminal wrongdoing, linked to the head of Soka Gakkai International that the group has established an independent site to refute allegations and rumors. Check out Clearing Up the Clearing House at http://clearingup.com/, where a rigorous defense is mounted against Soka Gakkai accusers. Or surf over to the Soka Gakkai page at http://members.aol.com/watchbuddh/sgi-link.htm, which is a user-friendly navigation guide to more than 100 Soka Gakkai international Web sites. This is a group with wide networks and multiple allegiances.

The Buddhist CyberPath

From the Dalai Lama to Soka Gakkai is a long chain of religious experience and expression. There is no single, or simple, view of Buddhism. It is richly expressed in contemporary American culture. Whether you check out movies, books, or actual Buddhist centers, you will hear echoes of Dharma. The diversity of expression should not overshadow the single aim. It is to point beyond the material world and its attachments. It is to strive for a higher inner world of peace and rest. It is to reach for nirvana, and among the many able exponents of the path to nirvana is a Thervadan monk, The Venerable Pannyavaro, shown in Figure 28.5.

The emergence of the Net offers a new opportunity to cybersavvy monks and lay persons. The Dharma Cat (www.dharmacat.com) may make you laugh, whereas Buddhanet (www.buddhanet.net) may make you rethink life through a Buddhist perspective. Enjoy these sights and more as you explore Buddhism on the Web.

Figure 28.5

The Venerable Pannyavaro is a Theravadan monk at home in cyberspace as well as on the eight-fold path.

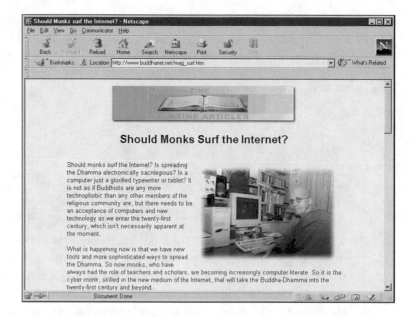

Rest and Remember

➤ Buddhists were among the first followers of a major religion to engage, explore, and embrace the World Wide Web.

➤ Buddhist sites on the Net are as diverse and as plentiful as the actual, ground level communities of Buddhist practitioners in the USA and abroad.

➤ The long-term influence of Buddhism in contemporary society will be in part determined through the CyberSangha and the many other colorful projections of Buddhist teaching in cyberspace.

Chapter 29

God Lives on the Ganges: Hindus

In This Chapter

➤ Developing for over 4,000 years and with the oldest scriptures in the world, Hinduism is represented by one in eight people on earth and is well represented on the Web

➤ Reform movements within Hinduism gave birth to Jainism (see Chapter 30, "God Does Not Harm: Jains") and Buddhism (see Chapter 28, "No Self, No God: Buddhists") long before Jesus was born

➤ Although traditionally limited to those of Asian heritage, Hinduism is attracting many adherents in the West

Just as India is bigger than all of Europe, Hinduism is also more varied than Christianity. It is also older, dating back more than 4,000 years in its earliest form, and it has continued to vary and adapt, while retaining certain essentials, through successive periods of history. I have tried to highlight some of its recurrent elements, and also some of its newer features, in this chapter.

From the Indus to the Ganges

Hinduism is a very ancient religion, and its origins can be traced to almost 2,500 B.C.E. Most scholars see two major influences on ancient Hinduism: the Indus Valley civilization and the Indo-European invaders who conquered and destroyed their cities. The hymns—called the Vedas—sung by these warriors provide the nucleus around which much Hindu literature developed. The sacrificial rites described in these ancient songs are still practiced by some Hindus today. The major deities of the Vedic hymns were Indra, a chariot-driving warrior; Agni, the god of fire; and Soma, the god of a drink that induced ecstatic states. The worship of the Vedas was primarily that of sacrifice, delivered to the celestial deities by Agni.

What Was the Indus Valley Civilization?

The sites of Harappa and Mohenjo-Daro on the Indus River (in modern Pakistan) are the two major sites that have been excavated by archaeologists looking for the oldest civilization in India. The cities were quite advanced, with running water to and sewage disposal from many houses and clear evidence of city planning. The inhabitants of the cities worshipped male and female deities, whose images are known from small statues and seals used to stamp documents. Some of these deities resemble those found in later Hindu temples. Unfortunately, the script used by the Indus Valley civilization has not been deciphered and what is known about their culture has to be derived from other remains. If you want to learn more about the civilization, check out The Indus Valley and the Raj at www.harappa.com.

At an early date, Indian sages began to ponder the reasons for sacrifice. How did it affect the cosmos? How was Agni, the fire god, able to appear in so many places at once? From these basic questions developed the sophisticated Upanishadic literature. This literature explored the relation between humans and the divine. One idea that developed became one of the foundation stones of later Indian religious thought: People are animated by the Self, which is the same essence as the underlying reality of the cosmos, known as Brahman. Most people are oblivious to the fact they are part of Brahman because their senses observe the illusionary world and not underlying reality.

A second foundation stone of Indian thought derives from observing the world. All Indian religions—Jainism and Buddhism as well as Hinduism—view the world as cyclical. Just as the sun sets and is reborn every morning and plants die in the autumn but re-emerge in the spring, so too are humans reborn repeatedly. Why does the Self choose to be reborn? It could be ignorance, because most people are not aware that they are part of Brahman. Or it could arise from karma. Karma is generated by desire, because desire goads people to action. Good actions produce good karma and bad actions produce bad karma. Thus, there are two main ways to escape the cycle of rebirth: Eliminate desire or achieve knowledge of the true nature of Self.

How Do You Know What Actions Produce Good or Bad Karma?

Knowing what activities produce good or bad karma is important, because when you die, you will be reborn according to the amount of good or bad karma you have accumulated. If you have a surplus of good karma, you will be reborn higher in the social hierarchy, but if your bad karma is greater, you will be reborn lower. And if you were really bad, you might be reincarnated as a dog, a cockroach, or even grass. Hindu sages produced law books describing the ideal behavior for people in various stages of their lives, because one's behavior is different when one is a student, a householder, or a hermit. Behavior also is different depending on one's location in the social hierarchy: Different rules apply to priests, kings, merchants, and servants. The texts describing these rules were called *smriti* texts and one of the earliest was the Laws of Manu. There are a number of translations of the Laws of Manu into English, but none are easily found on the Web.

Yoga

Many westerners think of yoga and picture people twisting themselves into uncomfortable positions! But *yoga* means unity (with the divine) and there are three main varieties of it in the Hindu tradition.

Hatha Yoga

When most Westerners think of yoga they think of uncomfortable bodily postures. But with practice, these postures can be comfortable, relieve stress, and improve health. A good site for this sort of yoga is The Yoga Site at www.yogasite.com. This well-designed site has relatively few graphics (a boon to those using slow modems) but has much to offer, including a list of yoga schools and teachers in the U.S., an extensive FAQs about yoga, information about publications on yoga, and offers yoga-related supplies (mats, books, videos) for sale.

Jnana Yoga: The Yoga of Knowledge

Typically, people accept the reality of their perceptions, but according to the Hindu sages, the real world is an illusion. To recognize the illusion, one has to meditate and practice detachment from the world. Eventually, with proper meditation, one will come to recognize the non-duality of underlying reality.

Wired Monk

What Is Vedanta?

Most people are blinded by their senses. They believe that their Self is different from the world. Thus, they see the world as in dualistic terms: Self verses Material. But according to Vedanta, the world is an illusion and the way to become one with the divine is to recognize the non-dual nature of reality, that the Self and the world are really the same. Getting beyond the illusion of our senses is difficult and you need a guide, like Ramana Maharshi, who became a holy man when he was a teenager and lived his whole life in a remote retreat. For more on his life, check out Ramana Maharshi and other advaita at www.sentient.org/amber/. The site has interviews and testimonials from people who are awakened. It also has a list of organizations practicing Vedanta and issues of a newsletter dedicated to discussion of the philosophy.

For a more detailed introduction to Vedanta, surf to Introduction to Vedanta at www.geocities.com/RodeoDrive/1415/veda.html. This site has a detailed description of Vedanta philosophy, as well as links to other yoga sites and other sites related to Vedanta.

Karma Yoga: The Yoga of Action

Karma is generated by desire, because desire causes people to act. Karma yoga seeks to eliminate desire by encouraging people to act appropriately, without concern for the consequences of their action, whether it is "good" or "bad." Not worrying about the outcome of your actions allows you to focus completely on the action itself, on the present, rather than fretting about the future results of your action.

Bhakti Yoga

Bhakti yoga developed into the most popular form of Hindu worship. Remarkably, although it is quite different from the older forms of yoga, it did not replace them.

Where Christianity defined itself in opposition to paganism and Judaism, Hinduism's tent encompasses an incredible diversity of ritual and belief. Thus, the yogic practices described previously continue to be practiced by some Hindus, although the vast majority practice various forms of devotional worship, known as *bhakti yoga*.

Devotional worship is described in the Bhagavad Gita, which advocates worship of Krishna. But many other gods and goddesses in India have their own devotees. This form of worship encourages people to offer prayers to a particular deity and to try to serve their deity every day and in every way. They chant the deity's name, pray, and try to surrender completely to the deity. In the Gita, which is illustrated in the Web page shown in Figure 29.1, Krishna promises that "he who acts for me, who makes me the highest goal, who is devoted to me, who has abandoned attachment, who is without hatred for any being, comes to me" (11.55).

What Is the Bhagavad Gita?

The Gita is the instruction given to Arjuna by Krishna, who was his chariot-driver. It is perhaps the most famous piece of Hindu scripture, but it is only a very small part of the larger epic poem, the *Mahabharata*.

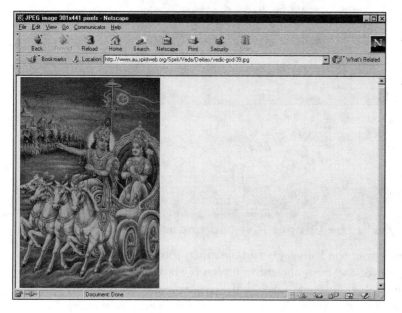

Figure 29.1

In this picture Krishna teaches Arjuna and gestures towards the opposing side's war-elephants.

Why is *bhakti* so popular? The older forms of worship require enormous sacrifices (akin to becoming a monk in the Christian tradition) and so are hard for many people to achieve. *Bhakti* is available to anyone, of any income level, and can be done while in the everyday world of raising a family, earning a living, and so forth.

Bhakti in India

In actual practice, many Hindus worship a variety of gods and goddesses, depending on their particular needs or desires. This form of worship encourages people to view images of the divinities. Iconography (which I'll discuss soon) and pilgrimage to famous temple sites become an important form of worship. One of the most important pilgrimage sites is the Ganges River. You can see this practice in the Web page shown in Figure 29.2.

Figure 29.2

Bathing in the Ganges River is supposed to be particularly purifying. Steps make it easier for pilgrims to enter the holy river.

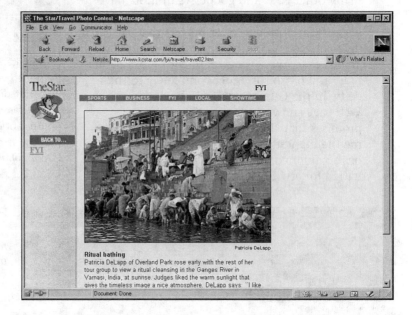

Why Is the Ganges River So Important?

The Ganges emerges from the Himalayas and meanders southeast to the Bay of Bengal. It is a large river and from ancient times has been regarded as holy. Today, there are many cities along its banks, each with temples and its own story about why the temple was founded there. Steps lead down the riverbank in many places, because bathing in the Ganges is supposed to be especially purifying. The most popular pilgrimage site on the Ganges (and probably in all India) is the city of Varanasi (or Benares). Varanasi is especially holy to Shiva and if one is fortunate enough to die in the city, one will attain liberation.

Bhakti in the West

Bhakti is popular in the West, especially after A.C. Bhaktivedanta Swami Prabhupada came to the United States. Prabhupada was a devotee of Krishna, who was dedicated to bringing the message of Krishna to English speakers. In 1965, he came to New York and founded ISKCON, the International Society for Krishna Consciousness, better known as the Hare Krishnas. The Hare Krishnas have many sites on the Web; if you are interested in learning more about them, a good place to start is The Hare Krishna Homepage at www.iskcon.org. This attractive site has information about the Hare Krishna's history, organization, provides a biography of the founder, describes ongoing projects (like building a Temple in India), and an online bookstore.

Is Hare Krishna a Cult?

The Hare Krishnas are viewed by some Westerners as a cult. They are accused of using brainwashing techniques to force people to join them. You can find lots of negative stories about the Hare Krishnas on the Web, but the basic problem for Westerners is that the Hare Krishnas are practicing a form of worship that is very different from Western religion, although it is fairly traditional devotional Hinduism.

On the other side of the coin, some Indians do not regard the Hare Krishnas as fellow Hindus. Some presentations about ISKCON argue that they are essentially monotheistic and hence, differ from mainstream Hinduism. For an example of this, see the discussion at OCRT, www.religioustolerance.org/hare.htm.

Hindu Scriptures and Mythology Online

Hinduism has a rich scriptural tradition explaining many of the previously mentioned traditions in great detail. If you can read Sanskrit, you are in luck, because many of these texts are available online at Sanskrit Documents (ftp://jaguar.cs.utah.edu/private/sanskrit/sanskrit.html). If you can't read Sanskrit, you will find that only limited selections from many important texts are readily available on the Web in English. But if you are really interested in Hindu myths, you can check out the Hindu Mythology Web site at www.indianmythology.com. The site currently offers stories about different Indian deities and links to other mythology sites. The author appears to plan to expand the site to include descriptions of the gods and goddesses, pictures, and additional information.

The following sites are good jumping-off points for the exploration of Hindu scriptural traditions.

Rig Veda

http://www.yoga.com/raw/readings/rig_veda.html

The Rig Veda is generally considered to be the oldest example of Hindu holy writing and probably reached its final form by around 1,000 BCE. For excerpts in English translation from the Rig Veda, check out this site, but if you want to get an overview of the Vedas and other parts of Hindu scripture, you might prefer to visit the Divine Life Society Web site dedicated to the Vedas. You'll find Swami Sivananda's basic introduction at www.SivanandaDlshq.org/religions/vedas.htm.

The Upanishads

The Upanishads record the philosophical questions of the ancient sages regarding the nature of the world and the divine. Much Upanishadic literature is over 2,000 years old, but literature with the title of "Upanishad" continued to be composed until the nineteenth century. A good site to begin exploring these texts is:

Upanishads: The Books of Knowledge

www.hindunet.org/upanishads

If you want to read excerpts from the Upanishads, you will probably need to go to your library. But this site will give you an idea of what you will find by providing excerpts from various ancient texts.

The Bhagavad Gita

Although the 200,000 verses of the *Mahabharata* are not all available on the Web, there are many sites devoted to discussion of the Bhagavad Gita. The Gita seems to have inspired some of the most creative and interesting Web sites. One of the most interesting is:

Bhagavad Gita

www.bhagavadgita.org

If you want to hear the Gita read in Sanskrit (using the RealAudio plug-in), surf over to this site. Also provided is a transliteration of the Sanskrit and a translation in English (also read aloud). You also can read (and listen to the translation) in many other languages.

The Ramayana

India has two extremely well known epic poems. The first, mentioned previously, is the *Mahabharata*, the second is the Ramayana. Again, it is easier to find versions of this poem on the Web than the older literature. A good site for the Ramayana is www.hscc.net/ramayana/. This site has several abridged versions of the poem, images of the characters in the poem, and links to sites offering character sketches for individuals in the epic.

330 Million Deities? Or Just One?

Hinduism has many gods and goddess, perhaps as many as 330 million! However, many Hindus would say that they are simply different manifestations of the ultimate divine, akin, perhaps, to a vastly multiplied Trinity. The three major gods are Brahma, who creates the cosmos; Vishnu, who sustains it; and Shiva, who will destroy it at the appointed time. Vishnu is often worshipped in his earthly forms (he has been incarnated as a human several times), especially as Rama and Krishna. Ganesha is Shiva's son and is easily recognized because he has the head of an elephant. There also are many female deities, including Parvati (Shiva's wife) and Lakshmi (Vishnu's wife). Kali (also known as Durga) is perhaps the most famous (or infamous) of the female deities: She wears a necklace of human heads and a skirt of human arms. Because seeing the divine is so important in Hinduism, the religion has an especially rich tradition of iconography. Gods and goddesses are depicted in pictures and sculpture. Some of these images are reproduced on the Web, as you can see in Figure 29.3.

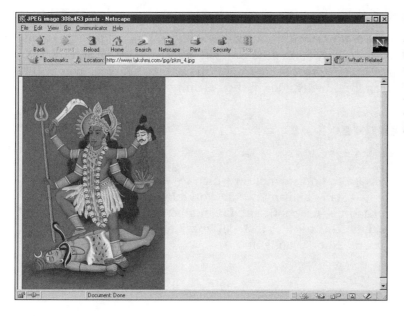

Figure 29.3

Kali is frequently depicted holding aloft the head of a giant, wearing her necklace of human heads, and skirt of human arms. She stands over the prostate form of Shiva, her consort.

Mohan's Hindu Image Gallery

www.geocities.com/SoHo/Lofts/6834/

Probably the most common form of Hindu iconographic artwork are mass-produced, very colorful images of various deities. These images illustrate the most popular stories about various god and goddesses. This site has a nice selection of images of different deities.

Images of Temples and Deities

www.geocities.com/Athens/Delphi/2627/page1.html

Hindu artists also decorated their temples quite richly. This site shows the statues of the deities that are located inside various temples.

Images of Temple Exteriors

www.hindunet.org/hindu_pictures/temples/temples.shtml

As well as providing images for the deities inside the temples, Hindu artists also lavished much attention to temple exteriors. The walls of many temples are completely covered with beautifully crafted sculpture. This site offers slide-shows of temples in 23 different locals.

Hindus Abroad

Indians and Hindus are found in every corner of the globe, not just India! Large communities of South Asians can be found in the United Kingdom, Canada, and the U.S., among other locations. There are a lot of sources on the Web to help members of the Hindu diaspora connect with other Hindus in their vicinity.

Directories of Temples

www.mandirnet.org/temple_list.html

If you are traveling and want to find a temple at which to worship, this site offers a list of temples in the United States and around the world. Information provided for each temple includes an address, telephone and fax numbers, a link to a Web site, and directions to the facility. This site also includes links to other South Asian religion centers—Sikh, Jain, and Zoroastrian temples.

The Harvard Pluralism Project

Part of the Harvard Pluralism Project (`www.fas.harvard.edu/~pluralsm/`) is an online database of over 3,200 religious centers in the United States. The project does not catalog Christian or Jewish sites, but if you are looking for Hindu, Jain, Buddhist, or Zoroastrian Temples, Islamic centers, or other world religious organizations, you might check The Pluralism Project Directory of Religious Centers, `http://icg.fas.harvard.edu/cgi-bin/pauldev/pluralism/directory`. You will need to spend some time learning how to change the search parameters, but if you are patient, you will get the data you want or need.

Hinduism Today

`www.hinduismtoday.kauai.hi.us/htoday.html`

This is the Web site for the printed monthly magazine, which records "the Modern History of a Billion-Strong Global Religion in Renaissance." The site contains text and graphics from the current issue of the magazine, as well as back issues (to 1996), and a search engine to facilitate finding information.

Rest and Remember

➤ Although it's the oldest religion in the world, Hinduism presents itself on the Web in a very modern guise.

➤ There are many forms of Hinduism, but bhakti yoga is predominant, both on the ground and on the Web.

➤ There is a preponderance of well-educated and technically savvy Hindus among the South Asian diaspora. As their number grows, expect Hindu sites on the Web to increase both in number and in depth.

Chapter 30

God Does Not Harm: Jains

In This Chapter

➤ Jainism was born long before Christianity and continues to project its distinct identity, now through the Internet

➤ Many of the Web sites on Jainism have an academic tone, but Jain computer experts also are learning to navigate in cyberspace

➤ Jainism shares many beliefs with other Eastern and Western traditions. Because of this, Jains aren't the only ones who can benefit from the rich information available on the Internet

It's hard to believe that there could be so many religions in one place, but in the Asian subcontinent, especially in the main part of it known as India, there is an immense diversity of spiritual expression. Jains are not as numerous as Hindus, nor as famous as Buddhists, but they are as authentically Indian as either Hindus or Buddhists. I will try to introduce the non-Jain reader to some of their major accents in this chapter, and I am assisted by the Jain cybernauts who have already begun to project their long standing religious outlook through the Net.

The History of the Jains

Quakers and Anabaptists, Hindus and Jains—what do they all have in common? A commitment to nonviolence. Although little known or understood in the Western world, the Jains are actually some of the world's strictest practitioners of nonviolence. Some go so far as to carry brooms as they walk to sweep away any insects they might harm by stepping! Their religious commitment also has led some Jains to avoid wearing any clothing at all! Where do these practices come from and why do they do it?

Well, Jainism shares characteristics with Hinduism and Buddhism and, like these religions, it is centered in India. Just as Hindus have their yogis and Buddhists have their Buddhas; Jains have their Jinas. In fact, there were a total of 24 of these Jinas or Tirthankaras throughout history. What are Jinas? Who are Tirthankaras? Well Jina loosely means conqueror and Tirthankara means a truly enlightened being. So, these guys were pretty powerful and unique. The first one was a giant who lived many millions of years ago. The most recent lived about 500 years before Christianity. His name was Vardhamana Mahavira; it was he who founded Jainism as a religion.

Who Was Mahavira?

Living somewhere around the fifth and sixth century B.C.E., Mahavira was the last of the Jinas. A truly devout man, Mahavira lived for several years with little to keep him alive. He might have almost died, but he also became enlightened. It was out of this enlightenment that he started the Jain community. How did he end up? At the age of 70 he deprived himself of food until he died, a truly devout action.

As you can see, Jain history is long and rich. Today the Jains have almost four million members, most of who live in India. If you are interested in learning more about Jain history, check out the following sites.

The Jain History Outline

www.cs.colostate.edu/~malaiya/jainhout1.html

This is a well-organized and useful outline with columns for Jain events, other events in India, and other events in the world. Not only does it give relevant information on Jains but it also puts this information into the context of other world events. Click the names of key figures and events and before you can blink, you'll see articles explaining their significance.

Jain Heritage

www.jainheritage.com

Along with beautiful pictures, this site, shown in Figure 30.1, provides a number of short essays about the uniqueness and history of Jainism. You'll find yourself on a beautifully illustrated and beautifully worded journey through the legacy of this tradition. You'll find it all at www.jainheritage.com.

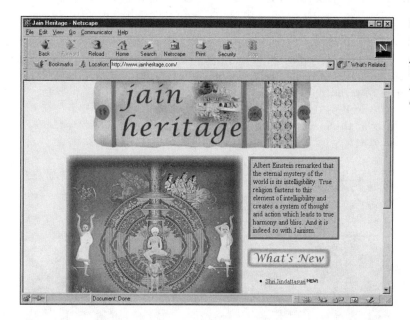

Figure 30.1

The beautiful pictures at Jain Heritage fit well with the almost poetic literary sketches of Jain history and culture.

Jain Beliefs and Scriptures

So what are the beliefs of this ancient philosophy? And where did these philosophies come from? Like most religions, the key doctrines came from the original teachers, in this case, the Tirthankaras. What they taught is set forth in the Jain scriptures, known as Agamas (precepts) or Siddhantas (treatises), and these scriptures guide Jains on their spiritual path.

So what is their philosophy? Well, unlike Western religions, they don't believe that a supreme being created the earth and will destroy it. The earth has always been, and will always be; it has no specific beginning, no predictable end. It is directed by nature, not a god.

Like Buddhists, Jains see suffering and pain in the world and seek to overcome it. They seek a higher consciousness through a simple life, no attachment to the materiel world, and deep compassion. Furthermore, they advocate ahimsa, or nonviolence. Ahimsa stresses the importance of not killing or harming another living creature in any way. One manifestation of this philosophy is vegetarianism. You can read more about the Jain philosophy of ahimsa and its connections to other philosophies of nonviolence at the very next Web site, Ahimsa: The Real Right to Life Movement.

Ahimsa: The Real Right to Life Movement

www.wizard.net/~ethan/ahimsa.htm

This site was created by Ethan Hamburg who, despite his last name, has been a vegetarian for more than 30 years. His page spans religious boundaries to show the universality of the nonviolence movement. With essays from Jews and Christians as well as Jains and Hindus, this page will give you a good feel for the philosophy behind ahimsa and ways to apply it in your life. Viewing only the first entries on this page, you might think it was a Christian page. Scroll down and you'll find essays on Jainism and the practice of nonviolence in this tradition. This shows the respect Jains have for other religions as well as their desire for the philosophy of nonviolence to cross all boundaries. After at this page, you will be switched over to www.wizard.net/~ethan/Source-Of-Peace.htm, which is shown in Figure 30.2.

Figure 30.2

This peaceful site about the philosophy of ahimsa begins with a picture of Jesus and several Judeo-Christian essays. Although the message is universal, the heart of this site is Jain.

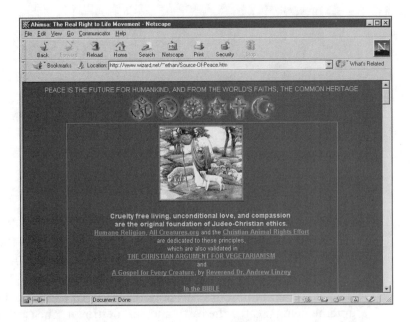

In addition to the idea of ahimsa, Jains like the idea of karma. Karma is a cosmic system of cause and effect that makes people accountable for their actions, be they good or bad. By living by these principles and more, Jains can attain kevala or moksha—liberation from the material world. It is at once a rebirth and an enlightenment.

The only differences among Jains concern who can attain enlightenment, and it comes down to clothes. There are two major groups. One favors wearing some garment; they also admit women to their ranks as world-renouncers. They are known as

Svetambara or white-clad. The other group, however, believe that nakedness is the only route to moksha or salvation, because even clothes impede the believer from practicing purity. They believe that only men can attain salvation, and so only men are admitted to the ranks of world-renouncers; women are excluded from their temples. These differences are important but also need to be kept within a perspective of common Jain accents on cosmology, ethics, and philosophy. For a very handy list to keep one's perspective, surf to the USAO Jainism page at `www.usao.edu/~usao-ids3313/ids/html/jainism.html`.

There are several other pages on the Internet that attempt to explain and explore the many aspects of Jain philosophy. What follows are some of the best.

Essence of Jainism: `www.angelfire.com/co/atmajyoti/`

Here you'll find almost every sort of writing and scripture you could want relating to Jainism. Be ready for some serious reading and some intense information. This site offers loads and loads of information that will expand and clarify your mind about specific doctrines and histories and more general moral ideas and standards. But be careful, only some of the texts are in English and all explanations are detailed.

Jaindarshan

`www.jaindarshan.com`

Jaindarshan is a clear source for explanations of the Jain philosophy. It summarizes various scriptures and introduces religious figures. For the beginner or non-Jain, the picture gallery might be the best place to start.

Resources

Still want to find out more? If you have any further questions about Jainism or are a Jain yourself and want to find more general resources, here are some sites for you. They range from the more general resource sites to lists of links highlighting specific needs.

Jain Study Circle

www.jainstudy.org

For the more academically minded Web-surfer, the Jain Study Circle provides a reading and writing intensive way to learn more about Jainism. This group comes from the publishers of the *Jain Study Circular* who began their word about 20 years ago. Here you can share your thoughts on various Jain scriptures and what others have to say about them.

JainWorld: www.jainworld.com

JainWorld works to reach the global Jain community and they seem to do a very good job! You can find everything here from recitation of texts to essays on ahimsa. Along with pretty pictures, you'll find subsections for philosophy, society, literature, education, and contributions. Click any of these and you'll find even more subsections. For example, if you click philosophy and then ahimsa, you'll find many essays on the philosophy itself and how to integrate nonviolence into your life. One great feature of this site is the devotional songs. Also a subset of philosophy, these songs come complete with a real audio recording! This is a great site for those seeking understanding and appreciation of the Jain culture and religion.

Jain Friends

jainfriends.faithweb.com

This is the site for socializing in the Jain community! This is a worldwide network of Jains and the opportunities for connecting with other Jains are endless. You'll find explanations of the Jain philosophy alongside a matrimonials link, chat rooms, and a directory of organizations, Web sites, and magazines related to the Jain religion. Another fun feature is the section that lists Jain names for your child!

Young Jains of America

www.yja.org

For younger Jains in America, this organization promises to create opportunities and connections for the next generation of Jains. The group and its Web site seem to be in the early stages but there are activities in the works and it has links to various regional groups across the country. Contact one of the members through the Web site to find out more.

Jainism Links: www.cs.colostate.edu/~malaiya/jainhlinks.html

Haven't found what you're looking for? This site, again from Colorado State, provides the best set of links out there on Jainism. Whether you are interested in Jain history and philosophy or modern lifestyle, you'll find the information here. You'll also find a stunning set of links to other Web sites.

Jainism is one of the three ancient Indian religions and its history is rich and diverse. The philosophy that shapes this religion overlaps with many other world traditions, but certain aspects are uniquely Jain. Although Jains are not widely recognized in Western culture, their philosophies have influenced it significantly. Anyone interested in fathoming the mystery of the universe and the depth of respect for all living creatures should check out Jainism, beginning with its several sites on the World Wide Web.

Rest and Remember

➤ Although many Jain sites have a philosophical content, others are geared to everyday needs, and most are interesting as well as informative.

➤ Jains use the World Wide Web, both to widen their influence and to educate those not familiar with the religion.

➤ When ancient religions use cyberspace, they provide all Net surfers with a wonderful opportunity. In this case, you have a wonderful opportunity to learn about the peaceful Jains and their dynamic history and beliefs.

Chapter 31

God Loves Long Hair: Sikhs

> ### In This Chapter
>
> ➤ Sikhs are part of the cluster of religious traditions that derive from India or South Asia. They are neither Muslim nor Hindu, although they share some common elements with each
>
> ➤ Sikhs are native to a part of northwest India, but they also travel abroad and often live in North America or England as well as parts of Southeast Asia
>
> ➤ Sikhs have been well represented on the Net, and there is much that both Sikhs and non-Sikhs can find out about the khalsa, or Sikh community, on the Net

If you've ever wondered how cyberspace works for religious self-expression, then visit some of the many, many Web sites constructed by and for advocates of Sikhism. Though much smaller than its Hindu and Muslim neighbors, the Sikh community of India is a vital presence, both at home and abroad. If you are not a Sikh, you can find out much about them by visiting some of their stops on the information superhighway. If you are a Sikh, I hope that you will find the stops or Web sites that I have selected in this chapter make your own experience as a cybernaut more enjoyable and beneficial.

Sikh and You Shall Find

Sikhs have existed for over 500 years. All Sikhs are monotheists: They believe in one God. They also accept 10 *gurus*, or teachers, as the definitive guides to God's Word. They also revere the teachings that have been revealed to their gurus. Known as the

Granth Sahib or *Adi Granth*, their scripture is held in such high esteem that it can be compared with the Torah in Judaism. It is the focal point of ritual practice as well as collective belief for almost 18 million Sikhs throughout the world.

What Is the Adi Granth?

After you click `www.sikhs.org/english/frame.html`, you will have the sacred text of *Sikhs* at your fingertips. You might not understand it at first, but you will note that it is long: almost 1,500 pages, it also contains nearly 6,000 hymns. Even if you have never heard of Sikhism before, you should bookmark this page; it contains the heart of Sikh devotionalism, and it is presented here in a very sophisticated format.

The First Guru

It was a prophetic teacher named Nanak (1469-1539), who began the religious movement we now call Sikhism. Nanak received direct revelations from God. How? According to Sikh tradition, Nanak disappeared into a river bordering the Punjab in North India (you can see where that is in the online map shown in Figure 31.1). Although people frantically searched for him, no one found him till he emerged safely from the water after three days. He claimed to have been in direct conversation with God; he had been told the truth of the universe. He then put in writing what he had heard. Known as the *Mool Mantra*, it set forth the nature of God as the Supreme Being and Creator of the Universe.

Where Is the Punjab?

If you look at this map of India, you can find the Punjab. You will see it as a large state between Jammu and Kashmir (far north) and Rajasthan (west). The Punjab is an agricultural state, with a prosperous infrastructure in industry and communications. Today the Sikhs are the largest group in that important region of North India.

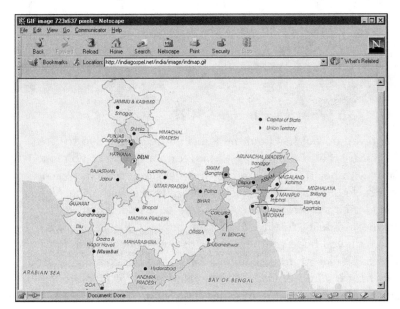

Figure 31.1

This online map depicts India, the birthplace of many major religions, including the Sikh faith, which originated in the Punjab region.

Sikhism might sound pretty much like other one-god religions, but there is a huge difference. Nanak taught his followers, whom he called *Sikhs*, or disciples, that all people could experience God, not just by priests or holy men. He thus rejected all class or caste markings. In effect, he argued that because God was universal, exceeding all human limits—of gender, of age, of creed, but also of class—the only true religion was one that was open to all God's people.

Nanak traveled throughout India preaching his message to both Hindus and Muslims. He even had a Muslim companion named Mardana. His message found a welcome audience among Hindus and Muslims, especially in the Punjab, and after his death his successor continued to solidify the new religious movement.

Guru Gobind Singh

Although there were nine other human gurus after Guru Nanak, the one who ranks at the top of the list in importance was the tenth guru, Guru Gobind Singh (d. 1708). It was he who gave the Sikhs their enduring symbols of identity. They are known as the 5 k's, which stands for kesh (uncut hair), kangha (comb), kara (steel bangle), kachcha (undershorts), and kirpan (short sword). Guru Gobind Singh not only blended them into the core of Sikh identity, but before he died, he declared that the Sikh scripture, the Guru Granth Sahib, would be his successor. Yes, that's right, there would be no further living teacher. Revelation ended with Guru Gobind Singh, and the point of reference—and reverence—for all Sikhs in the future became the Granth Sahib, the eternal, unfailing guru.

So What's with the 5 K's?

If you are not Sikh and you do not hail from the Punjab, it might be hard to remember the 5 k's. But try this: The uncut hair stands for purity. The comb represents cleanliness, along with healthy behavior. The steel bangle reminds its wearer that he is bound in a circle of loyalty with bangle wearers, that is, with other Sikhs. The undershorts remind their wearers that they are to be pure in deeds as well as thoughts, and purity means fidelity, fidelity to the faith but also fidelity to one's wife. And the sword? Well, you hope you never have to use it, but it stands for your willingness to go to any length to defend your faith and your community. And what about that turban? It is a further mark of Sikh male identity; it binds its wearer to other turbaned Punjabis, that is, to other male Sikhs.

Basic Beliefs of Sikhism: Equality of Men and Women

Because the 5 k's put so much stress on men's outlook and male behavior, one might think that Sikhism is a male tradition in which women have little say. That is not the case, however, for if you look at any cybersite on Sikhism, such as the one shown in Figure 31.2, you will find an up-front declaration that men and women are not only equal but they also have equal access to all the rituals of the Sikh tradition.

Figure 31.2

The Web site at www.sikhs.org summarizes the Sikh affirmation of gender equality.

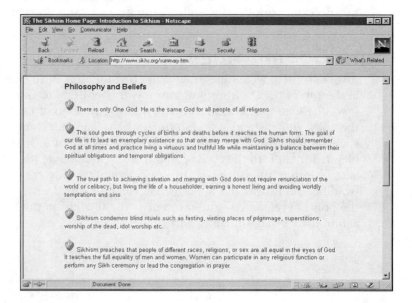

For those who are not familiar with other Indian religions, this last point that "people of different races, religions, or sex are all equal in the eyes of God" is worth stressing. Neither Hindu nor Muslim nor Jain nor Buddhist communities have public ceremonies in which women are permitted to lead all the congregants, including men, in prayer. It is one of the singular marks of the radical equality that Guru Nanak preached and that Guru Gobind Singh, along with later Sikhs, have upheld.

A Sikh Primer on Sikhism

Are you ready for a Sikh exposition of fundamentals? Well you might *not* be ready for www.sikhs.org. It is *the* Sikh home page, complete with bells and whistles. It contains the Guru Granth Sahib in translation. It has information about all aspects of Sikh beliefs and practices, including comparisons with other religious traditions. Not only does the home page jump out at you, but it also includes audio and animations at several points.

Suppose you knew nothing, and had not a clue, about Sikhism. You could scroll through this site, from the introduction to Sikhism, to the background history of Sikh origins and development. Then you could segue into the Sikh way of life before finding out more about Sikh resources and ending, where every Sikh would end, with Sikh scripture.

Were you counting? If so, you counted to five, and you might have guessed: there are 5 k's, and so this sequence exactly mirrors the 5 k's. Each of the markers for the five main sections of this home page is a clip art replica of one of the 5 k's, making its symbolic layout as well as its narrative content the perfect entry into cyber Sikhism.

Other Sikh Resources

Although it has almost everything a Sikh enquirer or a non-Sikh explorer might want to know about Sikhism, the Sikhism Home Page at www.sikhs.org is a huge site, with so much information that you do have to be patient surfing through its various channels. If you have more immediate interests, you might try some of the following.

Sikh Media Action and Resource Task Force

www.sikhmedia.org/main.html

Despite their impressive skills and global credentials, Sikhs are often not able to get across to non-Sikhs their perspective on many issues. For instance, many Anglo-Americans equate Indian with Hindu. They see Sikhs as just one more Hindu group. Even though Sikhism did emerge from medieval Hinduism, it rejected many Hindu beliefs, especially polytheism, and one indispensable Hindu social marker, the caste system. Yet Sikhs have to remind others constantly that they are Indian but not Hindu. SikhMedia is an impressive site providing practical resources to Sikhs as they continue to struggle for both racial and religious recognition within United States and Canadian societies.

Khalistan Movement: Burning Punjab

www.burningpunjab.com

This Burning Punjab site is not for everyone. It has graphic footage of the most disastrous public event in contemporary Sikh history: the 1984 Indian government attack on the holiest site of Sikh worship, the Golden Temple in Amritsar.

How did this happen? Well, ever since the Punjab was divided, or partitioned, between Pakistan and India in 1947, many Sikhs have wanted to have their own homeland, or Khalistan. In the early 1960s, Sikhs set up a political party, the Akali Dal, to mobilize forces and fight for national recognition. The movement for an independent Sikh nation reached a crisis in the early 1980s, and the Indian government responded with extreme force. Indira Gandhi, who was the prime minister overseeing the crisis, was later blamed for the damage to buildings, and the loss of life, inflicted on Amritsar, the capital of Sikh piety. Sikh bodyguards assassinated her in 1984, and then Sikhs were subjected to retaliatory massacre in the riots that ensued after Mrs. Gandhi's assassination.

What does this have to do with religion? A lot if you are a Sikh, and if you identify not only with the Punjab but with its recent history. For many Sikhs, even those living in Europe or North America, the future of India remains linked to the unresolved issue of Khalistan as a nation.

Other Sikh Sects

Up until now you might have thought that there was only one group of Sikhs, and they all fall into line behind the 5 k's, striving for a separate Sikh religious identity and perhaps also for a separate Sikh homeland in India. But there are other Sikh groups that do not identify with the majority group or Singh Sikhs (named after Guru Gobind Singh, or sometimes called Khalsa Sikhs.) Two non-conformist sects are the following.

Siri Singh Sahib

www.yogibhajan.com

This sect is identified with a twentieth century Sikh teacher, Yogi Bhajan. He began his movement in the 1960s, calling it the 3HO. Yogi Bhajan explained that the Order of the 3Hs stands for: Healthy, Happy, and Holy. The message befits a new age group that accepts its leader as both a teacher for the Aquarian Age as well as a master of White Tantric Yoga.

This group is very active in promoting global awareness of Sikhs as the custodians of Truth and harbingers of Peace. It has links to other Sikh sites, but they are all within the circle of 3HO Sikhs, and few are reciprocated by the majority of Sikhs.

Sikh Links within 3HO: www.yogibhajan.com/sss.html

Here you can find everything, from marriage proposals to shopping tips to free music downloads. Often you will find reference to other Sikh groups or Sikh-related links that are not directly connected to Yogi Bhajan, but the overall intent is to raise the profile of this minority group of Sikhs who self-identify with Yogi Bhajan and the 3HO network. A bit misleading, to say the least.

Also misleading is the name of the other server for this site: It is www.sikhnet.com. In other words, Yogi Bhajan has both its own named site and also a site that most surfers would assume refers to all Sikhs. In fact, Sikhnet is Yogi Bhajan by another name.

3HO is self-conscious of its minority status. It is possibly for this reason that it rates Indian Sikh sites such as the one exploring Sikh shrines in a South Indian state (Maharashtra). Check out the site at www.takhatsrihazursahib.org/home.htm, and you will see how tough it is to determine what are the criteria for evaluation, other than particular preferences of the Webmaster!

Nirankaris

Although they lack a Web site, the Nirankaris are much more objectionable to Singh Sikhs than the 3HOs. These are Sikhs who claim allegiance to Guru Nanak, the first guru, rather than to the last Guru, Guru Gobind Singh. They claim to pursue the worship of the pure name of God (Sat Nam), and not to be bound by other rituals, including the rituals that came to be established with Singh, or majoritarian, Sikhism. Their members emphasize the formless quality of God, Nirankar, and the importance of interior discipline. They also acknowledge the need for a living guru who can serve as a spiritual mentor. Their presence in Amritsar provoked a riot within Sikhism in 1978, one that has been described in gruesome detail in print media and now in cyberspace (see www.burningpunjab.com/pages/clash-1.htm).

Ironically, these minority Sikhs embrace nonviolence: They have criticized the Singh Sikhs (or majority of Sikhs) not only because they impose upon Sikhism a sectarian symbolism but also because they follow Guru Gobind Singh rather than Guru Nanak and therefore, in the Nirankari view, are predisposed to violence.

Who Are the Real Sikhs?

The Sikhs are everyone who claims to be Sikh. What I have tried to do is to give major attention to the dominant group, but also to allow some voice for those who oppose its views.

In general, Sikhs are among the hardest working, engaged, spiritually alert, and professionally nimble citizens, both at home and abroad. Sometimes they reside in their Indian homeland. Sometimes they come to distant places, such as the U.S. and Canada. Whether they come temporarily or permanently, they seldom fail to project their history and their faith in public spaces.

Rest and Remember

➤ Sikhism is an Indian religious tradition, with broad global connections, including high profile adherents in both Europe and North America.

➤ Sikhism is monotheistic, scriptural, disciplined, and egalitarian, with an effective presence on the Net as well as on the ground.

➤ While most Sikhs agree on their history, and share common hopes for the future, there are a few minority sects that dissent from, and oppose, the majority of their co-religionists.

Chapter 32

God Is Harmony: Taoists

In This Chapter

➤ Taoism is both a feature of popular culture and a deeply historical Chinese world view. It also has a practical face: the martial art of Tai Chi

➤ You can learn about either form of Taoism in cyberspace, though in one sense Taoism can never be learned, just experienced

➤ Popular Taoism and Tai Chi are better represented on the Web than their weighty counterpart: philosophical/religious Taoism

Of all the religious traditions that I explore in this book, Taoism is the one that stretches the mind beyond the cyber signs of the new information superhighway. It is not a religion so much as a practice, and it is a very, very demanding practice. Almost as if by design, there are fewer Taoist Web sites than, say, Buddhist or Hindu sites, and they also divide up into two very different avenues of exploration. I chart the more accessible and popular avenue first, before inviting you to join me on a journey down the historical and philosophical avenue of Taoist metaphysics.

Taoism Light: The Popular Take

All religious traditions have key concepts. If Christianity's is salvation and Buddhism's is enlightenment, Taoism's is harmony. Harmony with what? With self, with nature, with different sizes?

Different sizes? Yes, if there is one Taoist principle that separates it from many other traditions, it is the accent on the small, the seemingly insignificant, and the *big* role that what is small can play in each of our lives.

It is for that reason that an Oregonian naturalist (he prefers to prune trees for a living) has become the best-selling writer of popular books on Taoism. His name is Benjamin Hoff, and his two widely sold books are titled *The Tao of Pooh* and *The Te of Piglet*. Figure 32.1 shows *The Tao of Pooh*'s home page, `www.algorithms.com/users/belascot/pooh.html`.

Figure 32.1

The home page for The Tao of Pooh is an online shrine to the popular book.

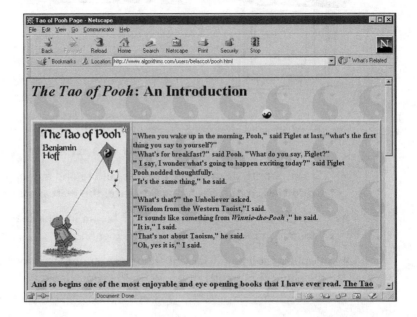

Many readers of this wildly popular book begin by saying: "It has changed my life," "I never felt better," "I can't believe it!" Even those who have never heard of Tao or Te—and that could be said of most Americans—have heard of Pooh and Piglet. It is not just because they rhyme more easily (actually, Tao and Te are pronounced daoh and deh, and elide even more seamlessly than do Pooh and Piglet). It's because most English-speaking Americans know the characters and stories created by a British cleric called A.A. Milne, whose book *Winnie-the-Pooh* was first published in 1926 and was followed two years later by a sequel, *The House at Pooh Corner*. And so the *Pooh* stories, which are all about getting it right and are told through animal characters with human qualities, have become classics for most young Americans in the twentieth century. Moreover, these characters are instantly recognizable as archetypes that Hoff asserts embody—or fail to embody—Taoist principles.

Learning Taoism from a Bear and a Pig

Hoff understood the connection of Pooh and Piglet to the deeper message of Taoism, so his books are both about the Taoist respect for very small animals. They translate that message into a wide-ranging ethic, not only for Taoist and Buddhist monks, but for everyone who wants to pursue virtuous conduct. The key concept is harmony: the idea that the most marginal people, like the smallest animals, play a role in the world's moral economy. Likewise, those who are the biggest, wealthiest, and most powerful are often the most unfulfilled and may actually have something to learn from the smallest, the poorest, and the weakest. The big bear and the little pig beckon human beings to take lessons from them about the game of life.

If the message of Taoism is harmony, it is harmony that can be achieved only by looking at the world turned upside down. When we flip the usual scheme of things and our taken-for-granted perspectives, we can try to restore our own balance. After we find inner harmony, we discover that the world also has found *its* harmony. It is a simple message to hear but a hard task to pursue. Put aside pride, prejudice, anxiety, power, and fear. Easy? Not quite. But in that reversal, or restoration, lies the power of Pooh and Piglet, as well as Tao and Te.

Pooh on Pooh!

Not everyone agrees or is happy with the link of Tao to Pooh or Te to Piglet. A number of attack sites have been created on the Net. To get a flavor of this opposite reaction to Benjamin Hoff's works, you might explore the Winnie the Pooh site at www.gaijin.com/void/pooh.html. The chief criticism at this site is that no one can be happy all the time; life really does have a downside. Taoists understood this, but, according to these critics, Hoff does not. The language is not only anti-Pooh, but even a bit raunchy. The author's a self-styled Taoist, and he disagrees with Hoff, who is also a self-styled Taoist. Who is right? Or is all this conflict itself eluding the harmony of the Tao? You be the judge.

Taoism Heavy: The Philosophical Take

Technically, Tao means "the way," Te means "the virtue," and both concepts can be traced back to a Chinese teacher known as Lao Tzu, who may have lived about 2,500 years ago, around the same time as Siddhartha or Gautama Buddha in nearby India. Lao Tzu became famous only when another Chinese scholar and teacher wrote about him 200 years after his death, saying that he was an elder contemporary of Kung-fu-tzu, also known as Confucius, and it was he who left the court where both he and Kung-fu-tzu served. He went west never to be seen again.

Another Chinese Sage, with a Long History

Are you wondering what happened to Confucius and Confucianism in this book? Well, you can write only so much about all the religions and religious activities that have sites on the Net. Even more than Taoism, Confucianism is a text-based tradition, and to grasp its general outline, you only have to click the Confucianism home page prepared by Ontario Consultants on Religious Tolerance, www.religioustolerance.org/confuciu.htm. Here you will find the best overview of Taoist rituals, schools, and scriptures. On the other hand, if you want a longer introduction to the texts themselves, and you are eager to learn how they cohere as a school or outlook, you might want to go to another home page on Confucianism that actually originates from Japan. See the Confucianism page at www.geocities.com/Tokyo/Springs/6339/Confucianism.html. Either way, you'll find that Confucianism is also a religious/philosophical tradition that has ancient texts needing a modern commentary.

Taoist Scriptures

Taoism originates from two sources: first, its legendary founder Lao Tzu and his later disciple Chuang Tzu and second, their joint literary legacy. The literary legacy consists of two main texts. One text, called the *Tao te ching*, is said to have been written by Lao Tzu. The other text, called *Chuang Tzu*, is said to have been written by—you guessed it—Chuang Tzu.

Tao Te Ching in English, Please

If you were eager to explore the Tao te ching and had some knowledge of Chinese, you could go to the Web and get a copy of both an English translation and the original Chinese text side by side. But suppose you wanted just a straight English translation. Well you can get no less than four of these by clicking over to `www.chinapage.com/laotze.html`. It provides one of the classical statements of a Chinese worldview, and it is worth your time to ponder it.

Other Aspects of Philosophical Taoism

Whereas the Net sites on Taoism are actually limited, as is Taoism itself in terms of number of adherents, a succinct overview is provided by our mother of all subject directories: Ontario Religious Consultants, aka Religious Tolerance. You could glean much of value about this ancient tradition just by surfing to `www.religioustolerance.org/taoism.htm`.

And if you were keen to finding other aspects of Taoism, especially those with an everyday spiritual appeal, you might go to the Daoist Depot, shown in Figure 32.2. No, that is not a typo, Daoists often spell their name Daoist, rather than Taoist (perhaps to bring the pronunciation into harmony with the spelling), and this is a remarkably friendly Daoist Depot.

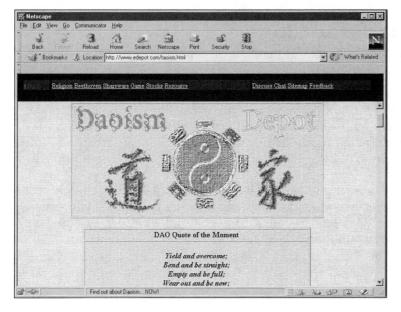

Figure 32.2

The Religion Depot, www.edepot.com/ religion.html, is a multipurpose religious site: It is Daoist, but it also has points of entry for Buddhists, Christians, Jews, Muslims, and Hindus.

What you find in these and other sites is that Taoists love the number two. They have a pair of founders: Lao Tze and Chuang Tze. They have twin scriptures: *Tao te ching* and *Chuang tze*. They also have two equal or twin concepts that inform their way of life and their outlook.

It is the most basic principle of twinning or harmonizing that is linked to China: *yin* and *yang*. The idea, very much like Benjamin Hoff's characters, is that two are much better than one, that nothing can succeed without its opposite. *Yin* and *yang* are poles. It is their combined force that represents the Way, or Tao, it is their combined use that leads to the Virtue or Te. In their most elemental description, *yin* is said to be cold, feminine, and evil, and *yang* is said to be warm, masculine, and good!

Yin and Yang, not Yin or Yang

Obviously, it is crucial for translations to work across cultures, and much of Taoism depends on translating or rendering into everyday life the functional complementarity, not the exclusive opposition, of *yin* and *yang*. What is evil without good, feminine without masculine, cold without warmth? If one thinks too much about the negative aspect of each element, the synergy, or their ability to work together, is limited or even eliminated.

The Practical Tao: Tai-Chi

After you've surfed through Taoism Light and waded through Taoism Heavy, you might be ready for Taoism in practice, or Taoism as a guide to everyday good health. That comes through Tai-Chi.

Chi means breath, and Tai-Chi is the way of breath, or the way of regulating the breath. And it is not just what you see or feel when you breath in and out. There is also the inner breath. It is vital energy that goes beyond ordinary air. The real purpose of Tai-Chi is not just physical, but metaphysical: to purify the inner breath through specific exercises. In Taoist language, it means to nourish the yang, or force of growth, and to limit the yin, or decaying energy. But it also means to keep both elements constantly in harmonious circulation, so that the yang becomes yin and the yin becomes yang continuously. Hence the primary movement of Tai-Chi is circular, because both elements are needed to sustain life.

Breathe Deep, Live Well

Breathing right is the key to living right for Taoists who pursue Tai-Chi. Breath nourishes the body if it is controlled though deep respiration. The Tai-Chi-adept breathe not only air, but also vapors or currents from deeper sources such as the sun, moon, and stars. The effort is to align oneself with the elemental force of all life—the Tao. Certain exercises, beginning with proper breathing, help good energies circulate through the body; they also counteract, or eliminate, internal blocks that may cause disease, illness, or death.

If you want to learn more about Tai-Chi, including its relationship to a Chinese worldview and Taoist metaphysics, you can visit any number of sites that are now available on the Net. One of the most informative is the Gin Soon Tai Chi Chuan Federation home page at www.geocities.com/RodeoDrive/4687/. It provides a thorough integration of yin-yang complexities with the physical exercise of Tai-Chi.

Another site, which is less complex but also intent on promoting Tai-Chi as a form of cross-cultural understanding, is the home page of the Taoist Tai-Chi Society-International. It has the simplest Web address of all, www.taoist.org. There you will find out about a wide range of activities that bring Tai-Chi almost to your doorstep. It bills itself as the world's largest nonprofit Tai-Chi organization, and judging by its ample Web site, it is certainly one of the best, if not the largest, of Tai-Chi societies.

Rest and Remember

➤ Taoism is among the oldest philosophical traditions in the world, and it is closely linked with a Chinese worldview.

➤ Popular Taoism is not for everyone, but neither is philosophical Taoism. However, you can explore both on the Web.

➤ The best-known practical aspect of Taoism is Tai-Chi, which has also found its niche in cyberspace.

Chapter 33

God's Persian Prophet: Zoroastrians or Parsis

In This Chapter

➤ Zoroastrians represent one of the world's oldest religious traditions, the grandfather of Abrahamic monotheism

➤ From cradle to grave, Zoroastrian ritual life encourages its followers to serve Ahura Mazda through the pursuit of good thoughts, good words, and good deeds

➤ Zoroastrians, although small in number, project their sense of community both on the ground and in cyberspace

---

Despite their very small size, Zoroastrians represent an ancient spiritual community, and now they have emerged with a presence on the Web. For those who are still astonished at how much there is to learn in cyberspace, the Parsi presence on the Net is yet one more cause for amazement, and applause. The digital image that we now have of the tiny Zoroastrians is clear, consistent, and engaging, as you will see in the Web sites noted in this chapter.

From Zoroaster (a.k.a. Zarathustra) to Zoroastrianism

Zoroastrians are heirs to the spiritual legacy of ancient Persia. Today they are a small but influential community. They maintain the fires of one of the world's oldest and most storied religious traditions.

The story of Zoroastrianism begins with the figure of its founder. But who was he? The details of his life remain obscured in myth and legend. Zoroaster is the Greek rendering of the Iranian name, Zarathustra. He might have trained to be a priest in ancient Persia. His birth and childhood were said to be marked by miraculous events, but the true miracle happened at age 30. Zoroaster was engaged in his priestly duties when he saw an angel who led him to Ahura Mazda and the Holy Immortals. You can see his portrait in the Web site illustrated in Figure 33.1.

Figure 33.1

The Web site at `www.ozemail.com.au/ ~zarathus/tenets33.html` *includes both an artistic rendering of the prophet Zarathustra and a description of his tenets.*

Who Are Ahura Mazda and the Holy Immortals?

Ahura Mazda, the Wise Lord, is the Zoroastrian name for the one true God. He is the eternal source of goodness and the creator of all living beings in the universe. The Amesha Spenta, or Holy Immortals, are mentioned in the sacred scriptures composed by Zoroaster. They are Divine Attributes that communicate between Ahura Mazda and human beings. There are seven of them: Good Mind, Order, Dominion, Devotion, Wholeness, Immortality, and the Holy Spirit. Some Zoroastrian thinkers have understood them as abstract concepts. Others view them as personified beings.

Zoroaster continued to have revelations in which Ahura Mazda instructed him to preach the true religion. His priestly peers resisted, but Zoroaster prevailed. Eventually he won royal support for his fledgling faith.

There are many other aspects to Zoroaster's life and legend. For a detailed look, dive into his biography at www.zarathushtra.com.

After the Prophet Zoroaster's death, the tradition struggled to survive. Alexander the Great conquered Persia in 330 B.C.E., burnt the royal capital of Persepolis, and destroyed the definitive copy of Zoroastrian scripture, the Avesta.

Wired Monk

What Is the Avesta?

Want to read a 2,500-year-old book? Surf over to the Zoroastrian Archives at www.avesta.org/avesta.html and discover the Avesta: the sacred scripture of the Zoroastrians. The Avesta is composed of hymns, prayers, and invocations. The recitation of this ancient text remains one of the primary ceremonial duties of Zoroastrian priests. Be sure to look at the Gathas, or songs. These are five sacred hymns in praise of Ahura Mazda. They are believed to be the direct words of the Prophet Zoroaster himself.

Despite these setbacks, the religion prevailed. Centuries later, Zoroastrianism reached its peak. It became the official state religion of the powerful Sassanian Empire. Zoroastrian temples were built and the Avesta was collected and codified.

Doctrine

Central to Zoroastrianism are the concepts of heaven and hell, the resurrection of the body, the arrival of the Messiah, judgement at death, and the Armageddon battle at the end of time. At the heart of this religious world is the supreme god, Ahura Mazda. By contrast, an evil spirit named Ahriman causes havoc, destruction, and suffering in the world. In Zoroastrian doctrine, the cosmic struggle between these forces of good and evil will culminate in a battle of Armageddon when Ahura Mazda will finally triumph over Ahriman and his followers.

The stylized figure known alternatively as Farohar or Faravahar, shown in Figure 33.2, is said to represent the ideals of Zoroastrian piety, reminding the faithful of the soul's journey towards union with Ahura Mazda. For a detailed explanation of this Zoroastrian symbol, see The Significance of the Faravahar at www.stanford.edu/group/zoroastrians/faravahar.shtml.

Figure 33.2

This figure, known as Farohar or Faravahar, is taken from a pillar at the ancient Persian capital of Persepolis.

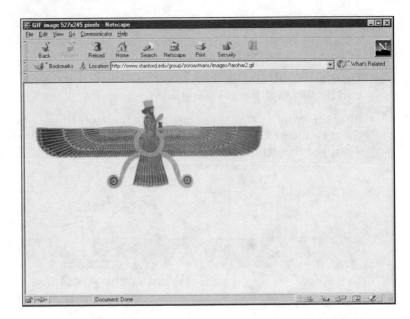

Literal or Figurative?

Not all Zoroastrians interpret this story of Ahura Mazda and Ahriman literally. One influential school of thought sees this cosmic battle as a metaphor for the moral struggle within the mind and soul of every human being. In fact, most modern Zoroastrians deny that the tradition is in any way dualistic. Instead, they stress the supreme power and goodness of Ahura Mazda, and emphasize the fundamentally monotheistic nature of their faith.

Until that final victory, human life itself is a battle between good and evil. Believers are called to serve Ahura Mazda through the disciplined pursuit of good thoughts, good words, and good deeds. At death, the human soul crosses over the Chinvat Bridge. The bridge widens so the righteous can enter paradise. It narrows for the wicked who tumble off its knife-edge into the torments of hell. In the hope of reaching paradise, Zoroastrians place great stress on personal honesty, integrity, and altruism in their daily lives. They view the pursuit of goodness as a reward in itself. For a summary of Zoroastrian beliefs, see the informative Zoroastrian section at our old friend OCRT, www.religioustolerance.org/zoroastr.htm.

Ritual Practice

Fire is the eternal source of purity, light, warmth, and power. For Zoroastrians, fire symbolizes divine presence, power, and purity. So guess what? The central space of worship for Zoroastrians is the Fire Temple. You can see one illustrated at the Web site www.zoroastrian.com, shown in Figure 33.3.

Figure 33.3

White-clad Zoroastrian priests gather to evoke the eternal flame.

Within the sacred space of the Fire Temple, Zoroastrian priests (all of them men) offer prayers on behalf of the faithful around an eternal fire. For a taste of this ritual space, visit a virtual fire temple at the Zarathushtra page, www.zarathushtra.com. Lay people also keep fires in their homes where they recite prayers drawn from the Gathas. For insights into a Zoroastrian's daily ritual routine, including prayers in English and Persian, check out the Zarathushtrian Assembly at www.zoroastrian.org.

From cradle to grave, a Zoroastrian's life is marked by ritual observances. Between the ages of 7 and 10, every Zoroastrian child is initiated into the duties of religious life in a ceremony called *navjote*, or new birth. Boys and girls each receive two sacred items. They are worn under their clothing for the remainder of their lives. One is a white undershirt called the *sudreh*. The other is a hollow woven wool cord known as the *kusti*. It is long enough to be tied three times around the waist.

Several times a day, especially after washing, the Zoroastrian reties the *kusti* while saying certain fixed prayers. Tying is also an important feature of the Zoroastrian marriage ritual. The officiating priest symbolically bonds the couple together by wrapping them in a long cord.

Even in death, the ritual concern with purity and propriety continues. At death, a body is considered highly polluted. Historically a corpse was placed on top of a *dakhma*, or

Tower of Silence, where it was exposed to the sun and vultures. For a discussion of this ancient burial custom, check out Dakhma-nishini at www.ozemail.com.au/~zarathus/dakhma33.html. Today this practice is no longer observed. Instead, the body is placed on a metal stretcher and buried in a cement box so that dirt can not pollute it further.

Community

With approximately 200,000 followers worldwide, today's Zoroastrian community is tiny. While a few survive in the religion's Iranian homeland, the vast majority of Zoroastrians live in the Indian subcontinent where they are known as Parsis.

Who Are the Parsis?

More than three-fourths of the world's Zoroastrians live in India. Known as Parsis, their ancestors originally fled from Persia during the Muslim invasions of the seventh century. They settled mainly in the western areas of Gujarat, and are especially prominent in the bustling city of Bombay. Parsis have had a disproportionate influence in India because of their high standards of education. They also are renowned as prominent business and political leaders. For insight into this tightly knit community, see the Parsi Personal Touch Services notice at www.zoroastrian.net. At this site a group of Parsi women are creating a virtual online community. They offer everything from wedding arrangements and prayer requests to party catering for Zoroastrian clients in the Indian cities of Bombay and Poona.

The Zoroastrians' success has a lot to do with their powerful sense of community. This bond is strengthened through worship, marriage, and personal and professional networks. These days, cyberspace also helps cement communal ties. For examples of how Zoroastrians are creating virtual communities on the Web, stop by the following sites.

Zoroastrian Matrimonial Page

www.ozemail.com.au/~zarathus/soulmate.html

This site declares its intentions from the start: Marry Inside Our Community and Save Our Religion. Whether you're in Bombay or Boston, this is the place to find a Zoroastrian significant other.

Zoroastrian Business Directory

www.zarathusht.com

What a large directory and what a huge variety! Here you will find an online link to Zoroastrian businesses. If you're looking for anything from arts and entertainment to real estate, manufacturing, and legal advice, this is the place to start.

Zoroastrian History and Culture

www.vohuman.org

For those who shun business but love books, this site offers a number of online essays and Web journals. It focuses on Zoroastrian history, religion, and culture.

Zoroastrian Groups in North America

www.fezana.org

This is the official Web page for Fezana, a federation of 22 Zoroastrian associations and 15 informal groups in the United States and Canada. This page illustrates that Zoroastrians are building a sense of global community, joined together by faith and culture.

Zoroaster Beyond Zoroastrians

The Prophet Zoroaster also inspired people outside of his faith. His name and his teachings have been evoked in a variety of contexts often with very new twists. The nineteenth-century German philosopher, Friedrich Nietzsche, brought Zoroaster to life in his famous book, *Thus Spoke Zarathustra*. For more on Nietzsche and an online translation of this influential book, check out the Friedrich Nietzsche Society at www.fns.org.uk.

In India, followers of the famous holy man, Meher Baba (1892-1969), recognized him as a divine *avatar*, or incarnation, of the Prophet Zoroaster himself. For Meher Baba's own words on Zoroaster, see The Life of the Avatar Zarathustra at www.cybertrails.com/babadas/Zarathustra.html.

While not all Zoroastrians would approve such appropriations of their Persian Prophet, these examples are proof of the enduring power of Zoroaster's message.

Rest and Remember

➤ Zoroastrians have ancient roots but a modern outlook.

➤ Zoroastrians observe ethical standards that they project with consummate skill on the Web.

➤ Zoroastrians are a global community and because many of them have become netizens, they now enjoy a representation on the Net that far exceeds their numbers.

Chapter 34

God Is the Devil: Satanism

In This Chapter

➤ Satanism is a modern religion that traces its roots back to its founder Anton LaVey

➤ There are two major sects within Satanism and both have a huge satanic Internet presence

➤ While some sites provide information for the uninitiated, there are numerous community-based satanic sites

There are some folk who would like to skip over this chapter and also distance themselves from its subject. Satanism? A religion! You must be joking! Well, actually there is quite a bit to say for the way that present day Satanists have rethought that old guy with the funny ears and the pitched fork. You might not even recognize the devil you thought you knew after reading this chapter. Of course, if you *are* a Satanist, all these Web sites will seem like natural, and welcome, stops on the information superhighway.

Sympathy for the Devil

Hello, and welcome to Satanism 101. Let's see, what is the first thing that comes to mind when you see the word Satanism. Anyone? That's right, Satan! Well, Satan only plays a minor role in the religion of Satanism. More importantly, it's not even the nasty Christian Satan that is recognized. The religion has almost nothing to do with evil at all. In fact, those who profess Satanist beliefs project a very tolerant worldview. Their beliefs deserve to be called Religious Satanism, which consists of two major sects: the Church of Satan and the Temple of Set.

The Church of Satan

This group is the dominant Satanist sect, and it has received a lot of attention, especially on the World Wide Web. A prominent Satanist home page can be seen in Figure 34.1.

Much of their religious practice centers on sex and sensual satisfaction. Members of the Church of Satan believe in the power and authority of the individual rejecting the power and authority of God. Additionally, they consider each individual to be his or her own redeemer and proscribe the fulfillment of one's lusts and desires. "What about the seven deadly sins," you might ask. Well, Satanists embrace and explore these "sins" in order to achieve personal euphoria.

The Satanic Network Home Page: www.satannet.com

Want to find out more than you ever wanted to know about Satanism? Just visit www.satannet.com. This wonderful site provides new initiates with an introduction to the religion. It also contains essays both about Satanism and about its presence on the Net. For the practicing Satanist, this site has chat rooms, message boards, and numerous links.

Figure 34.1

It's party time! According to this Web page, Satanists are all about having a good time and being happy.

Anton Szandor LaVey: The Satanist for This Age

The man most responsible for these attitudes is Anton Szandor LaVey. His writings, *The Satanic Bible*, *The Complete Witch*, and *The Satanic Rituals* form the core of Satanist text. They profess his belief in personal liberation through rigorous self-indulgence. LaVey formed the Church of Satan on Walpurgisnacht (Translation: April 30, 1966). There are numerous sites on the Internet related to this hero and founder and, while most Satanist sites talk about the man, the most relevant site is the following.

Whose Magick?

Yes, Magick had its creator, and he was Aleister Crowley, a twentieth century British magician and member of the Order of the Golden Dawn who pursued the Law of Thelema and invented his own religion. Neither Aleister Crowley nor the Law of Thelema should be confused with Anton LaVey-style Satanism, even though the word Magick frequently appears in Satanist texts and rituals. (Crowley spelled magick with a k so the word would contain seven letters.) Crowley's motto "do what thou wilt shall be the whole of the law" is also widely quoted. For more on Crowley and his practices, see www.religioustolerance.org/satanism.htm.

Anthony LaVey Home Page

http://hem.passagen.se/baphomet

Here you can find a biography of LaVey, some of his scriptures, a Satanism FAQ, a message board, and much, much more. You also can find LaVey's Nine Satanic Statements here—they sum up the average Satanists' beliefs.

The Nine Satanic Statements

According to followers of LaVey, Satan represents:

1. Indulgence rather than abstinence

2. Vital existence, not spiritual fantasy

3. True wisdom, not hypocritical deceit

4. Kindness for those who deserve, no kindness for those who don't

5. Vengeance

6. Personal responsibility

7. Man as the most vicious animal

8. Gratification of all personal desires

9. The best friend of the Christian Church because he keeps them in business

Satanism 101

www.satanism101.com

Satanism 101, shown in Figure 34.2, is a wonderful Web site that provides information about Satanism in a very straightforward manner. There's an overview of the basic tenets, Satanist news, an in-depth view of Satanic philosophy, and much, much more.

Holidays and Ceremonies

There are several types of Satanist ceremonies and several types of Satanist Magick. The holidays occur during and soon after the June/December solstices and the March/September equinoxes. Additionally, practitioners acknowledge Satan's birthday, Halloween, and Walpurgisnacht as holy days. Men usually wear black robes during ceremonies while women traditionally don sexually suggestive attire. Most also wear amulets with the famed Baphomet, such as depicted in Figure 34.3.

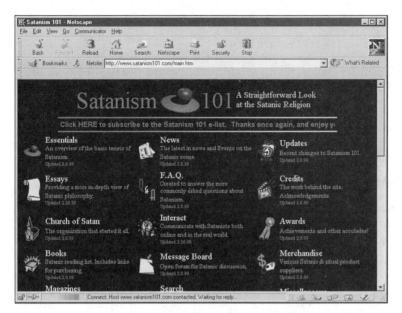

Figure 34.2

At www.satanism101.com you can learn about the basic tenets of Satanism or communicate with Satanists all over the world, and that's only the beginning!

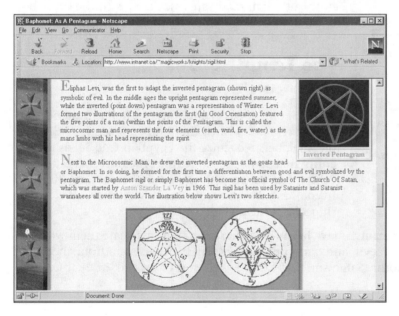

Figure 34.3

What's with the five-pointed star inside a circle? Well, the fancy name for that symbol is baphomet. *Satanists will wear baphomet amulets during ceremonies but they would never paint the symbol on public walls (despite what many believe).*

There are three types of Magick ritual performed during ceremonies. They include sex magick, a healthy or happiness ritual, and a destruction ritual (usually performed by a group).

Rites of Darkness

http://members.spree.com/lifestyles/azatoth

This site is packed full of information about satanic magick and rituals. Just click the eerie **dark rites of unspeakable evil** button to learn more about Satanic beliefs and ceremonies. This site even includes directions on how to perform your own Satanic ritual!

Where the Wild Things Are

www.maledicta.com/lavey

This is a great site. Check out the tributes to LaVey and the section on Satanic magick. Then, peruse the lovely art galleries and check out some interesting photos.

Although tradition calls for a naked woman to be used as an altar, most temples use something a little less animated like stone.

What Do You Call a Satanist Shrine?

There are many names for Satanist places of worship. They can be called grottos, pylons, or temples. But they're all the same thing!

The Church of Satan is highly decentralized because that's the way it wants to be. Each temple is its own entity although many are associated with the Church of Satan and all are followers of LaVey's teachings.

The Temple of Set

www.xeper.org

In 1975, one of LaVey's followers, Michael Aquino, left the church and formed the Temple of Set. In this temple, members recognize the Egyptian God Set as an entity that stands separate from the universe. Often depicted as a man with the head of an animal (like a hyena), as you can see in Figure 34.4, the God is worshiped as, well, a God.

Throughout history Satanists have been misunderstood. Most associate them with ritual killings, sacrifice, evil, and harm unto others. These beliefs stem from another form of Satanism, Gothic Satanism, that existed, well, sort of existed, in the fifteenth century.

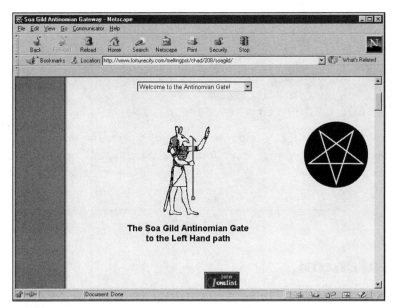

Figure 34.4

Here's what Set looks like (at least to this artist).

Gothic Satanism

Gothic Satanism is, in fact, completely imaginary. No, seriously, the Christian Church invented it way back in the fifteenth century. The church used Gothic Satanism to justify the many witch burnings of the period. Gothic Satanists were portrayed as evil, murderous, practitioners of black magic, and worthy of death. In essence, this "religion" was as anti-Christian as you could get. The problem was, there never were any Gothic Satanists. Christian opponents assigned the characteristics of pagan deities, such as horns and hooves, to the Devil. Though Satan is very articulate, especially when he appears to Job in the Hebrew Bible, he remains but a voice till the appearance of Gothic Satanism.

Wired Monk

The Online Temple of Set

The best site about the Temple of Set is its own, www.xeper.org. Here you will find information about the temple, its beliefs and practices, and links to affiliated temples all over the world.

The 600 Club: `http://the600club.com`

Here you will find the Satanic evangelist response to Pat Robertson. The non-profit site is dedicated to clearing up misconceptions about Satanism. Those who look down on Satanism as evil devil worship should check out the essays on this site.

Resources for Satanism

There are tons of Satanist sites on the Internet and their numbers increase almost daily. They exist for two audiences: those who practice Satanism and those only interested in learning about it. Here are some of the best.

Sites for Satanists

Of the many to visit I have picked two that seem to be at the top of the list, if not for everyone, then certainly for Satanists themselves.

The House of Satan

www.houseofsatan.com

The House of Satan provides various forms of entertainment for Satanists like a "den of indulgences". While this might sound wicked, the site is actually very funny. There is little in the way of Satanic teaching here but there are some very interesting examples of average Satanist interests.

The Satannet Frost

www.coscentral.net/frost

This community-based Church of Satan site boasts tons of graphics in several galleries and is home to poetry, literature, music, art, and links about Satanism. The site is under construction and is expanding daily. Visitors can add their own art to the gallery, which displays the works of several talented computer graphics artists. There is a lot of user-friendly information about the religion and the top 50 links to Satanism on the Internet.

Satanville?

Yes, it exists, at least in cyberspace, and at the address: www.satanville.com. Here you will find the self-proclaimed "online town for the Satanic internet community." It contains a tribute to LaVey and, after you join, you can sell your (or anyone else's) soul online. Additionally, members can choose the type of abode they would like in hell. I chose the two bedroom if anyone's curious. But please take note: Although the site is chock full of fun stuff, there are some sexually explicit pages; and if that's beyond the limit of fun for you, please be sure to skip along to the next site.

Sites for Interested Parties

If Satanism is a matter of curiosity for you, but not some group or outlook you want to pursue, then you might want to go to Web pages designed for 'friendly' outsiders to Satanville. Here are a couple of the best:

United Satanic Front (USF)

www.geocities.com/Athens/Parthenon/5947/usf.html

United Satanic Front is responsible for much of the growth of Satanism on the Net. The USF is dedicated to expanding online Satanist territory. It also has a chat room and several message boards.

Ontario Consultants on Religious Tolerance

www.religioustolerance.org

For an impartial and very detailed look at Satanism, you can't do better than this site. There you will find the history of Satanism, including brief biographies of its founding members. You also will find information about different types and styles of Satanist worship, and a clear explanation of the difference between Anton LaVey and earlier exponents of Magick. Be careful, though: not all the information here is up to date.

AvatarSearch

www.AvatarSearch.com

Finally, this is the best search engine of the Occult on the Internet. Just type in any topic of interest and wait: You will be swamped with great sites.

Rest and Remember

➤ Satanism came to life in the modern age and has embraced modern technology to the fullest.

➤ Almost every site out there talks about Satanic teachings or pays tribute to its founder Anton LaVey.

➤ Practicing Satanists will find their virtual community already well established, but anyone interested in Satanism also will be able to find a wealth of information about nearly every aspect of this very different religious group.

Chapter 35

God's Many Voices: Vodun

In This Chapter

➤ Vodun, also known as Vodou and Voodoo, is the major African-based religion practiced in the Caribbean and the U.S. that has sites now available through the Net

➤ Along with Vodun there are Afro-Caribbean religions that inspire devotees in their country of origin and also country of residence; they include Santeria, along with its offshoots, Orisha and Ifa

➤ None of the expressions of Vodun, or its sister faiths, should be confused with popular images. Too often popular images are distortions of actual beliefs and practices. Cyberspace is home to both the real Vodun and the false Voodoo

If ever there was a religious outlook and ritual practice that cried out for change via the World Wide Web, then it's Vodun. Too many folk still see it as some kind of weird magic, called Voodoo, but it really is a vital spiritual tradition with deep roots in the Caribbean but is also now in parts of mainland United States, and its preferred name is Vodun. I have tried to touch on some of Vodun's most evident features as they are projected by its real life practitioners in cyberspace. It makes for a good read, but also a clear rethinking of Voodoo as Vodun.

Vodun Is Not Just for Fun

Vodu or Vodun means divine spirit, and it refers to the divine spirit that guided African slaves who worked in Haiti starting in the seventeenth century. They had to practice their African-based religion in secret. They would be persecuted, even maimed, sometimes killed if their owners discovered them. Still they held covert meetings. They performed dances. They carried out funeral practices. They also experienced trance possession.

Vodun also has a political side: It inspired the slave revolt in Haiti, which eventually led to Haiti's independence, making it the sole black republic in the whole span of North, Central, and South America.

Ritual Practices

There are priests and priestesses in Vodun. The priests are called *hungan*, the priestesses *mambo*. The spirits are known as *loa* or *lwa*. They are both male and female. When one of the female spirits (such as Ezili) or male spirits (such as Ogou or Legba) possess an individual, they *mount* that person. He or she becomes a mounted horse, who then enacts a ritual that involves dance, song, and speech all directed by the spirit in charge.

What happens to the possessed individuals? They are able to heal, to ward off evil, to bring good or evil fortune, but mostly good fortune. In other words, they are agents of white magic.

Food for Thought

What Is White Magic?

Actually white magic is *good* magic. It helps people for whom it is performed. The contrast is with black magic, which is intended to harm the person against whom it is practiced. There are many Web sites that are linked to white magic, most often through Wiccans and Neopagans. For the latter, see Chapter 26, "She Is God: Neopaganism and Wicca," or skip directly to an example at Zaby's Book of Shadow. It is available in both French and English at www.geocities.com/Athens/Aegean/7510/.

Someone who is married to a spirit is protected by that spirit, but also has the obligation to nourish the spirit through ritual acts. It is an intense but reciprocal relationship: The spirit helps the devotee who feeds the spirit who keeps on helping the devotee, and so on.

The range of rituals in Vodun is enormous. It goes from simple acts of devotion like lighting candles and saying prayers to observances for the ancestral dead to feast-like, day-long meals that include drumming, singing, and trance dancing.

And all this ritual activity is directed through priests and priestesses. It is they who perform divination and healing rituals for individuals. They also oversee all training and all seasonal ceremonies. They are usually older, and they guide younger members in possession or trance dancing. In these dances, individual spirits are thought to be present. They are worshipped, and they in turn offer healing and advice.

Link to Catholicism

And so you think that all this sounds very African, or at least non-Christian, right? Well, actually it is closely tied to Roman Catholicism, the religion of the French slave owners in Haiti before independence. The Vodun ritual calendar follows the Catholic seasons and celebrations. Vodun spirits are associated, although not equated, with various Christian saints. Also, Vodun theology parallels traditional Christian theology. There is a high creator spirit, Bondye (or Bondieu). All the intermediary spirits act like Christian saints, able to intervene when needed. Many Vodun practitioners follow not only the Christian ritual calendar but also common Christian rituals of baptism, marriage, and even Mass.

But the flavor of Vodun remains authentically and persistently African. Consider the pantheon of spirits, known as loa or lwa. The lwa are divided into two groups: Rada, the generous and helpful spirits, and Petro, the violent, often terrible, spirits. Higher powers are linked to the directions or the planets or places such as springs or cemeteries. These higher powers can project the souls of demons and ancestral spirits, including sacred twins, from the spirit world to this world.

In the cycle of Vodun there is both requirement and free choice. The requirement is to venerate ancestors and spirits from one's own family. The free choice is to recognize individual spirits either out of need or because they correspond to one's own personality and outlook. In Vodun ritual the practitioner responds both to familial expectations and to open-ended options.

False Vodun or Voodoo

Just as Scooby Doo, the cartoon character, can be just another fun-loving dog, so Voodoo can be an innocent name for a major Afro-Caribbean religious tradition. The trouble is that Scooby Doo can also play tricks, and seem to have a mischievous side, and so can Voodoo.

Instead of emphasizing white or good magic, many people emphasize black or evil magic when they think of Voodoo. Sometimes this idea is linked to the term zombie. The notion is that a zombie has no will of its own, but is manipulated by others usually in ways that are harmful, either to the zombie or to those near it.

Voodoo dolls, like zombies, became widely known through horror movies, but voodoo dolls were thought to be more prevalent than zombies are. A sorcerer would stick pins in a doll that looked like a living person, and that voodoo doll would then effect the person whom it represented. It was a form of curse, and it was supposed to be especially prevalent in places of French-Caribbean culture, like New Orleans or Savannah in the southern United States. This notion has become so prevalent that there's now a virtual voodoo doll that you click, not stick, as you can see in Figure 35.1.

Figure 35.1

Even if you don't want or need a voodoo doll, the VVV Web site is alluring. Its Very Virtual Voodoo doll is an emblem of popular and now cyberculture.

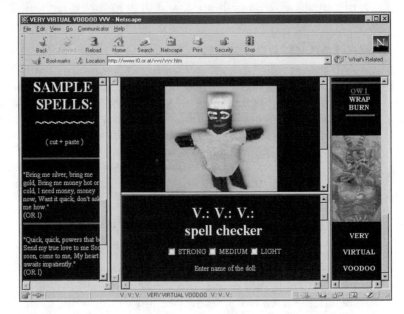

Check out any New Orleans Web site, and you'll find what seems to be a friendly notion of ghosts, spirits, and the dead. Wander over to the Voodoo Museum in the French Quarter at www.voodoomuseum.com, or slip into the tomb of the legendary Marie Laveau, also known as the crypt of the Voodoo Queen. It is featured in the Webcorps page of New Orleans Cemetery Images at www.webcorp.com/images/nocemeteries.htm. But you would still do better by going to a home page dedicated to Marie Laveau: www.neosoft.com/~nodust/ml.html, shown in Figure 35.2.

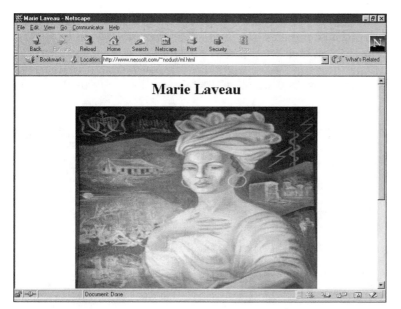

Figure 35.2

The Queen of Voodoo brought to life!

Sensational, Not Actual

Less true to the Vodun spirit are Web sites that pander to the sensational. They might even claim to give you a recipe for doing your own curse. Watch out for such appeals to the weird and not so wondrous side of popular Voodoo. There is the Very Virtual Voodoo Doll, also known as Very Virtual Voodoo (VV), at www.t0.or.at/vvv/vvv.htm. There you will find 10 steps to making a voodoo doll, along with sample spells to cast! This is Voodoo in name but not in spirit. Sorcerer, beware!

The Real Vodun Medium

Are you are ready for a full overview of Vodun culture from a Vodun perspective? Then you can do no better than visit The Vodoun Culture page at www.geocities.com/ Athens/Delphi/5319/. There you will find a Table of Contents that highlights the complex history of Vodun in both French and English versions. In addition you will find the Pantheon of Spirits, the Major Songs, the Sacred Dances as well as notes about language and ritual symbols. It is a masterful exposition of Vodun from the top down.

But maybe you want to find the authentic face of Vodun from the bottom up. If you want to see how a Vodun priestess projects herself in cyberspace, you ought to visit The Vodou Page of Mambo Racine sans Bout, shown in Figure 35.3. As she explains in her beautifully crafted and multiply linked site, there is a power within Haitian culture, and its roots, like her names, are *sans bout,* literally without end; they are deep and endless.

Figure 35.3

Race, gender, and politics all flow together seamlessly in the exposition of Vodun set forth in this site.

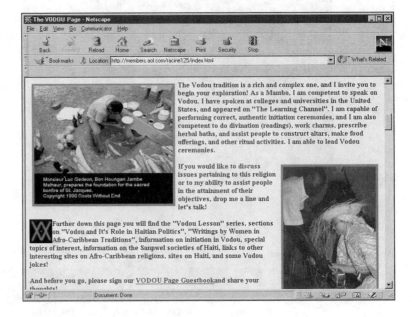

Santeria

Standing in its own right as an Afro-Caribbean religion is Santeria. It is as strongly linked to Cuban devotees as Vodun is to Haitian descendants of African slaves and their French overlords. It also embodies a ritual system and view of the world that depends on spirits, mediums, and followers. The spirits are not called lwa but orisha. Orisha can personify some aspect of nature or project the soul of an ancestor. They possess, or mount, certain human beings, who then become the mediaries or mediums through which they communicate to ordinary human beings. Like the lwa in Vodun, they also can sometimes be identified with Christian saints. But do not be fooled: Despite the links to Roman Catholic saints, and also to Christian rituals as well as holy days, Santeria stands apart from the official teaching of any Christian group.

Obatala's House

`http://members.tripod.com/Obatala/`

This is essentially an informational link site. It will allow you to connect to other Orisha sites on the Net. It is named after Obatala, one of the major spirits or powers in the Yoruban pantheon, who stands just below the ultimate creator god, Olorun.

OrishaNet

`www.seanet.com/~efunmoyiwa/ochanet.html`

Projecting both Spanish and English versions of its message, OrishaNet claims to receive a hundred thousand hits per month. If true, that would make it one of the most popular sites in the religion sector of the Web. Even while that claim might be exaggerated, it is no exaggeration to say that Orisha, the major spiritual forces of the Yoruban higher world, are well represented in this imaginative, bells and whistles site.

It provides extensive background material as well as a heap of practical advice. It is to Santeria what the home page of Mambo Racine sans Bout is to Vodun: the best place to start on the Net and the one to which you will return most often in exploring Afro-Caribbean practices.

Is Animal Sacrifice Religious?

According to Santeria, animal sacrifice is religious. Cuban immigrants to the United States who wanted to practice animal sacrifice were challenged in the U.S. Supreme Court in the early 1990s, giving the religion enormous, not always favorable publicity. What resulted was a Supreme Court ruling in favor of the Santeria practice of ritual animal sacrifice. It is a touchy subject, and a lot of folk have very strong feelings for and against allowing animal sacrifice for any reason, religious or commercial. To see the text of the Supreme Court decision, and also some of the controversy surrounding it, check out the Supreme Court Ruling on Santeria Practices available at OCRT, `www.religioustolerance.org/santeri1.htm`.

Ifa

`www.ifafoundation.org`

Though an independent group, Ifa fits into a Santerian worldview. It offers a practical philosophy of devotion to Orisha. Its main medium has put together a model Web site. The site provides a spiritual store of extensive ritual and divinatory items. It also includes information on initiations and divinations as well as an Internet Ile or way station, where you can stop, click, and connect to a range of other Orisha-minded netizens.

Rest and Remember

➤ The images of Vodun vary enormously depending on where you go and with whom you talk, either on the street or in cyberspace.

➤ Some of the best sites on Afro-Caribbean religious practices feature both Vodun and Santeria in their actual settings, with their authentic mediums and practitioners.

➤ The best way to think of Vodun and Santeria is to get beyond the negative images, either in popular culture or on the Net, and visit the Web pages constructed by and for their devotees in cyberspace. It's the real thing!

Chapter 36

New Religious Movements

In This Chapter

➤ People opposing them label many groups "cults". This term has negative connotations and should be used with caution

➤ There are many new religious movements beginning every day. Many of these find the Web a useful tool in communicating with members or attracting new adherents

➤ Some new religious movements are variations on older religions, but others are genuinely new, offering a radically different worldview to their members

---

No one has figured out how to talk about the many new groups that seem religious, often claim religious inspiration, and attract many followers with religious motives. Are they cults or new religious movements or both? I have tried to sketch some examples from the best-known groups, without prejudging them as good or bad, cultic or religious. Not every one will agree with my choices or my descriptions. But I do hope that you will come to the end of this chapter realizing how integral to religions online are those religious groups that are unconventional and creative, no matter how marginal they may seem to more traditional expressions of religious devotion and practice.

Cult or Religion?

New religions are springing up every day and the growth of the Web has accelerated the process. Are these groups cults? Are they religions? Are they serious or tongue-in-cheek? How should society regard them? These are difficult questions! For some true believers, Star Wars is a religion, as you can see in Figure 36.1.

Figure 36.1

This graphically intensive site illustrates how the characters in the Star Wars trilogy fall into familiar mythic patterns.

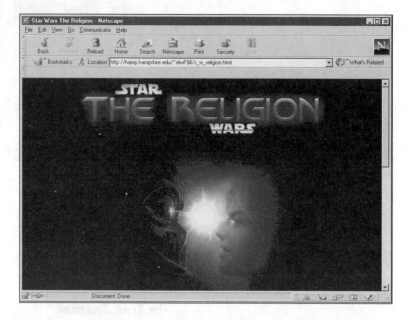

The Ontario Consultants on Religious Tolerance (OCRT) argue that there is a difference between groups like the Unification Church and Jehovah's Witnesses and those like Heaven's Gate and the Solar Temple. The first two are "high-intensity" religions, groups that require a greater commitment from their members than typical churches do. The latter two are "destructive cults," participation in which resulted in the deaths of many of their members.

In this chapter, we will discuss several of these groups, starting with the "high-intensity" religions of the Unification Church and Scientology. We will then briefly discuss the Heaven's Gate and Solar Temple cults and the Christian Identity movement.

High-Intensity Religious Movements

Some religions demand more of their adherents than do others! They might encourage their members to donate their goods to the church, to work for the church, or to recruit new members. People might find the network of other church members replacing that of their family and friends. This might lead their family to believe they have been "brainwashed" and indeed, this is the most frequent charge leveled against new religious movements.

The Unification Church

Sun Myung Moon, the founder of the Unification Church, was born in North Korea in 1920. He was raised in the Presbyterian Church, but was excommunicated in 1948. Rev. Moon's teachings are contained in his 1957 book *Divine Principle*. In 1972, Rev. Moon came to the U.S. and began a missionary campaign, including several large wedding ceremonies, where he married up to 2,000 couples. In 1984, he was convicted of tax-fraud and served 13 months in prison.

The Unification Church resembles other conservative Christian groups, but has some unorthodox beliefs. Perhaps the most important is that Eve is blamed for the spiritual fall of humanity, by having sex with the Archangel Lucifer; she also is blamed for the physical fall of humanity, by having pre-marital sex with Adam. For this reason, the Unification Church stresses the importance of marriage and family.

For information about The Unification Church, you can surf over to its Web site at www.unification.org. You will find a history of the church, messages from Rev. Moon and his wife, information on the church's teachings, educational outreach programs, and the inevitable links to other Unification Church sites.

> *Wired Monk*
>
> **Do You Speak Korean?**
>
> Want to learn Korean? Check out the **Introduction to Korean** section of the Unification Church Web site. It explains the alphabet and pronounces words for you to study. You can find it at www.unification.org/ucbooks/ kintro/index.htm.

As with many other "high-intensity" faiths, the Unification Church has been attacked as "cult-like." There are several Web sites created by former Church members decrying church practices and accusing it a variety of excesses. An example of this sort of site can be found at Xmoonies www.xmoonies.com. The author of this site was involved in the Unification Church from 1978 until 1993. He regrets his time in the Church and criticizes Rev. Moon's lavish lifestyle. He describes his own experiences and provides links to other sites, both those supporting (and promoting) the Unification Church and those strongly critical of it.

Scientology

Besides being famous actors, what do John Travolta, Nicole Kidman, and Tom Cruise have in common? They are all members of the Church of Scientology, along with Oscar-winning singer Isaac Hayes and Nancy Cartwright, the voice of Bart Simpson! Scientology, to say the least, has an interesting history and a controversial present.

History

L. Ron Hubbard, a pulp science fiction writer, created Scientology. After World War II, Hubbard wrote the foundational text for Scientology. Published in 1950, *Dianetics* argues that mental aberrations (or *engrams*) sprang from early trauma; "auditing," a process something like psychoanalysis, could cure them.

If you want to learn more about L. Ron Hubbard, you can surf to the L. Ron Hubbard Site (www.lronhubbard.org) for the Church's presentation of his life and accomplishments. According to the site, Hubbard was an author, educator, humanitarian, and artist. The site does not mention his problems with the IRS, which conducted investigations in the 1970s and concluded that L. Ron was skimming millions from the Church and stashing it in Swiss bank accounts. Hubbard went into hiding for five years, but died before the criminal case could be prosecuted. Interestingly, Hubbard continues to publish books although he has been dead since 1986!

Is Scientology a New Religious Movement?

Scientology denies that it is a religion and allows its adherents to remain Jews, Christians, or members of other faiths. But it sought and was granted tax-exempt status from the U.S. government as a religious organization. This shifty stance has raised caution signs in the minds of many people, especially given the Church's history.

Controversy

Scientology has generated a lot of controversy, because it encourages its members to donate large quantities of money for its services. Groups that oppose the Church or criticize it frequently find themselves sued or facing other legal assaults. The frequent use of lawsuits causes further controversy about the Church's tactics. *Time* magazine ran an article in its May 6, 1991 edition about the Church and its tactics. The article is available online at Scientology: The Thriving Cult of Greed and Power, (www.cs.cmu.edu/~dst/Fishman/time-behar.html). The article led to a five-year lawsuit against *Time*, which was dismissed in 1996.

Scientology is especially controversial on the Web because it has filed several important lawsuits against former members and others publishing criticism or documents relating to the Church on the Web. Scientology holds its literature under copyright.

The Church's home page can be found at Scientology (www.scientology.org). After scrolling past two pages of advertisements for books and other materials you can purchase, the page provides links to information about the Church, including an elaborate FAQs section written by the Church's president.

A good place to look for criticism of Scientology might be An Introduction to Scientology (www.modemac.com/cos/). This site, critical of the Church, includes links to the Church's sites, along with comments about them. It also has extensive links to Web sites documenting various grievances against the Church. Worried that all these sites have an axe to grind? There are also links to mainstream publications, like *Time*,

The Boston Herald, and *The Wall Street Journal*, as well as scads of public-domain legal documents (court filings, briefs, and so on). Read them yourself and decide.

What If You Want to Learn About Criticism of Scientology?

Well, don't try the Web page Those Opposing Scientology (http://opposing.scientology.org/index.htm), because it is owned by the Church of Scientology. Nor should you try the Cult Awareness Network (www.cultawarenessnetwork.org), because it was forced into bankruptcy in 1996 and bought by a member of the Church of Scientology!

Destructive Cults

Unlike "high-intensity" religions, there are some new religious movements that can be quite destructive, either to themselves or to others. Frequently, these groups are doomsday cults. Many of these groups read Revelation (the last book in the New Testament) and apply its scary messages about final battles to the present day. Examples of self-destructive or suicide cults include Heaven's Gate and Solar Temple. The Christian Identity movement, although not advocating violence itself, promotes a theology that can be interpreted to encourage violence against minorities and homosexuals.

Heaven's Gate

The members of the Heaven's Gate cult combined elements of the New Testament book of Revelation with a fascination with UFOs. They thought that aliens had visited Earth sometime in the 1920s and moved into human bodies. The leaders of the cult, Do and Ti, thought they were the leaders of the alien ship and the other members of Heaven's Gate were the crew of the spaceship.

Cult members lived together in a large house, which they called their monastery. They lived celibate lifestyles, dressed in black, and lived communally. They supported themselves by creating Web pages and used the Web as a recruitment vehicle, as you can see in Figure 36.2. This all came to an end when the Hale-Bopp comet appeared in the sky in 1997. The group thought the comet had a spaceship on it and the way for them to get to it was by committing suicide. Thirty-nine people died.

Figure 36.2

This page is a copy of the group's original Web page (their computers are now in the possession of the FBI), but here it has been updated to reflect the events in 1997.

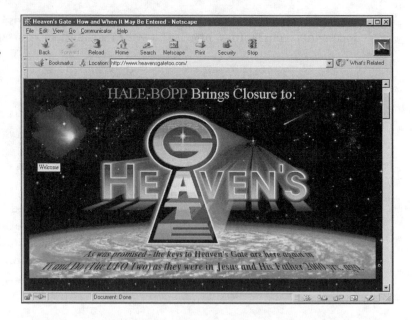

Some of the cult members did not commit suicide, and a copy of their Web site reflects the further thoughts of those who did not kill themselves. If you want to learn more about the group, check out their Web site Heaven's Gate at www.heavensgatetoo.com. You will find transcripts of their writings and theology, and you can purchase videos and tapes of the leaders of the group as well.

Solar Temple

Luc Jouret founded the Solar Temple cult in 1977. He taught his followers that he was the reincarnation of a member of the Knights Templar from the fourteenth century. According to the Solar Temple theology, death is an illusion—people continue to live on other planets. Between 1995 and 1997, 74 members of the Solar Temple committed suicide to reach other planets. Solar Temple does not seem to have its own Web site, but the suicides were widely covered by mainstream media.

Other Destructive Cults

If you are interested in learning about other destructive cults, you should check out the cult section of Ontario Consultants on Religious Tolerance at www.religioustolerance.org/destruct.htm. This site has information on several destructive cults or people influenced by cults including Aum Shinri Kyo, the Branch Davidians, the Family (Charles Manson), The People's Temple (Jim Jones), and others.

Christian Identity

Perhaps the only thing worse than a cult that destroys itself is one that encourages destruction of others. The basic premise of the Christianity Identity movement is that white people are the "true Israelites" and that Jews and people of color are sub-human "mud-people" or "children of Satan." The "mud-people" and the government will be destroyed in an apocalyptic battle. These organizations see the U.S. as the "New Jerusalem" and see themselves as patriotic, as the Web site in Figure 36.3 indicated; others might describe them as xenophobic and isolationist.

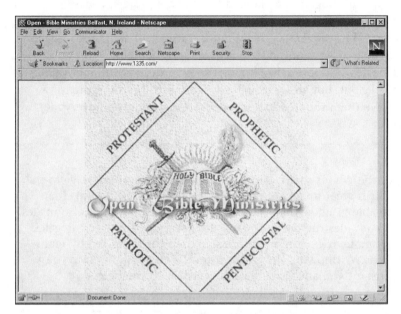

Figure 36.3

This picture clearly illustrates the religion and nationalism found in the theology of Christian Identity.

Although most Christian Identity sites do not advocate violence, they predict a coming battle in which the "mud-people" will be destroyed. Moreover, Christian Identity provides a coherent religious basis for hate groups that do advocate violence, such as the Ku Klux Klan, Aryan Nation, and Nazis. Christian Identity is not an organized religion, but rather has many groups that subscribe to its beliefs. Thus, although there are a large number of sites advocating "white power," they call themselves by a variety of names. World Church of the Creator (www.creator.org), America's Promise Ministries (www.amprom.org), and others are examples of different "churches" that subscribe to Christian Identity. There is nothing intrinsically Christian among any of these groups, but their appeal to prejudice, racism, and terror in the name of God is as loathsome as it is widespread on the Net. As long as cyberspace remains a frontier for self-expression, such groups will have license to hate, and to try to spread hatred. Information, rather than ignorance, is the best counter-assault.

While there are a large number of Web sites dedicated to Christian Identity, it has no overall organization, and so there is no "main" Web site. Ironically, the most complete lists of sites related to Christian Identity are those dedicated to opposing hate groups.

Monitoring Hate Mongers on the Web Is a Full-Time Business!

The best collection of links related to the Christian Identity movement is Hate Watch (www.hatewatch.org). Begun as a Harvard Law School project, it has become a full-time business. The site tracks hate on the Web. You can find hate organized by category (white supremacy, racist music, racist skinheads, neo-nazism, and so on), illustrations of the symbols different hate groups employ, lists of prominent hate advocates, and so forth. Although these groups are all motivated by hate, not all are religious, but all are equally dangerous to the principles of an open society which give them the freedom to oppose everything, and everyone, different from them!

One of the strengths of the Web is that it allows each person with a Web page to publish his or her ideas. This is great for small religions, organizations, or groups that might otherwise not be able to make their views known. Unfortunately, it also makes it possible for hate mongers, destructive cults, and other scary groups to create slick Web sites that look legitimate or even more impressive than those created by mainstream religious traditions. Winnowing the wheat from the chaff is not always easy for Web surfers, but constant vigilance is better than blissful abstinence!

Rest and Remember

➤ Many "cults" are new religions with old ideas. Some are dangerous and destructive, but others simply demand more discipline, submission, and payment from their members than do mainstream churches, mosques, or synagogues.

➤ On the Web, you can find as many anti-cult sites as pro-cult sites.

➤ If you are not sure about the credentials of a new religious movement, or are worried about the activities of a cult, take a (virtual) trip to Canada and visit the Ontario Consultants on Religious Tolerance.

God—Almost

When we come to the end of the many, many paths to *The Complete Idiot's Guide to Religions Online*, what do we find? Do we find God, at least a god resembling any thing like what we thought God was or should be before the advent of the computer and now the Net? Or do we find instead that the World Wide Web has become a substitute God, resembling a new idol that competes with the many idols of the past, whether Biblical or scientific?

You will have to find your own answer. The chapters of this book are meant to help you explore, to question, and to enjoy what is now a cornucopia of spiritual resources on the Web. But users beware! It will not replace ground level groups of believers or worshipers or likeminded folk. If it did, there would be very little information to exchange in cyberspace. Without activities on the ground involving real persons inter-acting face to face, religion would become very dull very quickly. Even the excitement of the Internet would soon turn to bitter disappointment.

If that's the bad news, what's the good news? The good news is the very real possibil-ity that we have arrived at the cusp of a new age. It intersects with the Age of Science, but is not identical with it. Modern science, as we know it, came from a broad range of experiments that began long before Christopher Columbus sailed the ocean blue in the fifteenth century and discovered the new world. Modern science springs from pre-modern alchemy. Alchemists were trying to make refined substances out of base met-als; they wanted to change lead and copper into silver or gold! By today's standards, alchemists might seem unscientific, but in their own day they were trying to use language, intuition, and reflection to transform the ordinary into the extraordinary. One of their goals is as modern as medicine: to achieve total health, which would prolong life, and maybe, just maybe, produce immortality.

Whatever happens in the Age of Science, we now seem to be retrieving some of the methods that alchemists once used. We are looking at the world of matter and saying: it is not enough. There has to be deeper purpose, other meaning, commitment to more than just money, sex, the good life. We search for a world of norms as well as forms, a world with moral values and not just price tags or commercial value. And we want to live as fully as possible for as long as we can. Even if there is no immortality, we'd like to wink at the Great Reaper, as the Angel of Death has been called, and tell him to bide his time!

Perhaps we will move from the Age of Science to the Age of Celebration. We will celebrate our rediscovery of the world as enchanted and magical. We will celebrate matter that is not merely mundane and physical but also porous, liminal, and spiritual. We will celebrate not the God against Nature, Man, and Hope, but the God within our deepest selves. It will be a God as much feminine as masculine, and finally neither feminine nor masculine, at least as we humans are. It will be a God evoking curiosity, wonder, and awe but a God who also requires commitment to justice, generosity, and beauty. It will be a God who marks the depth of pleasure and possibility, whatever lifespan we are granted.

Are we to pass from the Age of Science to the Age of Celebration via the Net? Can we all become cybernauts, all learn the language of netaphysics? Not easily, not quickly, and never totally. The hope that is held out in these pages confirms real people in the real world to pursue their religious dreams and to make of them the stuff of celebration. There will always be a large populace, either due to poverty or alienation or disinterest, who do not enter into this world, for whom none of these resources matter. And it is against the downside of the long-term future that one must be careful in saying: the human race is about to enter the Age of Celebration.

Yet those of you who find the cyberprofile of your spiritual search to be a cause for renewal, for connection, for hope, you are launched. You have already become part of an experiment that none would have thought possible a mere 10 years ago. Email was then unfamiliar to most, the Internet had not come into being, except for military minds, and the notion of *The Complete Idiot's Guide to Religions Online* had not been born. We still have much to learn from the alchemists. What they knew about matter as spirit, about outer form and inner will, matches our own urge to experiment, to play, and to grow. If the Age of Celebration has not yet been charted, it has at least become possible, and whatever the resource you glean from *The Complete Idiot's Guide to Religions Online*, might it make you a spiritual alchemist with light equipment and a happy destiny! Good luck! Find your elixir! Enjoy it! Live well!

Glossary: What You Can't Forget

bookmark   When you put it in a book or a folder, it was a piece of paper or a sticker that kept your place for future reference. The computer version does the same thing; only it keeps the location of a Web page you want to return to as memory in your browser, explained next.

browser   A browser is a piece of software that lets you view material on the World Wide Web. A browser is provided by a particular company, such as Netscape or Microsoft, and it can usually be downloaded for free. It lists the Web address or URL of the address you are viewing, displays text and images, and plays sound and video. It also gives you a Back and Forward button for navigation, and has bookmarks, allowing you to recall other URLs or Web addresses that you want to save for frequent use.

chat rooms   A chat room is a location on the Internet in which users communicate by typing instantly appearing messages to each other. It's like deciding that you and your best friend want to share some thoughts with others. In the real world, you'd have to call or write or fax to get together your bigger group of buddies. But on the Net you can go to a Chat Room, and find a fast start, ready made group of strangers who share your interests, and will give you feedback on problems or issues you want to explore.

cybernaut   This term is not for rocket scientists; it is for everyday folk who want to explore cyberspace, or the World Wide Web, the way an astronaut explores outerspace, the great universe of which the earth is but a speck. In the second information age, we have to think of ourselves as perched on the edge of discovery, and the image often used is cybernaut, an astronaut in cyberspace.

digital   Whether it's digital dharma, as in Hinduism, or digital divine, as in a cyber-church, digital refers to digits or bits of data stored on your computer as strings of ones and zeroes that you can access to find out more about God on the Web. Is the digital real or virtual divinity? Go check out the definition of 'virtual'!

domain name   They are the crucial names by which Web sites are identified. They are part of URLs or Uniform Resource Locators. It's often easy to think of domain names and URLs as parties and telephone numbers. If you know the name of the person you are calling on the telephone, it helps but you can reach her, him, or them just by knowing the dial number.

FAQs (frequently asked questions)   Some common questions come up for every issue or group that is linked to religion or spirituality on the Web. A FAQ is a text file containing these questions and their answers so newcomers can acquaint themselves with the knowledge participants are assumed to have. The best Web sites almost always include FAQs, to steer you into a firmer knowledge of the subject they present.

HTML   Short for *HyperText Markup Language*, the code that makes up Web pages.

hyperlinks   You can't find everything you want to know from one Web site. Hyperlinks offer links or connections to other Web sites with similar but more detailed, or differently packaged, information on the subject that interests you. Most Web sites have hyperlinks to other Web sites, and they allow you to jump around from one site to another at a dizzying pace.

information superhighway   One of the boldest images for talking about the Web or the Net as a new means of communicating more and faster and further than was ever conceivable 10 years ago. If we are on the verge of the second information age, we will all have to learn to travel, and to observe new speed limits, on the information superhighway.

Internet   The Internet, or the Net, is simply a worldwide network of computers connected by telephone lines. It combines software with hardware to allow you to seek out a vast array of data that just grows by leaps and bounds every day.

Internet service provider (ISP)   A company that will get you access to the Internet. Usually, you use your modem to dial up from your office or home phone; in this case, it is not a free service but it is essential if you are to benefit from the many facets of the Net. You also might have access to the Internet at work, in which case your employer is your ISP.

modem   A device that you need in order to connect to the Internet. It translates a computer's digital information into sound pulses that can travel over a telephone line. It is attached to your computer, and the computer uses it to dial up an Internet service provider over your home or company phone lines.

mouse   A pointing device that comes with most computers, it helps you to scroll through information fast, and access different options not provided by your computer keyboard.

Netscape   It's the name of a company, but it is also the name for the Internet's most effective Web browser: Netscape Navigator.

pathnames   The location, either on your computer's hard drive or on an Internet computer, of a file or Web page. If you go to a big search engine, like Lycos.com, for example, you need to click a particular pathname (Society and Culture) to find Religion. Alternatively, you can just type *religion* in the search word box and go straight to the category Religion.

plug-in   The software that allows you to use your Web browser not just to read stuff but also to hear and see and experience what comes from the sounds and sights as well as the words of the Web.

RealAudio   Software that allows you to listen to audio over the Internet, it provides all you wanted to hear, and couldn't believe that you'd get from the Net. It is a mine of sounds and songs and information that relate as much to religion as to any other topic. You need to download the RealAudio plug-in from realaudio.com in order to play audio files from the Net.

screen bias   It's nasty but alas, it's true: Most of us are lazy, and screen bias assumes that because we tend to be in a hurry when we want data, we will take the first site that comes from our Internet search. Sad to say, the choice of first site in some search engines is not innocent or objective, and you must be careful of screen bias on all subjects, but especially religion.

search engine   These are the work horses or the spaceships of the new information age. They are provided by commercial companies, and they help you to search the Web and find the data that matches your interest, or answers your question, or just lets you roam in a new world of images and sounds.

second information age   The first information age was launched by print, and the Bible was its showcase success. The second information age was launched by the Web, and it has no single showcase, but religion is among the many topics that seem to suggest it will be as important for future believers as the printed Bible was for folk in an earlier age.

surf   Surf means to skim over the depths, and when you surf the Net or the Web, you are shooting from one Web site to another, looking for data that gets you further down the road toward your goal or your hope or your next dream.

URL   Uniform Resource Locators, or URLs, are Web addresses, the key to accessing information by the Web. Often they begin and end with another set of initials: HTTP means HyperText Transfer Protocol. If you want to know what that means, you might have to take a course on the Internet, but it's easiest just to think of URLs as a huge phone book, and growing bigger by the moment.

virtual   It's the opposite of real, or else it is the really real. Either way, virtual reality, or virtual religion, is another way of talking about the digital divine, a kind of approach to spiritual ideas, persons, and pathways that are expressed, and explored, on the Web. Do they replace other kinds of reality? That is the central question of both this book and the second information age.

viruses   No one, but no one, likes to get sick, and neither does your computer. But because the information superhighway has some illegal drivers, they can interfere with others' travel, and they often do so by jamming sites or creating programs called viruses that will damage other programs and data. It is not a pretty or nice feature of the Net, but it is one that many folk are continuously monitoring. They use *virus protection software* to shield themselves.

Web page   Just one page on a Web site that connects to the World Wide Web. You couldn't have the Web without countless Web pages, but for many non-techies, the hardest thing to do is to construct even a single Web page!

Web site   It is the access point for the words or images or sounds that you are seeking. There can be Web sites with just a single page, but often they consist of many, many linked pages, and the best have dazzling graphics along with easy to use hyperlinks, connecting you to other Web sites.

Webmaster   Someone who puts together many Web pages and constructs a Web site is known as a Webmaster, although in at least some places a woman who does so—and many, many women do!—is known as a Webmistress. Either way, a Webmaster or a Webmistress, this person has provided the exponential growth to the World Wide Web, or the Internet, as we know it, and use it, today.

World Wide Web   For some folk it's the new Trinity, because it has three parts all conjoined, all equally important. It spans the world, it is wide in its reach, and it forms a web, connecting every one who has a computer, a modem, and an Internet service provider to all others with the same three pieces of hardware. The World Wide Web depends on the hardware but it has its tremendous impact due to the software, the programs that are constantly being revised and rewritten through Netscape and other Internet service providers.

Index

Symbols

C

D

J

S

417